Boeing 757 and 767

Boeing 757 and 767

Thomas Becher

First published in 1999 by
The Crowood Press Ltd
Ramsbury, Marlborough
Wiltshire SN8 2HR

British Library Cataloguing-in-Publication Data
A catalogue record for this book is available from
the British Library.

ISBN 1 86126 197 7

Photograph previous page: Boeing 767 (Boeing).

Cover photographs
Front: America West 757-200 (Darren Anderson);
Canada Airlines 767-300 (Joe Pries).
Back: Continental Airlines 757-200 (Bob
Polaneczky); Boeing 757-200s in production
(Boeing); United Airlines 757-200 (Turk Apps/
Flying Images Worldwide); Boeing 767 and 757
together (Boeing).

Typefaces used: Goudy (*text*),
Cheltenham (*headings*).

Typeset and designed by
D & N Publishing
Membury Business Park, Lambourn Woodlands
Hungerford, Berkshire.

Printed and bound by Redwood Books, Trowbridge.

Acknowledgements

This book would not have been possible without energetic support from Boeing. I wish to thank Debbie Heathers and Debbie Nomaguchi of the Everett communications office for their help in supplying background material and establishing contacts with the many people who worked on the 767 programme. Cheryl Addams, in the Renton communications office, was incredibly helpful in my quest to research the 757, and reach out to the wonderful retirees and employees who worked on the programme. I also appreciate the help given to me by Tom Lubbesmeyer, Boeing's archivist; he guided me through the many documents that tell the story of these two wonderful aircraft. Thanks also to Robert Hegge of Boeing's visual communications office for supplying the many photographs in this book. I am also grateful to my superiors Marcy Cain and Martin Kraegel at Pratt & Whitney, for supporting my efforts. Many thanks, too, to Nick Veronico, editor of *Airliners* magazine, without whom this project would not have been possible. Above all, I wish to thank my wife, Amy, for putting up with so many lonely nights while I completed this book.

Contents

Introduction

The world's airlines faced rising fuel bills as a result of the oil crisis of the 1970s. They demanded new aircraft that could carry more passengers for less fuel, and Boeing, the venerable American maker of commercial aircraft, had the solution – the 767 and 757, a new family of fuel-efficient, high-tech airliners. Their versatility and reliability would make them among the most popular commercial airliners ever made.

The efforts of the innovative Boeing engineers will be remembered not just for what they accomplished – the creation of the most advanced airliners of the time – but also for what they inspired: a new generation of aircraft that introduced aviation to the computer age.

This dynamic duo revolutionized air travel. Because of their range, economy and flexibility, the 767 and 757 were used by airlines to open new routes to more cities, enabling more people to fly than ever before. This family of airliners replaced larger, more expensive aircraft that could not profitably serve many cities. At the same time, they gave airlines the capacity to begin more point-to-point services, bypassing busy hubs.

It is no wonder, then, that air travel continues to flourish nearly two decades after the 767 and 757 entered commercial service. And, as older aircraft are retired, airlines around the world continue to look to these aircraft as the medium-sized workhorses of the new century.

A Growing Family

The miracle of flight is sustained every day at the Boeing Company.

In two oversized factories near Seattle, Washington, along the damp north-west coast of the United States, aircraft parts in every state of assembly – wings, tails, fuselage sections, noses, landing gear, and aluminium and titanium of all shapes and sizes – lie throughout the cavernous buildings, waiting to come together like some giant jigsaw puzzle. They are assembled into fuselage sections, which are joined together, riveted to wings and filled with hydraulic cables, electronics, wiring, seats, bins and carpeting. After forty-five days' work, an aircraft sits on its wheels, ready for painting and delivery to anywhere in the world. For more than forty years, this is how Boeing has produced the most popular commercial aircraft in the world – its famous 'Seven Series'.

Between the show-stopping 747 and the all-new 777, two dynamic models were designed and developed – the 767 and the 757 – ushering in a new era of fuel-efficient flight and cutting-edge technology. These workhorses of the skies evolved at a critical juncture in aviation history. With spiralling oil prices, rapidly expanding airlines needed to replace expensive, first-generation airliners. At the same time, new technology emerged that would help make the newest members of the Boeing family the most cost-effective, efficient and reliable airliners ever made.

The genesis of Boeing's 757/767 family is revealed in the company's 1972 annual report: 'We are studying new airplane types employing advanced technology that will make air transportation more efficient and more attractive. We have established a design investigative effort, designated the 7X7, to explore a possible new family of Boeing airplanes. Discussions of our design concepts are under way with a number of carriers.'

These were hopeful words at a difficult time. By the early 1970s, Boeing had sold twenty billion dollars' worth of 707s, 727s, 737s and 747s, but had yet to see steady profits. Less than a decade later, with cash finally flowing in, Boeing launched two new twin-engined aircraft: the wide-body 767 and its smaller, narrow-body sister, the 757.

These new additions to Boeing's aircraft family gave airlines the aircraft they needed to combat rising fuel prices, to feed a growing market demanding point-to-point service, and to modernize ageing fleets. The sleek 767 and 757 would go on to become the most fuel-efficient commercial airliners of the time, standard-bearers against which technology of future civil air transports were judged. Over time, their design hallmarks were incorporated into newer Boeing aircraft – the 747-400, the 777, and seven models of the popular 737 series.

The family's list of firsts is impressive. The 767 was the first twin-engined aircraft certified for transcontinental flight. It was the first commercial airliner to cross oceans on two engines. Both the 767 and 757 were the first aircraft with an all-digital flight deck, built specifically for two crew members. Both were built with a composite material that was lighter and sturdier than aluminium, and their all-new wing designs helped to set a number of twin-engine speed and distance records.

Both planes, thanks to their economical operating costs and technical reliability, gave airlines around the world the capacity to open new routes that would have been uneconomical to operate with other aircraft. In turn, the 767 and 757 have made non-stop air travel more convenient and affordable for air travellers. Today, the 767 is the leading aircraft across the Atlantic – more than thirty carriers use it on these routes – and the 757 is the most popular model on transcontinental flights in the United States, and a favourite of European charter carriers.

Similarities and Differences

Introduced within five months of each other, the 767 and 757 are very much alike. Both aircraft share the same technological advancements in propulsion, aerodynamics, avionics and materiel. Both burn less fuel and make less noise than previous airliners. Both aircraft are powered by two engines, and both have many of the same components, including an electronic flight deck that replaces instruments and gauges with video display terminals, giving rise to the term 'glass cockpit'. Pilots qualified to fly one model can fly the other with little additional training.

In fact, 35 airlines operate both types largely because such commonality reduces training and simulator costs, and spare parts requirements.

The 767's size is between that of a 757 and the 777. The two-aisle, medium- to long-range wide-body is available in five models: the 767-200 and -200ER (extended range); the 767-300 and -300ER, stretched versions of the -200; and the 767-300 freighter. The 767 family is being joined by a sixth model, the larger 767-400ER, itself stretched from the -300 derivative.

The smaller, medium-range 757-200, designed to replace the 727, retains a standard-body, single-aisle configuration. Its capacity is between that of the 737-400 and the 767, making it the world's largest narrow-body aircraft. The 757 is also offered as a freighter and as a combi. The 757-200 is joined by the 757-300, a stretched derivative. The 757-300, along with the 767-400, ensure that the aircraft family will grow and serve airports around the world well into the new century.

Every month, about four 757s leave the assembly line in Renton, Washington, destined for any one of 50 airlines in 27 nations around the world. More than 920 757s will be in service at the dawn of the new millennium. Thirty-five miles (56km) north of Renton, in the city of Everett, four of the larger, wide-body 767s roll out every month, adding to a worldwide fleet in service with 60 airlines in 39 countries. More than 825 767s will be flying early in the next century.

The 767 has already carried nearly 820 million people on more than 5 million flights over 20 million hours of service. The 757 has transported 1 billion people a total of 1.5 billion miles (2.4 billion km) – 16 times the distance from Earth to the sun.

Designing, developing and building both aircraft at once was no small feat. When the 767/757 programme was formally announced in the late 1970s, it was the most aggressive and ambitious new airliner programme ever. It offered a challenge that perhaps only one company, with a rich tradition in aviation stewardship, could meet.

A 767 and 757 together in an animated drawing. Boeing

CHAPTER ONE

History

From Seaplanes to Missiles

'Boeing ... The very word, cold in print but rich in association, invokes images as vivid as man's memories and imagination can create.

'Images of mighty jetliners, leaving white contrails frozen against the blue sky as they streak across continents and oceans, shrinking a world that now measures distances in hours, not miles.

'Images of the great bombers defending the nation.

'Images of an American corporation whose name has become synonymous with technical excellence and integrity.'

(From *Legend and Legacy*
by Robert J. Sterling, 1992)

The development of flight has been remarkable. In less than 100 years, powered flight has progressed from canvas, wood and a single passenger flying a few yards, to more than 400 people on one jet flying non-stop half-way around the world. At the same time, flying has become safer, cheaper and more reliable.

To understand the philosophy behind the Boeing 767 and 757, it is important to understand the history of their maker.

The Boeing legacy goes back to aviation's infancy. In 1915, just a dozen years after the Wright brothers flew 120ft (40m) on their first attempt to take mankind skywards – a distance shorter than the length of the 767-200 – a Seattle timberman, William Edward Boeing, was assembling his first seaplane in a boathouse. It was a humble beginning for a company that today produces more commercial jets than any other in the world, and prides itself on being the largest exporter of the USA.

The Boeing Company has been linked, step by step, with the development of aviation. It built fighters for the First World War, bombers for the Second World War and the first commercial transporters in the 1930s and 1940s. In 1954, Boeing developed the Dash 80, the prototype for the Boeing 707, ushering in the jet age of commercial air transportation.

It all began with curiosity about those incredible flying machines. In 1910, 28-year-old William Boeing travelled to Los Angeles to see the first American air show. He returned to Seattle excited and enthused, but found few people who shared his interest. At the time aircraft were unreliable and rickety, barely able to lift their own weight.

Undeterred, Boeing turned to Lt. Conrad Westervelt, a naval engineer based at nearby Bremberton Navy Yard, to create a new, more practical aircraft based on design standards for Navy vessels. Westervelt designed Boeing's first plane, which was named the B&W, for Boeing and Westervelt. The single-engined biplane, with two pontoons, was crafted from wood, linen and wire. It was completed in June 1916. Since there was no such thing as an aircraft worker, that first Boeing model was assembled by a ragtag team of shipbuilders, carpenters, cabinet-makers and seamstresses.

According to company lore, just before the maiden flight of the B&W, Boeing grew impatient when it seemed that the test pilot was late. He took the controls himself. As the tardy pilot hurried to the hangar, he could only watch as Boeing taxied to the end of Seattle's Lake Union, turned and took off. The first Boeing aeroplane flew for a quarter of a mile (400m).

Westervelt never designed another plane for Boeing. He was transferred to fleet duty. The first two B&Ws, unable to arouse the interest of the US Navy, were sold to the New Zealand Flying School for pilot training and used for express and air mail deliveries.

Boeing officially entered the aircraft business on 15 July 1916, with an enterprise initially called the Pacific Aero Products Company. A year later, the fledgling company became known as the Boeing Airplane Company. A visible reminder of Boeing's legacy in the region stands today on East Marginal Way in Seattle, in the form of a replica of the red wooden building that housed the original company. Boeing went after the best engineers in the

country to design new planes. In 1916, he employed 24 people. The lowest wage was 14 cents an hour and top pilots earned $200 to $300 a month. William Boeing used his own finances to guarantee a loan that covered all the wages – about $700 per week.

Navy orders during the First World War helped the Boeing company to grow. After the war, with demand dwindling, William Boeing decided that air mail was a way to get the business going again. On 2 March 1919, Boeing and pilot Eddie Hubbard took off in a Boeing Model C from Lake Union north across the Canadian border to Vancouver. The return trip to Seattle, with a pouch of Canadian mail, took three hours. It was the first international air mail flight from the United States. However, even this milestone was not enough to keep the company fluid, and it was teetering on the verge of bankruptcy in the 1920s.

After Charles Lindbergh's historic transatlantic solo flight, in 1927, the future of American aviation began to look considerably more rosy. Boeing took his company public in 1928. A year later, he became chairman of United Aircraft and Transport Corp., a diversified trust made up of some of America's early aerospace leaders. The group comprised Boeing and other aircraft companies Chance Vought, Stearman and Sikorsky; engine manufacturer Pratt & Whitney; propeller maker Hamilton; and United Airlines, previously known as Boeing Air Transport.

In 1934, the US Mail Act banned any connection between an aircraft or engine manufacturer and an airline. United Aircraft and Transport was forced to splinter into Boeing, United Airlines (today the world's largest airline), and United Aircraft Corp., the predecessor of United Technologies Corp., whose holdings today include Pratt & Whitney, Sikorsky and Hamilton Standard.

Boeing's tradition of building passenger aircraft began in 1928 with the Model 80, America's first airliner designed specifically for passenger comfort and convenience.

The Model 80 carried twelve passengers in a cabin appointed with leather seats, reading lamps, ventilation, and hot and cold running water. Commercial aviation did not immediately catch on, because of the high cost of flying and lack of airports. However, for those few people who could afford tickets, Boeing planes quickly began to earn a reputation for reliability and comfort.

The Boeing 247, developed in 1933, was considered to be the world's first modern passenger transport. The all-metal, twin-engined plane was the first with an autopilot, pneumatically operated de-icing equipment, a variable-pitch propeller, and retractable landing gear. It completed the trip between New York and Los Angeles in 20 hours, seven and a half hours quicker than any previous airliner. The Model 247 was the first in a long line of durable Boeing workhorses. Along with the DC-2 and DC-3 from rival Douglas, the 247 brought speed, reliability, safety and comfort in air travel to the world. Although the 247, and the improved 247D, were soon outclassed by the immortal DC-3, its place in history was secure.

Following the success of the 247, the Boeing Company began to concentrate on large aircraft, starting with the Model 314 Clipper and the Stratoliner. The Clipper, based on an experimental bomber, came about in response to a demand for an aircraft able to cross oceans; it was a four-engined, long-range flying boat. The Stratoliner was the

first pressurized airliner – a Boeing innovation without which commercial jet travel could not have happened. It was also the first plane to employ a flight engineer in the cockpit, a move later reversed with jets.

Perhaps more than its early successes in commercial aviation, it was the onset of the Second World War that vaulted Boeing into aviation history. Among its contributions were the B-17 Flying Fortress – the workhorse of the American and British bombing fleets – and the B-29 Superfortress, one of which, the *Enola Gay*, dropped the first atomic bomb to hasten the end of the war.

Boeing produced 60 planes a month in 1942, and 250 a month by 1943. Thousands of women, symbolized by 'Rosie the Riveter,' flooded the workforce, boosting production to an amazing 362 planes per month by March 1944. On one occasion, the Seattle plant rolled out 16 planes in 24 hours.

With the end of the war, commercial aircraft production flourished, using the technical innovations developed during the conflict. Boeing's Model 377 Stratocruiser, a design based on the B-29 bomber, set a new standard for luxurious travel, carrying up to 100 passengers in extra-wide cabins connected to a lower deck lounge by a circular staircase. Boeing built 56 Stratocruisers between 1947 and 1950. However, Boeing did not become a major producer of passenger transports until the dawn of the jet age.

The Jet Age

Boeing engineers had envisioned a jet-powered plane as early as 1943. Using engineering and manufacturing experience gained from building the B-29, and knowledge from the German scientists and engineers who pioneered jet aviation, Boeing designed the world's first swept-wing jet bomber, the B-47 Stratojet. That was followed by the eight-engined B-52, which is still in service today. These early jet successes gave Boeing the foundation to launch commercial jet service.

Boeing engineer Wellwood Beall returned to Boeing in 1950 after delivering an order of Stratocruisers to the British Overseas Airways Corporation. He told his colleagues how the British had developed a medium-range airliner, the de Havilland Comet. Although that plane largely failed to capture of the imagination of the airlines, Beall and other Boeing engineers became convinced that jets were the planes of the future. By then, propeller-driven aircraft were becoming difficult and costly to maintain. The high speed and efficiency of the jet made long-distance air travel more practical.

In a decision that would revolutionize air travel, Boeing announced, in August 1952, that it would invest $16 million, two-thirds of its post-war net profits, to build a prototype for a new long-range, jet-powered aircraft. This was to be known as the Dash 80,

The Boeing 247, developed in 1933, was considered the world's first modern passenger transport, including retractable landing gear. Pratt & Whitney

From the 707 on, Boeing believed in offering a family of aircraft. Pratt & Whitney

and was the plane that ultimately became the Boeing 707. The four-engined 707 was completed in 1954, before its primary competitor, the DC-8, hit the market. The timing gave Boeing an advantage that it never lost, and ultimately led to the merger of Boeing and McDonnell Douglas in 1997.

The 707, the first 'Seven Series' aircraft, cut air-travel time almost in half for flights from one US coast to the other. The plane flew high above turbulent clouds, and the noisy vibrations heard in the cabins of propeller-driven aircraft were reduced. The 707's relatively low operating costs brought air fares within reach of more people. The aircraft helped to create the new industry of international air travel. Three decades later, the 707's distant cousins, the 767 and the 757, would refine and sustain that tradition.

Boeing delivered 855 707s between 1957 and 1992, 725 of them for commercial use. Military versions are still being used as tankers and radar aircraft.

From the 707 on, Boeing believed in offering an aircraft family – planes with similar features and a common fuselage that, when used together, would give airlines the ability to fly from 100 to 500 passengers to the next city, or around the world. The 707's airframe influenced the design of future Boeing narrow-body planes, including the 757.

By 1960, Boeing faced increasing competition from the French Caravelle and Britain's Trident in the short-to-medium range of jetliners. The US company envisioned a high-speed jet that would replace the world's ageing turboprop fleet. The 727, the company had forecast, would have low operating costs, a durable airframe and reliable equipment – the hallmarks of later Boeing transports. It would also be able to use small airports, and to fly in bad weather, and would have quick turnaround times at airports. With the financial backing of several US airlines, Boeing unveiled the three-engined 727 in 1962. Originally, Boeing had planned to build 250 of the planes. They proved so popular that a total of 1,831 were produced by 1983.

In 1965, Boeing saw an opportunity for a small, short-range jet – the 737 – that would feature the same fuselage cross-section as the 707 and 727. 'Fat Albert,' as it was called, would go on to become the most prolific airliner ever built. Besides two early versions, the 737-100 and -200, Boeing produced the upgraded -300, -400 and -500 series. Three 'Next Generation' 737 models have entered service, the 737-600, -700 and -800, ensuring this type will dominate the skies on short-haul routes far into the next century. A longer derivative, the 737-900, not much smaller than the 757, will be the longest 737 when it flies early in the new century.

Boeing has delivered more than 3,000 737s, and more than 1,000 more are on order and being built side-by-side with 757s in Renton. Since the 737's debut, in 1967, more than 280 airlines in more than 100 countries have ordered the aircraft. Boeing likes to point out that more than 800 737s are in the air at any time, with one taking off every six seconds.

Arguably Boeing's most famous model, the 747 jumbo jet, was developed at a time when air traffic was growing, fares were falling and higher-thrust engines were developing. When Boeing approached the airlines about a 550-seat jetliner in 1966, the reaction was positive. Launch customer Pan Am placed a $525 million order almost immediately.

The 747s are produced in the same building – the largest on earth, by volume – as the 767s and the all-new 777s. Boeing followed up an already huge 747 with an extended upper-deck 747-300 and a longer-range 747-400. A total of more than 1,200 747s have been built.

Despite the rapid succession of new planes, a recession in the early 1970s forced Boeing to reduce its workforce from 80,400 to 37,200. A billboard outside Seattle read, 'Will the last person out please turn out the lights.' The company went 18 months without a new domestic order. This sour economic period, influenced by rising energy costs, inspired a new generation of airliners – the 767 and 757 – which would become Boeing's most fuel-efficient aircraft. The advances of these new planes secured Boeing's future and influenced its later models.

The 727 was Boeing's answer to short-haul travel. The 757 was designed more than 20 years later to replace the 727. Pratt & Whitney

The World's Largest Aerospace Company

On 1 August 1997, Boeing, also a maker of military fighters, space rockets and missiles, merged in a $16 billion deal with another American aviation powerhouse, the McDonnell Douglas Company, to create the world's largest aerospace company. The acquisition turned the world's leading manufacturer of commercial jets into the biggest maker of military aircraft as well. At the time, McDonnell Douglas was producing only a handful of commercial planes – the MD-80, MD-90 and MD-11. Boeing decided to halt production of these models, but to continue making the MD-95, a shorter version of the MD-80, itself a derivative of the DC-9. The MD-95 was later renamed the Boeing 717-200.

The merger gave Boeing customers in 145 countries, generating $45 billion in revenues in 1997. In 1998, Boeing delivered 563 jets, surpassing the 1997 total of 375. It takes the effort of a nation – with a great deal of help from suppliers around the world – for every Boeing jet to take flight. The giant aerospace company employs 200,000 people in 27 US states and two Canadian provinces.

Today there are more Boeing planes flying than any other manufacturer's.

Numbering

The designation of Boeing's 'Seven Series' commercial fleet had always increased by one number over time, each model distinguished by a different middle numeral. The 707 was followed by the 727, then came the 737 and 747. The 707 should have been the 700, if the tradition of earlier Boeing aircraft whose numbers began with 2, 3 or 4 had been followed (the numbers 5 and 6 were used for missiles and pilotless aircraft). According to company lore, Boeing's first jet-powered commercial airliner was known as the 707 rather than the 700 because the public relations department thought it a good idea.

No matter what the story, the model numbers 757 and 767 were out of sequence. Why? Since both planes were designed around the same time, it was seen as necessary to define one model as smaller than the other. The 757 is a smaller plane and therefore was given the lower middle numeral. The wide-body 767 actually predated the smaller 757 in final design, first

The Missing Model

Whatever happened to the 717, the 'missing' model number in Boeing's 'Seven Series'?

In January 1998, Boeing renamed the MD-95, a plane it inherited from its merger with McDonnell Douglas, as the Boeing 717-200. This struck aviation historians as peculiar, since the model number 717 showed up in Boeing history as a military plane. The moniker was originally assigned in 1956 to the KC-135 Stratotanker aerial refueller, a 707 lookalike, of which nearly 200 are still in service with the US Air Force.

In the 1950s, Boeing began assigning a set of numbers to each of its product lines – 600 for missiles, 700 for commercial jets, and so on. Every significant initiative in a series was assigned a number, even if it was just a sketch. When the 707 came out in 1954, the marketing people decided they liked the sound of '707' so much that every 700-series jet would end with a 7.

The 717 was also to be the name of a shorter-range 707, but that was later changed to the Boeing 720. The first 'new' 717 enters service in 1999.

flight and entry into service. Despite separate developmental paths, though, the two programmes soon merged to become one complementary dynamic duo that would redefine commercial aviation.

CHAPTER TWO

Design and Development

Origins

The 767, Boeing's second wide-body and fifth 'Seven Series' aircraft, was known in its infancy as the 7X7 – a name that once had been assigned to a brand-new aircraft Boeing was to build with Aeritalia of Italy. When that project was dropped, the 7X7 evolved in the mid-1970s into a transcontinental airliner sized between the 727 and the 747, yet smaller than the McDonnell Douglas DC-10, or its similar-sized rival, the Lockheed L-1011. The 767 was also the prime competitor of a new airliner being introduced by a scrappy new European consortium, Airbus – the A300 – and is often confused with it. The 767 targeted high-density routes, and its prospective customers were large US airlines. It was originally envisioned by designers as a potential wide-body version of the 727, complete with the 727's hallmark tri-engine design.

The 757, meanwhile, was originally known as the 7N7. Boeing's fourth narrow-body, or standard-body, model, it began as an airliner study project in 1976. Strictly a derivative of the 727, it was intended as a replacement for the 727. The only difference between the 727 and the 757 was that the 757 was to have two wing-mounted engines instead of two on the aft fuselage and one on the tail. In time, however, an all-new aircraft was born. The 757, which at first was not supposed to be similar to the 767 except for the Boeing name, ended up with many of the same features as its larger cousin, including an identical flight deck.

Introducing two new models five months apart was something no other aircraft manufacturer has ever done. (Boeing did roll out the 737-400 and 747-400 on the same day in 1988, but both planes were derivatives.) The risks were great, and the rewards uncertain.

The early and mid-1970s brought many new challenges to the aviation industry. In the United States, the airline industry was weak, and no carrier had sufficient funds for a new aircraft programme. Even when US airlines began to make money again, in 1976, the scars of recession and high fuel prices remained, and it was not until the middle of 1978 that the all-new 767 programme could begin. The aim was to reduce costs per seat for the first time, without having to build a bigger airliner.

With vivid memories of sky-high fuel costs, airlines demanded a fuel-efficient aircraft that would boost their bottom line. They were also looking for a plane that would fill capacity gaps between the Boeing 727 and the larger wide-bodies, the DC-10, L-1011 and the 747.

Another factor contributed to the need for a new model. In the 1970s, the US Civil Aeronautics Board (later disbanded) initiated moves allowing for more airline competition in the USA. This led, in December 1979, to the passing of the Airline Deregulation Bill, which eliminated route control and gave airlines permission to fly anywhere they pleased. With more frequent flights to more cities, the airlines needed more planes.

Early Orders

Despite the perceived demand, many in the aviation industry were sceptical about plans for new medium-haul airliners, feeling they might detract from the highly successful 727. Boeing's intention was that, instead of buying the 767 to expand fleets, as had been the case with the 747, airlines

A British Airways 757. BA was a launch customer for the model. Peter Sweeten/Aviation Images Worldwide

Specification – 767-200/-200ER	
Engines (two):	Pratt & Whitney PW4056; General Electric CF6-80C2
Dimensions:	Overall length 159ft 2in (48.51m); height 52ft (15.85m); wingspan 156ft 1in (47.57m); cabin width 15ft 5in (4.7m); cabin height 9ft 5in (2.87m); cabin length 111ft 4in (33.93m)
Passengers:	181 (three class), 224 (two class), up to 285 for charter
Cargo volume:	2,875 cubic ft (81.4 cubic m)
Fuel capacity:	16,700 gallons (63,200 litres); 24,140 gallons (91,400 litres) for extended-range model
Weights:	Plane weight 177,500–186,000lb (80,510–84,370kg); max. take-off weight 300,000–335,000lb (136,080–151,956kg), 345,000–395,000lb (156,492–179,172kg) for extended-range model; max. payload 38,010–43,200lb (17,240–19,595kg); max. landing weight 270,000lb (122,470kg), 285,000lb (129,275kg) for extended-range model
Performance:	Max. speed 0.80 Mach Max. landing speed 157mph (252km/h) Max. operating altitude 42,000ft (12,800m) Range 3,636–4,430 miles (5,852–7,130km), 5,869–7,675 miles (9,445–12,352km) for extended-range model
Take-off field length:	5,900–6,500ft (1,798–1,981m); 7,900–8,900ft (2,408–2,713m) for extended-range model

would use the 767, and later the 757, to replace older planes in their fleet. Boeing knew from the start that the 767 would not sell as briskly as the 747 had in the 1960s, but they optimistically projected sales of between 1,000 and 1,500 767s by 1990. In fact, 343 models were delivered by 1990. By 1998, more than 700 had been delivered, all but 250 of them the stretched -300 model. While the airlines had bought 225 747s in the first five years of their production, Boeing delivered just 156 767s in that programme's first five years.

When the 757 debuted, Boeing forecast the need for 1,400 such airliners into the 1990s. By 1990, just 332 757s had been delivered; more than 800 were in service by 1998, with another 100-plus on order.

Early orders for the two aircraft were relatively low because the recession of 1980-81 made airlines cautious. In addition, despite the perception of an increase in demand for new aircraft following deregulation of the US airline industry, the changes in the system initially had the opposite effect. One of deregulation's major legacies was the build-up of the hub and spoke system, begun by Delta Air Lines at Atlanta. The carriers established hubs in the USA by feeding traffic into various cities where passengers connected with other flights to their final destination. The hub system gave airlines greater schedule flexibility and increased flight frequency, but it also cut down on the number of non-stop, point-to-point flights, many of which had provided long-haul services between major cities. This hurt the 767 and, to a degree, the 757, but it boosted sales of the smaller, short-hop 737.

In light of this situation, the planes, in fact, sold better than many experts had predicted. The 757, in particular, was a surprising success, although Boeing was criticized for introducing a new narrow-body plane at a time when wide-bodies were so popular.

Boeing worked for more than four years on the design of both aircraft before they were launched officially. They became known as Boeing's 'New Generation' aircraft – light, efficient, powerful and comfortable.

Specification

The 767-200, the first 767 model, is 159ft 2in (48.5m) long, with a wing span of 156ft 1in (47.6m). Its cabin is 15ft 5in (4.7m) wide. The 767-200 can carry 181-224 passengers (up to 285 in a single-class, charter configuration) for up to 5,260 miles (8,465km), at speeds of .80 Mach, or 530 mph (848km/h). The 767-200ER (extended range) can fly up to 7,660 miles

Specification – 767-300	
Engines (two):	Pratt & Whitney PW4056; General Electric CF6-80C2; Rolls-Royce RB211-524G/H
Dimensions:	Overall length 180ft 3in (54.94m); height 52ft (15.85m); wingspan 156ft 1in (47.57m); cabin width 15ft 5in (4.7m); cabin height 9ft 5in (2.87m); cabin length 132ft 5in (40.36m)
Passengers:	218 (three class), 269 (two class), up to 350 for charter
Cargo volume:	4,030 cubic ft (114.2 cubic m)
Fuel capacity:	16,700 gallons (63,200 litres); 24,140 gallons (91,400 litres) for extended-range model
Weights:	Plane weight 192,100lb (87,135kg), 199,600lb (90,535kg) for extended-range model; max. take-off weight 345,000–351,000lb (156,490–159,213kg), 380,000–412,000lb (172,368–186,883kg) for extended-range model; max. payload 52,200lb (23,675kg), 45,780lb (20,765kg) for extended-range model; max. landing weight 300,000lb (136,080kg)
Performance:	Max. speed 0.80 Mach Max. landing speed 162mph (251km/h) Max. operating altitude 42,000ft (12,800m) Range 4,603 miles (7,408km), 6,760 miles (10,880km) for extended-range model
Take-off field length:	8,100–9,000ft (2,469–2,743m)

(12,330km). The stretched 767-300 is 180ft 3in (54.9m) long and can carry 218-269 passengers for 4,300 miles (7,340km); for the extended-range version, that distance is up to 6,830 miles (10,990km).

The 757 is the about same length as the 727-200 and shares the same cross-section, but it can carry more passengers. The 757-200 is 155ft 3in (47.3m) long with a wingspan of 124ft 10in (38m). Its cabin measures 11ft 7in (3.5m) across. The 757 can carry 201–231 passengers up to 4,520 miles (7,240km), at speeds of .80 Mach flying at 34,000ft (11,333m).

The first 767 rolled out of the factory on 4 August 1981, and flew for the first time on 26 September 1981. The 767 entered service nearly a year later, on 8 September 1982. The 757 was unveiled on 13 January 1982, and first flew on 19 February 1982. It entered service on 1 January 1983.

Specification – 757-200	
Engines (two):	Pratt & Whitney PW2037 or PW2040; Rolls-Royce RB211-535E4
Dimensions:	Overall length 155ft 3in (47.32m); height 44ft 6in (13.56m); wingspan 124ft 10in (38.05m); cabin width 11ft 7in (3.53m); cabin height 7ft (2.13m); cabin length 118ft 5in (36.1m)
Passengers:	178, 186, 202 or 208 (two class), 214, 220, 223, 224 or 239 (one class)
Cargo volume:	1,790 cubic ft (50.7 cubic m)
Fuel capacity:	11,276 gallons (42,684 litres)
Weights:	Plane weight 127,810lb (57,975kg); max. take-off weight 220,000–255,500lb (99,800–115,900kg); max. landing weight 210,000lb (95,255kg);
Performance:	Max. speed 0.86 Mach Max. landing speed 152mph (245km/h) Max. operating altitude 42,000ft (12,800m) Range (186 passengers) 3,200–4,520 miles (5,150–7,240km)
Take-off field length:	5,875ft (1,791m)

The 767 made its debut five months prior to the 757, Boeing's other fuel-efficient twin jet. Boeing

CHAPTER THREE

Evolution of the 767 and 757

The Needs of the Market

Boeing's fortunes were at a low point when the first steps were taken towards the launch of the 767. The shape of that first new aircraft was far from certain when Boeing's New Aircraft Programme was formulated, in 1970–71. The initial objective was to establish likely aircraft market requirements for the next decade, and to see how the company might respond to those needs by developing one or more new types to complement or replace such models as the Boeing 707 and McDonnell Douglas DC-8.

Why develop a new aircraft? With the world's commercial fleet rapidly ageing, Boeing recognized the availability of a decade's worth of new technology. At the same time, there was an urgent need for energy-efficient aircraft that could operate under stricter noise regulations. The aviation industry was also a changing market that demanded new capacities. Boeing spelled out these needs in an early internal memo with these arguments for a new plane:

'A significant US market exists for a 180-passenger, transcontinental-range airplane.'
'Improvements in noise and fuel productivity are important.'
'Two-aisle comfort level and standardized cargo containers are required.'
'Airline economics are of paramount importance.'

During 1971, a whole range of possible new airliner designs was examined. In August 1971, the company released an artist's impression of a possible 'advanced technology transport', which it described as 'one of several possible configurations now being studied for future application to long-range air routes'. The aircraft featured a narrow fuselage with accommodation for 200 passengers, a highly swept-back wing with supercritical airfoil, two engines on the rear fuselage and one under each wing, and a Mach .98 cruising speed. It was given the designation 767, but it was actually unrelated to the eventual design. This was just the beginning of a long process.

The 7X7 Series

Earlier in 1971, Boeing had concluded an agreement with Aeritalia for the joint development of a quiet, short-haul Short Take-off and Landing (STOL) airliner for 100–150 passengers – the Model 751. The plan was that the plane would be in service by 1975, delivered from assembly lines established simultaneously in Italy and the United States, but the project was dropped a year later.

Boeing and Aeritalia next collaborated on a proposed QSH (Quiet Short Haul) jet transport that could operate at close-in airports with short runways. This objective was based on the marketing hypothesis that new technology – high bypass-ratio engines, improved acoustic materials and unique configurations for noise shielding – would achieve a significant reduction in noise. This version was given the names Model 751-207A and 751-612A, but this proposal did not materialize either. Instead, in September 1972, the QSH venture evolved into one advanced aircraft programme, for which the designation 7X7 was used for the first time. (The 'X' was given because it was uncertain what the range of the new aircraft would be.) The objective of the programme was to 'determine the appropriate new aircraft which will complement the present Boeing product line and be sized to meet airline requirements beginning in the mid-1970s'.

The adoption of the 7X7 designation emphasized that the new aircraft, when launched, would be a member of the Boeing family. In early 1973, Boeing made presentations to a number of airlines, showing a family of related designs in the 7X7 series. The target date for the launch was 1 January 1974, with service entry in 1977. However, it would be another four years before the 7X7 was finally defined, after many permutations, into the shape of the 767. No less than 240 different configurations were considered in moulding the first 767 model, the 767-200.

Early 7X7 configurations included a small, medium-range twin-jet with 140 seats, known as Model 751-651. Initially, this version had engines mounted on top of the wing, to project noise upwards and away from the ground. For longer-range variants, which drew the interest of airlines, a three-engined 7X7 was proposed by 1 May 1973 (Model 751-666), bearing two engines underwing and one in the rear fuselage in a 727-type installation. Seating capacity would be about 200, but in these early proposals Boeing demonstrated an open mind on fuselage cross-sections, showing possible cabins with six- and seven-abreast layouts, and even an eight-abreast, high-density arrangement.

To serve long routes, another version of the 7X7 was studied, this time with four overwing engines. This version included Models 751-802, 751-882-1 and 751-892-1. (By January 1974, the wing placement on this version was switched to underwing, nacelle-mounted engines for reduced fuel consumption.) All were intended as all-new aircraft, with no commonality with existing Boeing aircraft. As a result of the OPEC fuel crisis in 1973, the primary design objective changed from minimum noise to minimum fuel burn.

In its first round of airline briefings on the new model, Boeing contacted thirty-seven airlines in an attempt to establish an acceptable specification for the 7X7, including cockpit, interior, engines and nacelles. From this point on, the eventual launch customer, United Airlines, played a key role in the 767 definition. However, in 1974–6, airlines were struggling to recover from recession and the first fuel crisis in 1973, and, while Boeing constantly refined its 7X7 proposals, no consensus could be found on which one to launch as a final design.

By this time, a realization of the economic realities was setting in. The impact of the fuel crisis was making itself felt, as prices doubled, or even tripled, around the world. Inflation rates were growing, and interest rates rose. Boeing saw short-haul airline traffic increasing at the expense of long-haul and international traffic. Previously grounded wide-bodies were returned to service, and older aircraft were being retired.

On 20 August 1974, Boeing agreed on a seven-abreast, low-tail tri-jet with 201 seats, known as Model 751-741. At the 1975 Paris Air Show, the aviation industry's largest biennial trade event, Boeing indicated possible options, which included a seven-abreast layout for 175–201 passengers, and a 283-passenger version with eight-abreast seating. By 25 November of

Boeing's new aircraft programme. With strong 727 sales, the company tended to favour three-engine layouts for its new aircraft; three engines, it was felt, would in any case be needed by operators for long, over-water routes. However, Airbus was at the time gaining support for the concept of a big twin, the A300 – bigger, in passenger capacity, than the 7X7 was expected to be – and it was accepted that the decision between twin-jets and tri-jets would in the end be made by airline customers. While Boeing's plans remained fluid, the three large engine manufacturers – General Electric, Pratt & Whitney and Rolls-Royce – busily prepared low-noise powerplants to

which at the time was powering the L-1011.

By the beginning of 1976, another new aircraft designation emerged, the 7N7, which would become the 757. Presentations later that year indicated that the 7X7 remained under study as a medium-range aircraft for 180–200 passengers, but that a 212in (538cm) fuselage diameter was now projected to permit comfortable eight-abreast, two-aisle seating. The 7X7 was now viewed as a medium- to long-range aircraft, with two or three engines. Variables yet to be decided included the exact fuselage width, length, tail position, engines and payload-range capability. By

An early 767 proposal in American Airlines colours. Note the T-tail, later abandoned. Boeing

that year, two new versions evolved: Models 751-770/771, seven-abreast low-tail tri-jets, and an alternate Model 751-954 twin-jet, all with 201 seats.

There were times when the impending launch of a stretched version of the popular 727, the 727-300, would further delay

cover every possible thrust requirement. The 7X7 tri-jet version was based on new engines that were never built: the Pratt & Whitney JT10D and General Electric's CF6-30D. Early twins were based on the Pratt & Whitney JT9D and GE's CF6-6D. Rolls-Royce was offering the RB211-524,

this time, the 7X7 had completed nearly 2,000 hours of wind-tunnel testing to verify the overall aerodynamic characteristics of its layout. Aeritalia was still a full partner with Boeing on the 7X7, on which more than $50 million had been invested by mid-1976.

Design Decisions and Variations

In May 1976, Boeing established a Twin/Tri-jet Task Force to look at three of the biggest issues to be decided: two engines vs. three, a low tail or a T-shaped tail, and seven-abreast or eight-abreast seating. As a result of these discussions, Boeing came out, on 10 August 1976, with two variants: a tri-jet Model 751-336 and twin-jet Model 751-251, each with eight-abreast seating capacity of 203. These further evolved, by November 1976, into the March 1977, Boeing had unveiled a tri-jet with eight-abreast seating, known as the Model 751-424. This was followed a month later by the 751-434, an alternate tri-jet with a T-tail and eight-abreast seating.

Between mid-1976 and the spring of 1977, Boeing made a major configuration change, adopting a T-tail for both the 7X7 and the 7N7, a design used on the 727. The two new programmes, running parallel, had grown closer, with the 7N7 taking advantage of the extensive work on advanced wing design already completed

The hope that management could make a go-ahead decision in October 1977 was found to be over-optimistic, largely because the US airlines that would be likely to launch the aircraft continued to have different opinions on the vital subjects of body width and number of engines. In an attempt to broker a compromise, Boeing reverted, later in 1977, to a 198-in (503-cm) fuselage, and to the 'twin first, tri-jet later' philosophy that it had pursued earlier in the programme.

In August 1977, two more seven-abreast proposals emerged: a twin/tri-jet family

The 767 as it looked prior to the decision to drop the T-tail configuration. This model is shown in the colours of 767 launch customer United Airlines. Boeing

Model 751-377, another tri-jet, and the Model 751-275A, a twin.

The 7X7 programme evolved rapidly by this point into a series of proposals that incorporated all the vexing design decisions. On 14 January 1977, Boeing presented tri-jet and twin models with a low tail and eight-abreast seating for 203 passengers. By 1 February, the wings had been revised to feature a 33-degree sweep, 150ft (45.7m) span and double-slotted flaps. By

for the 7X7. At this point, the 7X7 was to have an eight-abreast fuselage. Boeing said that 'considering the payload/range, critical field operations and over-water flying requirements of some of the key prospective 7X7 customers, the initial version was expected to be a tri-jet'. Out of this, on 22 May 1977, emerged the Model 751-440, a T-tailed, eight-abreast version.

In June 1977, Boeing was still having trouble finalizing the design of the aircraft.

known as Model 751-2016 and Model 751-3006. By October, a twin-jet with 190 seats (Model 751-2042), and a tri-jet with 210 seats (Model 751-3011) were offered.

In the same month, Boeing determined that the new plane would have a seven-abreast cross-section. In December, that configuration was revised to provide for eight-abreast charter seating. A seven-abreast design was deemed to be more efficient for a 200-passenger transport, with less drag and, subsequently, 2 per cent less fuel burn, compared with an eight-abreast cabin.

Boeing considered the seven-abreast, two-aisle body to be a major technological advance, and this configuration later became an industry standard. In addition to the weight and drag reductions achieved, it offered a measure of the passenger comfort and favourable cabin arrangements that Boeing hoped would gain the attention of travellers.

'That was a key decision on the programme,' says Joe Sutter. Regarded as one of the world's pre-eminent aircraft design-

the highest levels in the company: 'What was always pretty certain was the passenger requirement, 180–220 people. We were looking more at the passenger comfort end of it. The seven-abreast set-up seemed to fit well with the two-aisle concept. And two aisles seemed very popular with the airlines.' Mock-ups would later confirm that.

That decision was not easy. Engineers were in dispute over whether the new aircraft should have a larger or smaller configuration. 'After a while, people became convinced that the seven-abreast format

like T-tail. This version was shown to Boeing's board of directors for approval on 22 December 1977.

Initially, the 767 was offered as a short version, the 767-100, and a longer model, the -200. The -100 was offered to satisfy American Airlines' requirements for 175 seats, the -200 to address United Airlines' need for at least 190 seats. The -200 later won out, and the -100 was never built. 'We were proposing the -100 to them, but time caught up,' Sutter says. 'The -200 was actually getting too popular and grew too fast for a -100 to be developed.'

An example of the proposed yet never built 767-100. Boeing

ers, Sutter retired in 1986, having achieved the position of Boeing's executive vice-president overseeing all civil airliner engineering and development. According to him, 'the seven-abreast set-up was the most economically attractive'.

Everett Webb, director of technology for the new programme, who went on to become vice-president of engineering for the 767 programme, says that consideration of the seating configuration went to

was the most favourable,' Webb says. Boeing expanded the proposed fuselage to allow it to squeeze in eight-abreast seating for charter flights and cargo containers if the 7X7 were to become a freighter. The resulting change gave the aircraft better proportions.

With that key decision made, a version similar to what would become the 767 finally evolved. This was the Model 751-2050, a seven-abreast model with a 727-

A decision was finally made about the tail design, and, on 23 May 1978, the low tail was adopted in Model 751-2085C. The low tail features lower cruise drag, a reduction in fuel burn of 2.7 per cent, and increased range. It also allowed easier maintenance and resulted in a shorter overall aircraft length, which improved the ramp and parking characteristics of the 767.

Sutter was in charge of design when the issue of the T-tail came up. 'Boeing had

Configuration comparison.

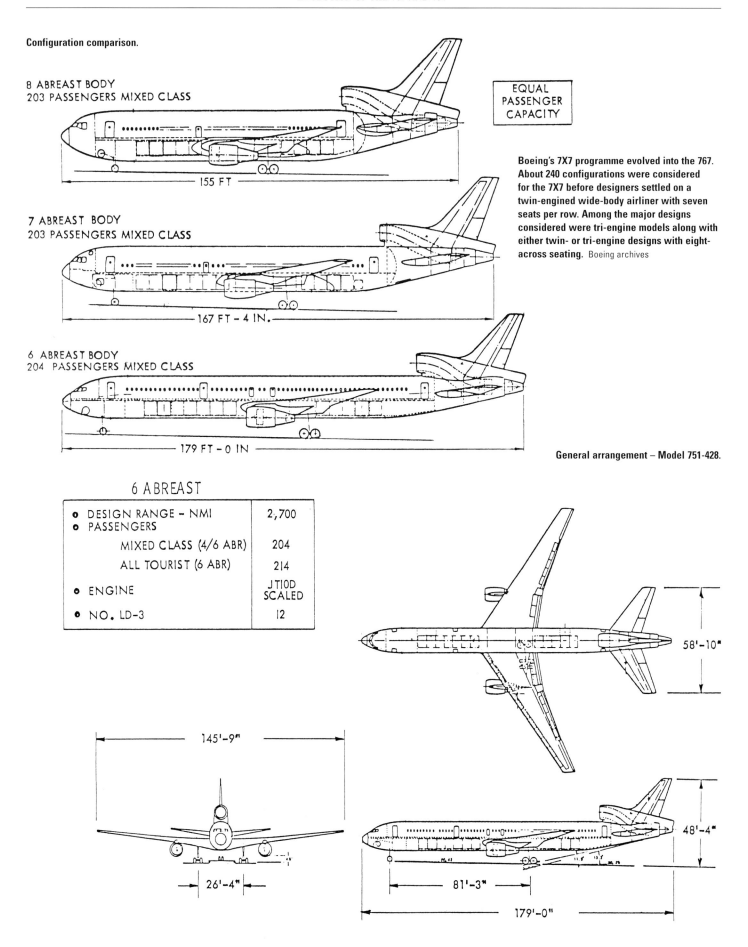

8 ABREAST BODY
203 PASSENGERS MIXED CLASS

155 FT

EQUAL
PASSENGER
CAPACITY

Boeing's 7X7 programme evolved into the 767.
About 240 configurations were considered
for the 7X7 before designers settled on a
twin-engined wide-body airliner with seven
seats per row. Among the major designs
considered were tri-engine models along with
either twin- or tri-engine designs with eight-
across seating. *Boeing archives*

7 ABREAST BODY
203 PASSENGERS MIXED CLASS

167 FT - 4 IN.

6 ABREAST BODY
204 PASSENGERS MIXED CLASS

179 FT - 0 IN

General arrangement – Model 751-428.

6 ABREAST

DESIGN RANGE – NMI	2,700
PASSENGERS	
MIXED CLASS (4/6 ABR)	204
ALL TOURIST (6 ABR)	214
ENGINE	JT10D SCALED
NO. LD-3	12

58'-10"

145'-9"

26'-4"

81'-3"

48'-4"

179'-0"

General arrangement – Model 751-424.

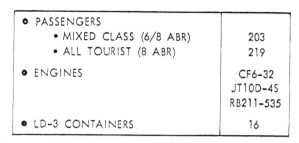

● PASSENGERS	
• MIXED CLASS (6/8 ABR)	203
• ALL TOURIST (8 ABR)	219
● ENGINES	CF6-32
	JT10D-4S
	RB211-535
● LD-3 CONTAINERS	16

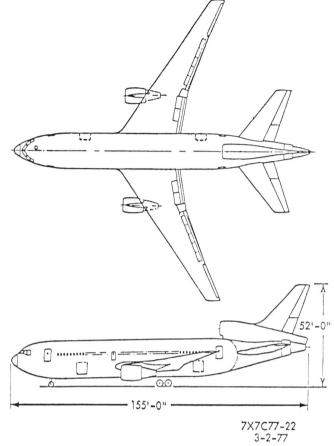

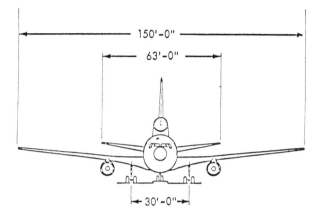

7X7C77-22
3-2-77

Medium range Tri-jet –
Model 751-691 (1973)
Model 751-721
(study configuration – May 1974)

	MODEL 751-691	MODEL 751-721
● WING (SQ FT)	2,250	2,250
• SWEEP (DEGREES)	27°	22°
• ASPECT RATIO	7.8	10
● THRUST (SLST – LB)	26,600	22,800
● TAKEOFF GR WT (LB)	270,000	264,400
● PASSENGERS (MIXED CLASS)	201	215

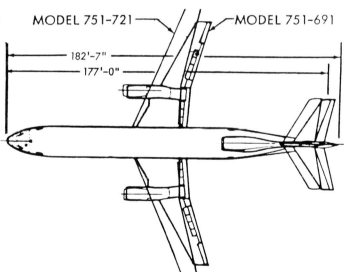

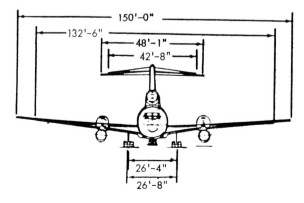

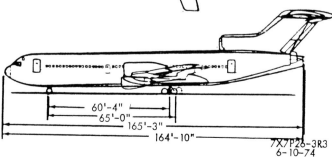

7X7P26-3R3
6-10-74

26.2

Examples of early 7X7 versions that would evolve into the 767. Boeing

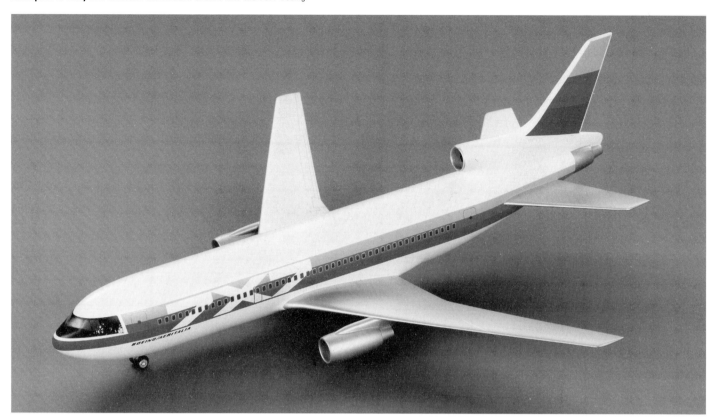

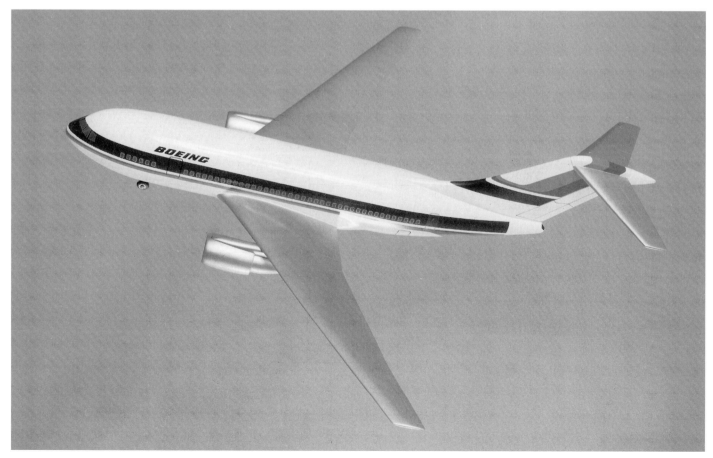

always had a procedure that, when something important is done, why not have others look at the design? On the 767, T-tails were somewhat in disfavour, while others said low tails might have more drag,' he says. 'There was a separate study, starting with the 767, looking at alternatives. That went on for quite a while. I didn't want to lock into the decision. The results ended up saying you could do the problem either way. The decision on the

signed a contract with United and had a big get-together and press conference with [Richard] Ferris [United's chairman at the time]. The day before I was given an *Aviation Week* article about the launch and asked to check it for errors. It was 100 per cent accurate, but the cover showed [Tex] Boullioun [Boeing commercial aircraft group president] and Ferris holding a model – still with a T-tail. Well, overnight, the guys built a model with a low tail to

757 and 767 had been allotted to the new projects that were being offered.

In early 1978, the 767-200 emerged as the central project in Boeing's new aircraft plans. A final round of evaluations took place in May and June, by which time the company was satisfied that the 767-200 met its requirements, and could beat the Airbus A310-200. (A shorter derivative of the A300 was being developed at around the same time.)

An early version of the 767-200, prior to the decision to go with a conventional tail. Boeing

767's tail came down to the fact that maintenance would be easier and that the characteristics of the low tail were more understood. It produced some hard feelings because people chose sides. I got in the middle of that ruckus.'

Interestingly, when the 767 was launched, a cover drawing on the July 1978 issue of *Aviation Week & Space Technology* magazine depicted the new plane with the T-tail, well after the horizontal stabilizer was shifted from the T-tail configuration to the low, conventional location. Sutter relates the story: 'We finally

make sure there would be no mistaking the decision.'

Launch and Production

On 5 January 1978, Boeing announced plans to expand the Everett plant in order to handle the new programme, saying the company would have to begin building at once to be ready for a possible go-ahead decision at mid-year. This important development was followed in mid-February by the announcement that the designations

The 767 programme received the official go-ahead on 14 July 1978, when the board of directors of United Airlines, the largest airline in the United States and a loyal Boeing customer for a long time, announced that it would order thirty 767s equipped with Pratt & Whitney JT9D-7R4 engines, in a deal worth $1.2 billion. The 767 would join the 727, 737 and 747 in United's fleet. United had begun a serious evaluation of the 200-passenger medium-range aircraft in October 1977. They had looked at the A300 and a future McDonnell Douglas version, the DC-X-200, and

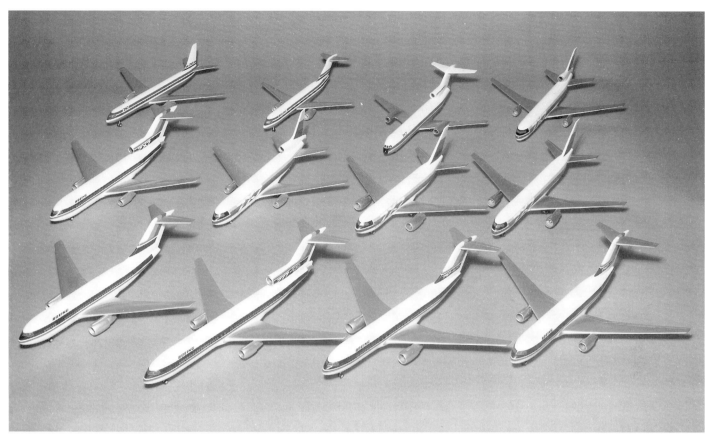

A collection of the various 7X7 proposals, along with two 7N7 versions (back row, first and second from left). Boeing

Three examples of the many different variations of the 7X7. Boeing

Artist's impression of an early version of the 767. Note the T-tail and the short fuselage. Boeing

had nearly selected the A300 over the 767. Airbus, eager to sell its first plane in the United States, offered an attractive financing and support package, but United had been convinced that the 767 was a better aircraft. (Incidentally, Eastern later became the first US airline to fly the A300.)

With production now getting ever closer, the 767's landing gear was changed, in August 1978, to cater for a request by American Airlines to meet requirements at New York LaGuardia Airport's short runways. The aft body arrangement and contours were refined in December 1978, and the final specifications for the interior arrangement were settled in April 1979. Construction of the first 767 began on 6 July 1979.

The United order, with an option for thirty-seven additional 767s, nine of them converted in October 1980, allowed Boeing to put the new aircraft into full-scale development and production. The Everett facility was expanded by 2 million square feet (666,000 square metres) to provide space for the 767 final assembly line. Aeritalia, a prominent partner in early 7X7 design, assumed a 15 per cent share, and was responsible for the design and manufacture of wing control surfaces, the fin, rudder and elevators, wing tips and nose radome.

United's interest did not exactly open the floodgates. It would take another four months after the launch decision before American Airlines and Delta would place an order for 767s, valued at nearly $2 billion, in November 1978. Following these orders, Boeing dropped plans for a three-engined, 219-seat 777. Years later, the idea of a new long-range model evolved into what would, in 1995, become the 777, the world's longest twin-engine aircraft, whose genesis can be attributed to the 767.

In its early days, the 767 captured the attention of eight airlines – United, American, Delta, Air Canada, CPAir (now Canadian Airlines), Pacific Western (now part of Canadian), All Nippon Airways and TWA. Between them, they ordered a total of 135 of the airliners, with options for 128 more.

In an article in the February 1980 issue of *AIR International* magazine, it was considered that the 767 is 'destined to be one of the most important tools of the airline trade in the forthcoming decade'. However, after the initial orders, much work was needed to prepare the 767, Boeing's first new model since the 747 rolled out in 1967, for its first flight.

Twin vs. Tri

While the 757 had always been envisioned with two engines, the number of powerplants on the 767 was a topic of much discussion. As late as the spring of 1978 – well into the design stage – Boeing was still talking about a three-engined 767. The company even distributed a rendering of a plane with a 727-type centre engine and two engines under the wings. It looked just like the L-1011, except for a T-shaped tail, which was later dropped.

The potential buyers – the airlines – helped to determine the end result. United Airlines wanted two engines and American Airlines preferred three. So, in keeping with its tradition of seeking always to please the customer, Boeing announced two versions in February 1978: a twin-engined wide-body carrying 180-200 passengers, and a longer-range, three-engined version.

In the end, the will of Ed Wells, a consultant during the 767's development, who patented the 767's landing gear, played a significant role in deciding that the 767 should have two engines, not three. Boeing had conducted exhaustive studies of the three- vs. two-engine quandary. Generally,

it was found that twin-jets have more total sea-level thrust than tri-jets, resulting in a higher, more fuel-efficient cruising altitude; in addition, the development time would be shorter with a twin. However, studies also found that twin-jets are more limiting in bad weather, due to different emergency-landing field requirements.

Other issues – engine pod size, potential design changes, range, weight and fuel burn – were also debated, making the decision a difficult one. Boeing's headquarters pushed for a twin. 'We went to lots of technical meetings on the weight benefits of the twin vs. tri-jet,' says Everett Webb. 'The twin would have to have at least 48,000lb of thrust for the engines, offering better performance and lower noise. The main thing was that the maintenance and spares would turn out much more to the advantage of airlines, so in many ways the

cost advantage swung the deal. For that to happen, the engine companies had to come up with an improved engine. When we started out – and this programme had a long birth – early in the game there was a big push to come up with an optimum engine of 25,000lb of thrust. With the size of airplane we had, that would have needed three engines.'

Looking back, Webb says the decision to go with two engines on the new plane was vital. 'Going to the twin was probably the most important decision in the programme,' he says.

Besides the economic advantage, the 767 was designed with two engines, in order to keep up with – or beat – the competition. In Europe, Airbus Industrie was developing the A310 – a shorter but longer-range version of the A300 – around the same time as the 767. The A310,

The Everett plant had to be expanded to accommodate the 767, which was to be assembled in the same mammoth building in which the 747 came together. Boeing

essentially the same size as the 767, was a bit pudgier, however, with eight- rather than seven-abreast seating.

A defining moment came in 1976, when engineers pondered a pair of proposed 767 models. One had three engines, the other two. Three engines, some argued, would provide more range, and offer the flying public peace of mind, in case of engine failure. On the other hand, a twin-engine plane would provide airlines with savings in purchase price, maintenance costs and fuel efficiency. Wells called the meeting in a conference room in Renton. As recounted in the Boeing history, *Legend and Legacy*, both models were on display. According to the book, Wells told them, 'I know what's going on. You're spending money on that three-engine project and paying lip service to a twin. You've got it backwards – you should be spending money on the twin and paying nothing more than lip service to a tri-motor.'

Wells, who died of cancer in 1986, felt that the 767's chances for success would ride on fuel efficiency, and that no tri-motor could beat the economics of a twin. In addition, Boeing knew the intense competition

between McDonnell Douglas and Lockheed in the three-engine wide-body market. The market was not big enough for two almost identical planes, let alone a third entry.

'The engines available at the time made the decision for us,' recalls Joe Sutter. 'Compared with the reliability of early engines, these were 20 times more reliable. That got people thinking that you don't need four engines, or even three. The simple reliability of the gas turbine engine made the decision easier. We realized we had to take advantage of that.

'The idea of using twins over water came from the Boeing gang. It was a carefully thought-out process. Selling it first to the certifying authorities and then to the public was going to be a tough job. At the time, everyone liked to look out and see four engines out there. We determined that twins over water were a natural,' Sutter says. 'We were looking at what the plane could do, at least to make it a good North Atlantic airplane.'

The results of 7,000 hours of wind-tunnel tests made the case for a twin-engine plane. They showed that this version would have superb aerodynamic performance. A

combination of generous span and wing area, wing thickness and decreased sweep promised lower fuel consumption with adequate range and speed. It was clear why the twin 767 prevailed.

The 757 Joins the Family

New aircraft are developed when new factors – increased demand, for example, an energy crisis or new technology – appear in air transportation. Noise and fuel were the two primary issues faced by airlines in the 1970s, and the two factors that contributed the most to the rise of the 757.

The energy crisis in late 1973 began with the Yom Kippur War in the Middle East, which spiked jet fuel prices from 11 cents a gallon (4 litres) to $1.10. To address potentially disastrous fuel costs, Boeing's 707/727/737 division in 1974 began to study numerous ways to develop advanced and fuel-efficient aircraft for the future.

This led to the proposed 727-300, a stretched 727-200, which nearly began production in late 1975 with the blessing of

A proposed 757 design, prior to the nose redesign and deletion of 727-like T-tail, shown in the colours of launch customer Eastern Airlines. Boeing

An early 7N7 example. Note the nose's resemblance to the 727's. Boeing

United Airlines. The 727-300 was to have been 20ft (6m) longer, with 35 more seats than the 727-200, along with new engines, leading-edge wing flaps and landing gear.

Large US airlines indicated that, even though the 727-300 was to add capacity, they needed an aircraft that could operate with the same versatility as the 727-200. That meant designing an airliner that could operate with equal aplomb from high altitudes and short runways. To do that, Boeing extended the leading edge of the 727-200 wing, lengthened the wing and added a double-slotted inboard trailing-edge flap. Wind-tunnel tests with re-fanned Pratt & Whitney JT8D engines showed that the 727-300 would save 13 per cent in fuel cost per seat, compared with the 727-200. Noise requirements were also met. In addition, the 727-300 was to have sported new twin four-wheel main landing gears; these eventually became the basis for development of the 757 landing gear.

In the end, airlines found the 727-300 configuration changes expensive, with the improvement in fuel burn per seat insufficient to cover the costs. In addition, even though the model met noise requirements, it was uncertain whether it would survive more stringent restrictions in the future. The age of deregulation in the United States also made airlines unsure of their equipment needs: were smaller planes needed to feed new, point-to-point routes,

or did they need larger aircraft, to build up hubs? The expected return on investment did not warrant the risk. United, the biggest potential customer, backed out after extensive development and review. The 727-300 programme was scrapped in August 1975.

According to Duane Jackson, at the time Boeing's configuration design manager for derivative aeroplane programmes, 'It was a bitter blow to stop the programme after five years of evolution.' Jackson was later involved in the development of the 757.

Towards the 757

The abandoned 727-300 cost Boeing $50 million, but the investment was not in vain. The design evolution proceeded through the 7N7 study programme, which lasted from early 1976 through 1977, and developed in 1978–79 into the 757, a new twin-engined narrow-body that could eventually replace the workhorse 727. During that evolution, Boeing focused on new wings and new high-bypass engines to meet the performance criteria demanded by the airlines. The extensive development work and airline feedback created under the 727-300 programme gave Boeing the necessary direction for their next step.

'We had quite a bit of input from the airlines on what kind of planes they wanted,' says Joe Sutter, known for developing the

747 family and for deciding to mount the engines of the 737 below the wings. 'After a lot of testing on a 727, Boeing determined that a bigger step had to be taken, and that an all-new plane was needed.'

With the 727-300 destined to remain a blueprint, studies of a new aircraft began in January 1976 under the designation 7N7. (It is believed that the 'N' reflected the involvement of Bob Norton, the product development director at the time.) The objectives of this new plane were to meet airline size and performance requirements, to keep costs low, to minimize fuel burn per seat and to reduce noise. In short, a low-cost alternative was being sought in an industry where expenses were mounting daily.

'We rationalized that the 757 could be a reasonably priced derivative approach,' Jackson says. 'It seemed to be a reasonable thought that we could save a large part of the forward section of the 727 and much of the aft body and systems.'

The first step towards the 757 was known in the design stage as Model 761-161. The body of this aircraft was a combination of the 727 and 737, along with new sections. The tail was derived from the 707 and 737. Three engine models appeared as possible powerplants for this new aircraft: the Rolls-Royce RB211-535 and the General Electric CF6-32, both derivatives of engines powering existing wide-body aircraft, and the new Pratt & Whitney JT10D (an engine that never went into production, but evolved into what later became the PW2000). The passenger capacity and low fuel burn of this new plane resulted in outstanding economic improvements compared with the 727.

The 164-passenger Model 761-161 was designed to share the same structure, tools and body systems as the 707/727/737 family. To take advantage of commonality, Boeing decided the aircraft should be developed with the 727's T-tail. Much of the 727's fuselage could then be used in this new model without significant changes, although the centre engine's removal would require a new aft body. This was reflected in Model 761-164, which featured a new-technology wing, high-bypass engines, new landing gear, a modified vertical tail, and seating for 165. Its fuselage was also extended from that of the 727-200.

'Some wanted to preserve the characteristics of the 727,' Sutter says. 'Very late in that design, I called over there and said, "Why don't you look at all of the things considered when going to the low tail on the 767 and then decide?" For the same reasons as on the 767, we came up with the low tail on the 757.'

By January 1978, Boeing began showing this version to Eastern Airlines and British Airways, two carriers that had expressed an interest for a low-cost 727 derivative. Eastern told Boeing it preferred the 165-passenger, dual-class design, while BA was looking for a plane that could seat 190 passengers in a single-class configuration. After much discussion, including many talks between the two airlines, Boeing increased the seating from 165 to 175 seats, achieving 190 in a single class. Both airlines agreed to buy the aircraft; this was a coup for Boeing since BA, still linked to its government, was obliged to consider ordering Airbus planes. At this point, US airlines were forecasting increased market growth and wanted to increase passenger capacity.

The Model 761-164 was then stretched, from 165 seats to 180, and became known as the Model 761-177, which formed the basis of the 757 development. By August 1978, Boeing had a handshake deal with Eastern and BA to launch the aircraft, confident that it would not interfere with sales of the larger 767.

Meanwhile, additional studies continued to refine the wing geometry and control requirements. This developed, by December 1978, into the Model 761-280, a 178-passenger version with an all-new wing

swept back 25 degrees, a reduction of 5 degrees, introduced as a result of improved technology in airfoil design. With the new model's engines under the wings, the wing could be built slightly lighter; the weight of the engines could be used to counter the bending forces created by lift.

This model was designated the 757-200 because of the possibility, which was never realized, of a shorter -100 version. (The 757-100 never appealed to airlines because of higher seat-mile costs – it would have been nearly the same weight as the -200, but carrying just 160 passengers. Years later, Boeing instead developed a stretched 737-400 model, which could seat 150 passengers, in order to satisfy the needs of that market.)

At the press conference announcing the launch order for the 757 from Eastern Airlines and BA, Boeing showed table models of its new aircraft, which bore an uncanny resemblance to the 727. It had a T-tail and the same nose section; the only major difference was that it had two wing-mounted engines.

By April 1979, the 767 had evolved to include a conventional tail. The 757, initially considered to be just a derivative of the 727, also had a T-tail at first. While either a T-tail or low tail were acceptable on the 757, many engineers preferred the stall-recovery characteristics of the conventional tail. Others preferred the lower drag of the T-tail. Eventually, it was decided that the 757's tail would be like the 767's. The 767's vertical tail was used for the rationalization of a low tail; the 757's tail came closer to the 767's, leading to an all-new horizontal tail. The change shortened the 757 by 18ft (6m), while offering a performance equal to that of earlier designs.

Once the 757's low-tail design was settled, the plane's aft body was re-lofted, retaining the wide aft pressure bulkhead, which would enhance the passenger cabin.

The initial customers were happy with the result. From January to April 1979, Eastern and British Airways had been closely involved in detailed discussions, represented at daily meetings and kept abreast of major changes and galley designs.

Commonality

With the 767 programme advancing rapidly, Boeing began to re-evaluate the 757's original philosophy of retaining commonality with the 727. 'It became clear,' Jackson says, 'that we had to decide to change

the 757's focus on commonality with the 727 to be more common with the 767.'

As the 7N7 and 7X7, both the 757 and 767 had begun to share common equipment and technology. A decision was made to use several components of the 767 programme in the 757, including the auxiliary power unit, the air-conditioning system, the avionics, the flight management computer, and more. Until then, only the 727's lower-tech components had been considered. Now, the new plane emphasized commonality with the 767.

'In early spring 1979, a lot of discussions and studies were going on about this, and the decision was not easy,' says Doug Miller, who served as chief engineer of the 757 for seven years. 'The consensus was that the airplane would become obsolete in a few years had we not gone this route, and there were cost benefits for both programmes to use the same production base of expensive systems that were going into the 767.'

Using common components and systems would ease the burden of designing two new aircraft, while providing operators with the benefits of reduced maintenance and support costs. At the same time, Boeing realized that having complementary aircraft would enhance the saleability of both types.

'British Airways and Eastern Airlines wanted a low-cost airplane, and frankly I fought real hard to keep it to around 160 seats, but the 757 was pushed closer in capacity to the 767 than we at Boeing wanted,' Sutter says. 'We always felt the customer was right. We looked at the 767 as an over-water plane. The reasons for doing two airplanes was that there were two requirements at the time: a low-cost 727 replacement and a new but smaller wide-body that could cross continents and oceans. When the customers wanted quick action, we felt we had better work hard to make the airplanes common.'

Now, on the verge of rolling out a new pair of jets within five months, Boeing engineers set out to make the 767 and 757 as similar as possible. This new strategy introduced dozens of new challenges that would have to be resolved before the new aircraft family could ever fly. At the same time, both the 767 and 757 were about to go through hundreds of thousands of design stages – from the way the doors opened to how much the aircraft should weigh – before they would take to the skies. Only after years of exhaustive studies and continuous improvement did final plans emerge.

Further Developments and Improvements

Cockpit Conversion

One of the most dramatic moves was Boeing's decision to convert the 767 cockpit, designed for a crew of three, into a flight deck seating two pilots. That meant ripping each production model apart and redesigning its sophisticated 'glass cockpit' flight deck right in the middle of aircraft production.

In the post-deregulation period of the late 1970s, US airlines were facing heavy price competition on routes that had been opened up to new rivals. Meanwhile, aircraft reliability, redundancies in aircraft

The 767/757 glass cockpit introduced commercial aviation to the computer age. Boeing

systems, and the exceptional record of the two-crew 737 led Boeing to examine the possibility of expanding the two-crew flight deck to the 757 and 767.

The 767 was designed to be flown by two pilots, but the prototype and the first few production models were built with an additional flight engineer's station in the cockpit, at the insistence of launch customer United Airlines. While the airline's pilots had agreed to fly 737s with two cockpit crew members, they figured that a flight engineer was also needed for such a heavy aircraft. United also opted for a three-person crew in order to reduce the risk associated with being the first to put the 767 into revenue service. Boeing's argument was that its sophisticated flight controls would simplify the work of flying an aircraft. The plane had about 140 computers and microprocessors on board, performing various navigation and monitoring tasks.

Despite United's insistence on a traditional flight deck, Boeing continued to develop a second, two-crew flight deck as an option for later customers. Contacts with major suppliers for the two-crew flight deck were established as early as October 1978. By March 1980, Boeing revealed publicly that all future flight decks would be built to accommodate two-crew cockpits (although the 7X7 had always been planned with a two-man crew).

While researching the benefits of a two-member cockpit in the early days of the 7X7 programme, Boeing came to the following conclusions:

- a two-crew operation is significantly cheaper to operate;
- two-men crews are no less safe than three-member crews;
- technical developments placed a high emphasis on easing pilot workload and on increasing safety;
- since airline management would determine the number of crew members for their operations, Boeing would design the aircraft to be operated safely by two pilots.

Airlines were certainly interested in two-crew aircraft. Airbus was marketing its A310 and McDonnell Douglas the MD-80, both with two-pilot crews. Boeing believed that, if its new models were to be viable in the long term, they would need the two-crew flight deck, at least as an option. The Airbus A300 was changed from three- to two-member cockpits long after it entered service, and many airlines believed it would have sold better if it had always been offered with the two-crew option.

Dick Taylor, a former Boeing vice-president, says that the company was convinced that a two-member flight deck, a set-up established with certification of the 737 in 1967, would work. 'We had a lot of fundamental knowledge of crew workload and what the pilots looked for,' he says.

The invention of the microprocessor in 1975 made it possible to consider building the 767 with a high-tech cockpit for two. 'I saw the potential value of doing all the monitoring through microprocessors,' Taylor says. Such tasks as managing electrical and hydraulic systems and fuel were well within the realm of the new technology. At one quarterly vice-presidents' meeting, Taylor remembers listening to the head of Boeing's computer division. 'At the end of his presentation,' he recalls, 'I brought up the notion that the new microprocessor was likely to be a tool that we could use to monitor all the systems and that would do a better job than a person could do eyeballing all the instruments.'

Armed with data from 737 crews, which showed that the safety record of two-member crews was better than that of three-member crews, and that two-member crews were not overworked – a common argument from pilots – Taylor visited airlines around the world extolling the virtues of two-member crews. In many cases, he faced a crowd of angry pilots with many questions. 'The design of the airplane was very good and therefore we could answer those questions,' he says.

The debate on crew sizes brought on by the 767 and A310 reached a crescendo in 1981, when the US Presidential Task Force on Crew Complement was commissioned (headed by John McLucas), to determine the safety of two-crew operations for large wide-body aircraft. After months of hearings and extensive human-factor and safety data analyses, the task force concluded, in July 1981, that two-crew operations could be conducted safely. The task force's report was delivered less than a month before the first 767 was due to roll out of the Everett factory, and 10 months before the aircraft's scheduled certification.

Dick Taylor was among those who testified before the task force in favour of a cockpit crew of two. His arguments included the following:

- the advance of technology made the flight engineer's job extinct;
- all controls and displays would be accessible and visible to both crew members, eliminating the need for a third person;
- no in-flight actions would be needed for maintenance;
- automatic switching would guard against the loss of critical systems without the need for crew action;
- the flight system would indicate appropriate corrective action in the event of a system failure; and
- the crew would be alerted to any unsafe conditions.

Taylor's simple argument was that flying would be easier and safer with all the new technology, leading to reduced workloads and fewer cockpit errors. 'The fact that a third, unmonitored crew member can be a safety hazard was on our minds,' Taylor says.

Following the decision of the task force, United Airlines' pilot union agreed to fly a two-crew 767, and the last major hurdle was therefore cleared. Eleven of the 12 airlines that had ordered three-crew 767s immediately changed their orders to the two-crew design. That change had enormous implications for 767 production and certification. By September 1981, Boeing had come up with the necessary plans to retrofit aircraft already produced with the three-crew flight deck, and to incorporate the new design into the production line, beginning with the thirty-first aircraft. With the presidential commission's ruling in hand, Boeing announced, in an unprecedented move, that it would modify the first thirty production 767s, so that those planes scheduled for delivery six months later would have the latest, state-of-the-art cockpit. One 767 was modified in time for flight testing, while others were converted prior to delivery.

The conversion was a huge undertaking, involving Boeing's engineering and manufacturing organizations, as well as vendors. Converting the flight deck for two-crew members meant replacing the forward instrument panel and flight engineer's panel. Forty-nine subsystem panel modules were replaced and twenty-two new ones were relocated to the pilot's overhead panel. Sixty conventional instruments and the caution and advisory system were given new controls and displays. The flight engineer's seat, seat track, oxygen equipment and lighting were removed. Linings and floor panels were changed. The aft aisle stand was replaced with a new unit to provide additional panel space. About a third of the aircraft's wire bundles were removed. Two flight-deck computers and a new equipment rack were installed in the electronics bay. Flight-deck air-conditioning and cooling ducts were also changed.

The first 767 to fly had a three-member cockpit. In fact, it was not until 27 May 1982, eight months after the aircraft's maiden flight, that the 767 first flew with a two-member crew. This was the beginning of a test programme that led, in March 1983, to certification of the 767 with the two-crew configuration. United, the first 767 operator, took delivery of three-man cockpit versions beginning in September 1982, but later retrofitted the planes for two-person crews.

The two- vs. three-member cockpit issue never affected the 757. That aircraft was designed with a two-member crew and was, in fact, the first of Boeing's new twin-jets to be certified with a two-member cockpit.

Even after a two-member crew cockpit received regulatory approval, Boeing offered the option to airlines to convert their flight decks into three-member configurations. No airline took up the offer.

The midstream cockpit conversation affected the 767's aggressive flight-test schedule. A seventh test aircraft was added to the certification programme after it had been retrofitted with the new flight deck. Boeing used the aircraft configured for three crew members to conduct certification tests that did not depend on the flight deck configuration. Crew size, workload

and operational testing was conducted using the retrofitted two-crew test aircraft.

The decision to convert the flight decks of the first thirty 767s so late in the programme had quite an effect. Among the impacts of offering a two-crew flight deck were the costs of modifying thirty aircraft, the cost of the original design and installation of the three-person cockpits, and the delay to the delivery schedule. (Boeing delivered twenty 767s in 1982, eight fewer than planned.) With the exception of three 767s for Ansett Airlines of Australia, all 173 of the first ordered 767s were supplied with two-crew flight decks. Thirty of them, bound for seven different airlines, were converted from three-member decks just prior to delivery, and these included United's first six models. 'We lost money

---

Australian Three Crew 767s

Ansett Australia airlines received five 767s configured for three cockpit crew members – the only ones fitted with a flight engineer's station to enter service.

Ansett was one of the first airlines to order the 767, signing up for five in March 1980. At that time, Australian pilot's unions insisted that the aircraft be operated by two pilots and a flight engineer. The flight engineer's panel would be an advanced side-facing arrangement incorporating an Engine Indicating and Crew Alerting System (EICAS). Interestingly, it was also agreed that if in the future Ansett were to order the narrower

757, those aircraft must also be delivered in the same configuration – an impossibility since the 757 was always designed with a cockpit crew of two.

With flight engineers being phased out throughout the 1980s, Ansett acquired five additional 767-200s with the conventional two-member flight deck. This led to a non-uniform fleet. The first aircraft to be converted was VH-RMG, which entered the company's Melbourne maintenance hangar in February 1998. Five days later it no longer had a flight engineering station. Four others also were converted in 1998, ending a quirky era for the 767.

Ansett Australia first received its 767-200s designed for three crew members. It later converted its fleet to accommodate the two crew members the aircraft was designed for. Peter Sweeten/Aviation Images Worldwide

A United Airlines 757-200, showing a nice view of the model's unique nose. Darren Anderson

Another view of the drooping nose, on a **Northwest Airlines** 757-200. Darren Anderson

on that, but it's not like stripping out the entire cockpit,' notes Joe Sutter.

The two-person cockpit changed the way commercial airliners are flown. Pilots, in effect, became system managers rather than hands-on operators.

Small Body, Wide Cockpit

While engineers faced the daunting task of converting 767 cockpits into two-member configurations in the middle of production, the 757 team had an equally menacing challenge: how to shoehorn the same cockpit, designed for a wide-bodied plane, into the standard-body 757.

Following the decision to make the 767 and 757 as similar as possible, with many common parts and systems, focus immediately turned to the flight deck. As the design progressed, a Boeing engineer suggested that, if the cockpits were so similar, a potential existed to get a common pilot type rating. 'At that point, we no longer had a 727 derivative but a totally new airplane in a design class of its own and many features common to the 767,' said Ernest Fenn, the 757 division manager at the time.

While there were internal disagreements over the virtues of two engines vs. three on the 767, and over the T-tail configuration, engineers readily agreed that a 767 cockpit design was needed in the 757. One rather large problem stood in the way of the quest for commonality. The 767's flight deck cab was an all-new design, while the 757 retained, at the time, the configuration used on the 727. In a move rarely made after the launch of a programme, Boeing began to reconfigure the 757's nose section. Borrowing the identical 767 forward windshield and related structure, the 767 cab geometry was tailored on to the standard-body 757 fuselage.

The 757's nose design was altered in the summer of 1979 after nine months of exhaustive studies. The new-look nose – until then identical to the 727's – gave greater flight-deck visibility, and increased the crew working area, as well as providing more galley and lavatory space for passengers, and additional passenger seating.

Perhaps the most interesting feature of the 757 is its distinctive, 'droopy' nose. The 757 nose cone evolved into its own look after engineers merged the 767 cockpit into the narrower 757. The 757 nose curves upwards more dramatically than

that of the 767, and the point of the nose is well below the centreline of the fuselage. 'The decision to go with the 767 flight deck in the 757 essentially created the 757's nose design,' says Doug Miller, later chief 757 designer. 'We had to maintain the relationship of the instrument panel and the 767 windshield. That means matching a 767 crown line with the centre of the 757 body, leading to a drooped nose. It's a unique nose as far as Boeing aircraft go. It looks more like a Douglas plane.' Squeezing a 767 cab into the 757, Miller says, 'was the biggest controversy of the entire programme. What drove the decision was the fact that pilots would have a common type rating and would be able to fly both jets.'

Making the 767 and 757 cockpits identical involved many challenges, and an informal committee drove the process daily. 'When we took the 767 cab and adapted it to the narrower body, we wanted the pilot to sit in his seat and not know what plane he was in,' Taylor recalls.

The cockpit design provided the 757 flight deck with more light and space and better visibility than the original. 'Now we had a cockpit where you could see more light,' Taylor says of the finished product. 'Under low visibility, we also had a safer cockpit. Then we wrapped the 767 structure [outside the instrument panel] to match the narrower body of a 757. The 767 instrument panel and windshield are identical, so it gave us a physical structure that would be the same for either.'

The windshield then had to be tested, to make sure that it could withstand bird strikes during flight. The windows passed with flying colours; the crown of the 757 failed, however. Dead birds fired at the windshield during testing struck the top of the plane and damaged the crown. As a result, the crown had to be redesigned.

Matching the cockpits was particularly challenging in an organization that was planning two new transports at once. Taylor says that people in both new programmes met frequently to make sure they did not divert from the design. Commonality became a way of life. 'Similarity was the top priority,' Taylor says. 'For instance, some wanted to put more fuel capacity in the 757, but we said no, because then it wouldn't be the same as the 767.' Ensuing design reviews eliminated the auxiliary fuel tank idea, instead making the extra capacity a part of the main wing tank; this meant that the pilot did not have to take any action to control fuel.

The resulting internal geometry of the flight deck led to a number of advantages for the 757. The external visual field was improved and became identical with that of the 767. Aerodynamic noise, long a cause for complaint in the 727 cab, was reduced by six decibels. The wider cockpit also provided better air-conditioning airflow patterns, more room, and more storage space. Adopting the 767 cab allowed for more space at the front of the plane, providing space for a lavatory and a large galley. In fact, the new nose design created the most spacious two-crew flight deck in commercial aviation; it was 24in (60cm) wider at the pilot stations than the flight decks on previous standard-body airliners. Despite all these advantages, however, it was agreed between Boeing executives that the most important feature of the 757's flight deck was its commonality with the 767.

Meanwhile, the combination of aft and forward body changes resulted in a reduction of 20in (50cm) in 757 cabin length, while increasing seat count by one. The new length was about the same as that of the 727-200, but the new aircraft could carry 32 per cent more passengers at the same comfort level, with 20 per cent less fuel burn and nearly 39 per cent less fuel per passenger. In addition, the 757's aerodynamic and weight savings would be worth an additional 10 per cent in cost savings.

With these changes, the 757 completed its progress from a modest derivative of the 727 to an all-new aircraft, which deliberately shared a great deal of commonality with its larger sister. At the same time, the 757 delivered the fuel efficiency required by the airlines. Although the 727-300, with re-fanned engines, would have improved fuel consumption by 11 per cent relative to existing 727 engines, this would not be enough to offset development costs. The 757's new engines offered a 26 per cent to 31 per cent improvement.

By March 1981, two years after the 757 received the go-ahead, the Renton facility employed 11,000 people on the 757 programme alone.

The 'Glass Cockpit'

Long before the difficult cockpit layout and design issues were resolved, Boeing was preparing to put plenty of brains into its new planes.

The 767/757 flight deck introduced computer technology to commercial aviation. Airlines taking delivery of the dynamic duo were purchasing the most modern cockpit of all time. It was loaded with computers, which could virtually fly the plane on their own, from take-off, through approach and to landing. And all the time, the computers were able to ensure that flight crews operated the airliners efficiently. The aim, simply, was to meld the latest technology with a safe, spacious and comfortable place to work. New-generation avionics, automatic guidance controls, systems monitoring and malfunction alerting brought about a significant increase in cockpit automation, and a corresponding decrease in workloads. This permanently eliminated the need for a flight engineer.

These two planes, developed at the dawn of the computer age, gave birth to a new term in commercial aviation – 'glass cockpit' – used to describe a flight deck boasting an array of video screens constantly displaying information tracked by the aircraft's computers. The concept was so ground-breaking that later Boeing models universally adopted the technology introduced on the 767 and 757. Likewise, Boeing's chief competitor, Airbus, also made cockpit automation – its 'fly-by-wire' system – a hallmark of its designs.

Boeing veterans agree that the digital flight deck was perhaps the planes' most significant contribution to aviation.

'It was a big jump to go digital, a real breakthrough,' recalls Dean Thornton, former head of the 767 programme. 'It was a natural evolution of technology. Of course, one of the biggest challenges was to make all the computers work, and work with each other. The greatest advantage to the digital flight management system is that it makes flight navigation more efficient and reduces the crew's workload of all the things that go into flying an airplane. There are fewer tasks and they are easier to do.'

'The glass cockpit was at the cutting edge at the time,' adds Everett Webb. 'Our

The 767/757 flight deck. Boeing

concern was that nobody had committed that technology to a commercial airplane. In order to do that, we felt we had to have very good specifications early in the game to get some suppliers to put in their own money and develop components.'

Although Boeing employed digital equipment and systems on earlier planes, the technology was nowhere near as pervasive and interactive between subsystems as on the 767 and 757.

Features of the flight deck, outlined in more detail later, include:

- six colour cathode ray tube (CRT) displays;
- an electronic attitude director indicator (EADI), providing a multicoloured display of information – artificial horizon, flight path, flight control, groundspeed and windshear detection;
- an electronic horizontal situation indicator (EHSI), offering an integrated multicoloured map of the airliner's position relative to VHF stations and instrument landing system (ILS) beams. Wind direction and velocity are shown at all times. The airliner's horizontal situation, present and predicted, and the aircraft's deviation from a planned vertical path are provided. A colour radar display can even be superimposed on the map, to show the location of bad weather;
- a flight management computer system (FMCS), which integrates navigation, guidance and performance data functions. When matched with the automatic pilot, the system provides accurate engine-thrust settings and flight-path guidance during all phases of flight, from immediately after take-off to final approach and landing. It can predict the speeds and altitudes that will result in the best fuel economy, and command the aircraft to follow most fuel-efficient or shortest-time flight paths. Flight planning, terminal area procedures and route information can be stored and retrieved;
- the Engine Indication and Crew Alerting System (EICAS). This provides full-time monitoring of engine parameters and aircraft systems through the use of a computer and display system.

The 767/757 flight deck evolved from concepts developed by Boeing and leading electronics firms in the late 1960s and 70s. In the early 1970s, Boeing conducted studies

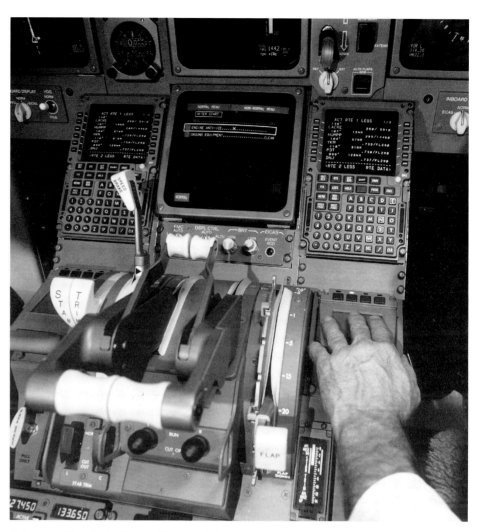

A close-up of the electronics found in the cockpit. Boeing

of various systems display alternatives, culminating in a research project called the Advanced Systems Monitor (ASM). The ASM used a 737 simulator with two centrally located CRTs that displayed engine and subsystem information, and flight crew procedural cues, in the form of checklist data. While that proved to be a remarkable step, the ASM study found that the absence of colour in the monochrome CRTs of the 1960s was a serious handicap; without different colours, pilots could not accurately and, therefore, safely assess operating conditions.

Quickly developing technology then introduced two key elements that would make the glass cockpit feasible: the microprocessor and the colour monitor. The microprocessor made possible the hightech wizardry. Colour screens made the system usable.

'When we decided to use TV screens, the initial decision was to go with black-and-white tubes because colour was not yet available,' says Joe Sutter. 'We were scared we'd come out with this new plane and then have to replace all the tubes with colour. We put pressure on designers. We had some sleepless nights.'

CRT technology was moving so fast that the 767, five months ahead of the 757, almost missed the chance to incorporate the new glass cockpit. The 757 was actually the first of the two to fly with a glass cockpit; the first 767s, those used on early test flights, actually incorporated only a few features of the new flight deck.

'Thank goodness the technology for the glass cockpit was moving faster than we could move so it developed in parallel with us,' says John Armstrong, the 757's chief test pilot.

Designing and Developing the Glass Cockpit

In designing the glass cockpit, Boeing was able to benefit from its broad military knowledge. Much of the technology being considered for future airliners was already being implemented in the company's radar and missile products and military jets. 'My proposition was that we take some of the electronic people on the military side and make them part of the design team,' Taylor says. 'There was only a small group of people who did this. We needed electronic people who understood physical databases, and they weren't that prevalent at the time.' This military *savoir-faire* led to the 767/757's flight management computer system.

Taylor recalls the trials and tribulations of developing an all-new concept: 'It was a typical engineering effort with something brand-new. There were arguments over the arrangements, technical problems,' he says. 'We argued over where to put the key arrangements and then there was a big discussion over what colours to use in the tubes. The process went on for months.'

The burgeoning system was not without its troubles, Sutter remembers. 'It was trial and error,' he says. 'But if you do trial and error with very smart people, they know how to fix the problems.'

Early designs of the glass cockpit took into account the views of major airlines and their pilots, as well as the experience gained from operating two-crew 737s.

'There were lots of meetings held where we were getting input from airlines and suppliers,' says Webb, who, along with Joe Sutter, Ron Brown and Ken Holtby, is credited with developing the glass cockpit. 'Our biggest problem was that we thought it was easier than it really was. The reason is we didn't have the experience to learn how tough it was. It took a dedicated effort from suppliers and our folks internally to get through that. In the long run, look where it's led. It seems like it was worth it.'

The 767 project test pilot, Tom Edmonds, had worked with Boeing designers since 1972 on a new generation of cockpits, consulting with airline pilots and flight engineers. He spoke with them at various stages of the design process to ensure that

The flight deck is both a comfortable working environment and a high-tech array of computers that can virtually fly the aeroplanes automatically. Boeing

developments met the requirements of those who would be flying the plane.

The glass cockpit survived the many evolutions of the 7X7 programme. Even in 1972, while the aircraft was constantly undergoing revision, Boeing had developed an advanced flight deck concept that looked remarkably similar to the cockpit that was finalized a decade later.

EICAS

One feature in the glass cockpit that had always stood out was EICAS, the Engine Indication and Crew Alerting System. The development of this system, which interfaces with many aircraft components and

evident that the increased systems-to-crew interaction provided by the displays and computers would have to be carefully implemented. The objective of such a system was to enable the flight crew to operate the aircraft systems as efficiently and simply as possible, with a minimum of human intervention, and to provide maximum knowledge of system status and health. It also meant that the systems monitor should not demand pilot attention for minor trends, only for system malfunctions that required pilot action during flight. 'This was developed so that we can show the pilot on a screen what the malfunction is, so that he can take action,' Taylor says.

In early 1979, bolstered by support from initial customers, Boeing management

that took place during the development of EICAS.

One of the most difficult projects was assuring avionics reliability in the 767's digital cockpit. 'All those black boxes had to talk to each other,' Holtby says. 'We spent a lot of time in the lab trying to make all the units play together, and the problem was that there were about six different vendors involved. Getting all the systems to function together was a major problem with the 767. By the time the 757 came along, we had the bugs ironed out.'

Old-school pilots initially had some trouble accepting the new technology. 'The biggest obstacle was convincing pilots in the airlines that these modern things, like CRTs in colour, were an advantage to them,'

United Airlines was the launch customer of the 767. The airline played a key role in the definition of the aircraft. Ed Davies

subsystems, benefited from a number of research projects undertaken in the decade before its introduction. It played a major role in the development of the 767 and 757 flight decks, both technically in the configuration and politically in the debates that surrounded two- vs. three-member cockpits. EICAS was the single most important technical advance towards allowing these planes to be flown without a flight engineer.

Boeing quickly learned more about CRT displays and systems-monitoring techniques, particularly the importance of minimizing required crew actions. It became

authorized EICAS to proceed, as an integral part of the 757 two-crew flight deck. The 767 three-crew programme was, at the time, too far advanced for a change to EICAS. However, after two-crew cockpits were allowed, all 767s received an EICAS two-crew configuration as part of the three-to-two cockpit switch.

Since the 757 was planned with EICAS, the attitudes of the first two 757 customers – Eastern and British Airways – had a significant effect upon how it was implemented. Both airlines were positive and encouraging during the many meetings

Armstrong says. 'We tried to keep the basic philosophy so that people who flew the old analogue cockpits could fly these planes. We made it a plan to keep it very logical and make the flight deck instrumentation look like the older planes so a pilot could understand the instrumentation.'

Customer Input

As the 767 and 757 programmes progressed from design into production, Boeing constantly sought feedback from potential customers. Unlike today, when manufacturers gather input from dozens of airlines, the decade of the 1970s was a time when just a handful of industry leaders decided the characteristics of a new aircraft. The 767 and 757 were configured around comments from such industry leaders as Dick Ferris of United Airlines and Frank Borman of Eastern Airlines. Both would later place the first orders for Boeing's new aircraft. 'In those days, when it came around to the basic design, the airlines defined the requirements and helped us to achieve it,' Sutter says.

While Boeing's family was still in development, airlines throughout the world, in particular in the USA, reacted positively. They liked the low fuel burn per seat, the modern flight deck, the commonality between the 767 and 757, and the new interiors. Still, selling an all-new aircraft was not easy. Boeing was competing with the MD-80, a derivative of the DC-9, and cheaper to produce, and the A310, also a derivative, funded by four European governments.

United Airlines

United participated actively in defining the 767 design, as it had done on the 727 programme. In one of the most dramatic examples of how Boeing were prepared to cater to customer demands, the maximum gross weight of United's first 767 was increased by about 10,000lb (4,536kg). Boeing veterans say that Boeing and United worked out the airline's needs in greater detail than had ever been done on a new aircraft programme. 'We knew exactly what to build,' Sutter says. 'They had defined their mission requirements more precisely than ever before. This was the most complete aircraft, the most thoroughly tested, the most complete specifications with a first customer that we had ever accomplished.'

Ferris, United's chairman from 1976–87, says that the 767 was created to fulfil a mission. Before buying, the airline undertook extensive research, focusing on the market, flight frequencies and optimal

sizes. United collaborated with Boeing on the design, constantly discussing what United needed in its next new plane to fill the gap between its DC-10s and 727s. 'We wanted a Chevrolet, not a Cadillac,' said Ferris, referring to United's quest to keep costs down in an era of some austerity.

While United was involved in broadly defining the 767's dimensions and capabilities, the company contributed in even more detail to decisions on the cabin interiors, including size and locations of galleys and toilets. During one meeting, Ferris saw a demonstration of an old-fashioned toilet and the 767's vacuum toilet. He picked the vacuum toilet.

United's biggest challenge in the 767 programme was to convince the powerful pilot's union to accept the planned two-crew cockpit. United was still staffing smaller 737s with three crew members, at a time when other airlines were opting for two. 'We had to convince them it was acceptable and safe,' Ferris says.

Completed 767s on the flight line in 1982, featuring the model's first two customers – United Airlines and Delta Air Lines. Boeing

Even as United was working with Boeing to define the specifics of the new plane, the airline was entertaining offers from both Airbus and McDonnell Douglas for new wide-bodies. In the end, Ferris picked the 767. 'It was faster, more fuel-efficient and had a bunch of new technology,' he says today.

United was not the only airline to show confidence in the new model. The 767 programme received a huge boost on 15 November 1978, when the second- and third-largest US carriers, American Airlines and Delta Air Lines, set a single-day Boeing sales record. In an order worth $2 billion in total, American ordered 30 aircraft and Delta 20. Both airlines needed the new aircraft to expand their US coast-to-coast service and to replace 707s and DC-8s. Each aircraft cost $25 million in 1978 dollars. The order – combined with United's launch – gave Boeing 80 firm orders and 79 options for a backlog of $3.1 billion; it was enough to recover the development costs. Assembly on the first 767 was able to begin in April 1980, with final assembly being completed a year later.

Eastern Airlines

The 757 became a fully-fledged production programme when Eastern Airlines and British Airways signed, on 23 March 1979, contracts for 21 planes, worth $1 billion. The airlines had agreed in August 1978 eventually to take delivery of a total of 82 models of the type.

Eastern Airlines (now defunct) had shown an early interest in the 757, even when it was known as the 7N7, with a view to replacing its ageing fleet. In the late 1970s, Eastern had the oldest fleet in the business, with first-generation DC-9s and 727s, and even a few Lockheed Electras. 'We desperately needed to upgrade our fleet,' recalls Frank Borman. 'We were competing in dense markets. We needed an airplane that combined low seat-mile cost with low overall airplane cost.' Sixty per cent of Eastern's fleet was inefficient, and the airline was competing with Delta, which was in the middle of a fleet-modernizing programme. The airline also needed to bridge the seating capacity gap between its 727s and the Airbus A300. 'We went to Boeing and said, "Hey, we need a new plane",' says Borman.

The first plane offered was the 727-300, but, when that proposal was dropped, Boeing came to Borman with what would have been the 160-passenger 757-100. 'We said we didn't want it,' Borman says. 'It wasn't big enough. We gelled their design team and told them to try again.' Eastern consulted a great deal with Boeing during the 757's design evolution. 'It's a great tribute to Boeing,' says Borman. 'We wanted the cheapest plane we could get and they accommodated us.'

The 757's greatest feature – the all-new digital flight deck – was not on Eastern's wish list, partly because of the airline's need for thrift. Eastern was planning for a conventional flight deck before the decision was made to give the 757 the glass cockpit. As Borman recalls, '"T" Wilson [Boeing president] called me one day and said, "Hey, you've got to come out here, I've got a deal for you." I was in no rush to travel. I had just had hand surgery, and my hand was hurting.' The trip to Seattle was worth it, though. Boeing showed Borman the plans for the newly designed cockpit. The technology-loving Borman, an ex-astronaut who had commanded the Apollo 8 mission that had orbited the moon in 1968, and an Air Force test pilot, was hooked. Wilson, eager to please the 757's first customer, made a deal with Borman: Boeing would put the glass cockpit in Eastern's batch of planes at no extra cost.

Months later, Tex Boullioun, president of Boeing's commercial aircraft group, was attempting to close the deal with Frank Borman after several days of meetings in Miami. They had reached an impasse. Borman decided to go to the airport with Boullioun. The car bounced over some railroad tracks and Boullioun suddenly said, 'OK, Frank, you've got a deal.' It was as if the bump had jolted him finally to make the agreement.

The agreement for the first 757s was based on what was known as Safe Harbor Leasing, a new tax bill that enabled companies heavily in debt, as Eastern was, to sell tax write-offs to profitable firms. Borman planned to finance the 757s with cash raised from Safe Harbor income, but, after the contract was signed with Boeing, the media began to criticize Safe Harbor as a refuge for inefficient companies. By 1981, Congress revised the law, putting Eastern's $560 million order in jeopardy. After a meeting in Seattle, Borman left with Boeing's promise to provide sufficient financing for the new planes.

At the contract signing, Borman confirmed how pleased he was with the new aircraft: 'With this order, Eastern takes another major step toward compiling the fleet of fuel-efficient, environmentally acceptable, highly productive aircraft essential to any successful airline between now and the end of the century.' (Unfortunately, his statement was to prove to be ironic, with Eastern ceasing operations in 1991.) He went on to say, 'The 757 is a classic example of how airlines are co-operating with aircraft designers and manufacturers to make the most of technology in conserving fuel and maintaining the lowest possible fares through operating efficiency.'

Like United on the 767, Eastern was closely involved in designing the new plane. The airline's flight attendants, for example, played a role in selecting galley locations and participated in mock-ups at Boeing. 'Everyone was looking forward to the airplane,' Borman says. 'It was customer-friendly and the cabin crew just loved it.'

By 1980, after British Airways had signed up for 757s, Boeing started to feel pressure. It had only two customers a little more than a year before the plane was scheduled to roll out of the Renton factory. Boeing began to focus its marketing efforts on another large US carrier, Delta Air Lines, which, as Eastern's prime competitor, was reluctant to buy the same plane. In another good example of how airlines can influence the make-up of new aircraft, Boeing worked with Delta to design a version to their liking; they came up with one that had new overwing exits, and a number of galley amendments. By this time Pratt & Whitney came out with its PW2000 engine to power the 757, and this brought Delta on board. The airline agreed to buy 60 planes in 1983, giving the programme a huge shot in the arm.

In launching the new planes, Boeing spent $2.5 billion on new machinery and buildings, including $500 million on computers and computer-controlled manufacturing. The Everett plant, designed to assemble the mammoth 747, was expanded to accommodate the 767. At the same time, the Renton facility grew to make the 757. Understandably, launching two planes at once affected Boeing's cash flow. The big challenge for Boeing management under president 'T' Wilson (Thornton Arnold Wilson, known to everyone as 'T') was to develop the 767, while planning simultaneously for the 757 programme, and keeping production lines humming for the 707, 727, 737 and 747.

The Airbus Factor

In many ways, the 767 was a competitive response to Airbus Industrie's growing line of wide-bodied, twin-engine aircraft.

When the first A300 took off, on 28 October 1972, the term 'air bus' was a generic one adopted by the industry to describe a short- to medium-range airliner proposed to meet increasing demand on busy European routes such as London-Paris. No European manufacturer could compete with Boeing or McDonnell Douglas. In

Concordes, which was grabbing headlines around the world. Yet, while the sleek supersonic may have turned heads, it was the A300, the world's first wide-body twin-jet, that heralded a new future for Europe's civil-aircraft industry.

Just as Boeing opted for two engines on its new 767, Airbus made the strategic calculation that a twin was essential for meeting tough airline requirements on operating economics. The A300 included the first two-person flight deck for a high-capacity airliner, introduced into service

for its function than any previous design, addressed two important requirements – a 4,300-mile (7,000-km) range and efficient short-range performance. However, unlike the 767's wing, the A310's small wing hindered the aircraft's ultimate long-range capability. 'In hindsight, I think we should probably have put a larger wing on the A310,' says Adam Brown, Airbus vice-president of strategic planning. 'The smaller design lacks the fuel volume and area needed to provide the very long range sought by customers in recent years.'

The 767 initially competed in the marketplace with the Airbus A300, the world's first wide-bodied twin-engined commercial aircraft. Airbus

late 1965, a French-British group published the specifications for a 200- to 225-seat aircraft. By December 1968, the design of the A300 crystallized, with construction beginning in September 1969. The first A300, dubbed the A300B, entered service in June 1975 with Germanair. Airbus followed the A300 by launching the A310, a shorter version, on 6 July 1978, just eight days before United Airlines announced its launch order for the 767. The first A310 flew on 3 April 1982, just behind the 767, which first took to the skies on 26 September 1981.

When the first A300 rolled out at Toulouse, France, in September 1972, it received less attention from the assembled crowd than it perhaps deserved. Parked opposite it was one of the prototype

by Indonesia's Garuda in 1982. Eastern, which had ordered the first 757, also gave the A300 credibility in Boeing's backyard when its first A300 entered service, in July 1977.

By the mid-1970s, Airbus was considering three derivatives based on the A300 fuselage, called the B9, B10 and B11. The first was a major stretch of the A300, the second a short-fuselage version, and the third a four-engine, very long-range aircraft. It was decided that the B10 would be first, and, following a failed attempt by Boeing to convince Airbus to develop the aircraft jointly (when the B10 became, briefly, the BB10), the A300-B10, later known as the A310, was launched in July 1978. The A310's wing, which featured a distinct twist at the root, and was smaller

Boeing's Joe Sutter agrees. According to him, one of the main reasons why the 767 was more popular than the A310s was because of its larger wings. The smaller wings have contributed significantly to the fact that the A310 is virtually out of production today.

Other innovations on the A310 included new, smaller horizontal tail surfaces with a carbon-fibre composite main structure, carbon-fibre composite fin and common engine pylons, which were able to accommodate for the first time both GE and Pratt & Whitney engines. The A310 also went into service with a digital flight deck based around six screens, just like in the 767/757. New, push-button technology was introduced, combining many of the tasks previously needing separate operations. A

The Airbus A310 followed the A300. Although similar to the 767, it has not sold nearly as well as the Boeing model. Airbus

longer-range version, the A310-200, was given the go-ahead in March 1983, and entered service in December 1985. It was followed in 1987 by the A310-300.

Meanwhile, Airbus decided that the technology in the A310 should be included in the A300 in much the same way as Boeing decided that the 757 and 767 should share common technology. The result was an aircraft with at least twice the productivity of the original A300, featuring the improvements from the A310, and a new, ergonomic cockpit designed by

Porsche. This model, the A300-600, was launched in 1980 and delivered in 1984. Besides offering total commonality with the A310 cockpit, the A300-600 featured increased use of composites, a major aerodynamic clean-up to reduce drag, and common brakes and wing tips. Today, orders for the A300-600 and A310-300 continue to be placed, but they trickle in. While these planes combined have sold less well than the 767 (about 240 A310s and 440 A300s), they greatly influenced Boeing's decision to launch and continually refine the 767.

Fuel Efficiency

Both the 767 and 757 were a result of economic necessity as much as technological innovation. Rising oil prices, environmental concerns and inflation had airlines scrambling for solutions in the 1970s. In 1973, fuel represented 24 per cent of the operating budget of every airline. By 1982, the year the 757 was rolled out, fuel made up 56 per cent of the budget, before costs finally eased. Clearly, carriers needed quiet, fuel-efficient and cost-effective jets.

In more than 30,000 hours of wind-tunnel testing, from 1970 until the 767's rollout, in 1981, Boeing had refined a new cross-section for subsonic wings. It is slightly fatter on the lower surface and thicker through the centre, changing the air flow over the wing for better distribution of lift.

In a break with Boeing's tradition of using relatively small wings, with sophisticated leading and trailing edges, the 767 and 757 are built with the all-new oversized wings. (The 767 wing is larger than that of the L-1011, a plane which seats at least fifty more passengers.) The 757's are slightly more swept back, and about two-thirds the area of those of its larger sibling. While the wings may not look very different from the wings on earlier Boeing aircraft, their design helps to make the 767 and 757 among the most fuel-efficient commercial jets.

Most notably, the 767/757 wings are more than 20 per cent thicker than a 727's, providing an efficient structure, increased fuel volume, more lift and a substantial reduction in drag. With more fuel capacity, the aircraft are able to fly further, or to use extra fuel to reach airports with special conditions, such as high altitude, high temperature, or both. A thicker wing also enables Boeing to lengthen the wing span. The longer span works on more air, producing less drag (the force acting against the wing surface) to slow the aircraft.

The family's wings are also designed differently in respect of how the air passes over them. All wings generate lift because of the way they are curved. At some point, as the air passes towards the back of the wing, the air no longer flows in streamlines, but breaks away in eddies. These cause aerodynamic drag. The higher the drag level, the less efficient the aircraft. Less drag means higher speed for the same amount of fuel burned. Alternatively, it means a combination of more payload carried further on less

fuel at the same speed. Less drag also means the wing can be swept back less for any speed. Besides being a more efficient fuel tank, a fatter wing that is less swept is easier to design.

Another feature of the family's wings is a sharper leading edge, forcing on-rushing air to turn less as the wing cuts through it. This, along with a simple wing-flap system, means less drag and lower engine power requirements, and, therefore, less noise on take-off and approach.

The advanced-technology wing design enables the 767, in particular, to climb more quickly than any other medium-range jetliner to cruising altitude, where the thinner air imposes less drag on the aircraft, allowing maximum efficiency. This accounts for a portion of the aircraft's fuel savings – the time required from take-off to cruise is key to a jetliner's fuel consumption. The new wing shape accounts for about 5 per cent (of 35 per cent) of the 767's fuel-saving advantages over airliners of earlier design. In addition, using composite materials on the wings leads to an 8 per cent improvement in strength and fatigue characteristics over previous wings.

Unlike the 727, the 757 was initially designed for economical, short-haul routes, where speed was less vital. Boeing calculated that climb consumed 60 per cent of the fuel that the 757 would use on a 575-mile (920-km) trip. It was therefore expected to spend almost as much time climbing and descending as cruising. As a result, the wing

To test the wing, Boeing put it through rigorous testing. During the final static test of the 767 airframe, a load test was conducted that pulled the wingtips up 15.5 feet (4.7 m) over the top of the fuselage at a pressure of 1.2 million pounds (544,320 kg). The wing did not break. Boeing

was optimized for a Mach .80 cruise. The 757's big wing houses double-slotted flaps on the rear and a series of slats that run the full length of the front. These flaps combine to produce outstanding take-off and landing characteristics, which are virtually unmatched, even today. The wing is slanted upwards at 5 degrees.

The 767/757 wings are made up of the following components: outboard low-speed ailerons; inboard high-speed ailerons, which droop in unison with flap extension to reduce fuselage angle of attack during approach; flight and ground spoilers on the wing; and conventional rudder and elevators. The leading-edge flaps are in six sections on

each half-span, and can be set at varying positions as a function of the trailing-edge flap position, in order to achieve best performance throughout take-off and landing. Single-slotted flaps occupy the trailing edge between the two sets of ailerons, and between the inboard ailerons and the fuselage. The spoilers are electrically commanded; other control systems are conventional.

The 767's revolutionary wing is a key to the model's fuel efficiency. Boeing

As fuel prices rose, older jetliners, such as the 727 and 737, became increasingly more expensive to operate. World-wide concern over noise pollution also required new jetliners to be quieter. (Both the 767 and 757 are among the quietest in the world; the sound of one of them taking off is equivalent to average street-corner noise.) Boeing now had two aircraft that could help cut fuel bills and add to the airlines' bottom line. When salesmen began to show the planes to the airlines, fuel efficiency was the biggest selling point: the 767-200 could replace the 727-200 and offer a 50 per cent increase in payload without burning any more fuel. The 767 would be 54 per cent more fuel-efficient than the 727-100, and 29 per cent more fuel-efficient than a 727-200. Replacing older 707s and DC-8s with the new twin-jet would lead to even more savings.

The 757 was also an easy sell. It could carry 186 passengers on 15 per cent less fuel than a 143-seat 727-200. In other words, an airline operating twenty 757s can carry the same number of passengers as twenty-six 727s. The combination of extra seats and improved fuel efficiency results in savings of 850 million gallons (3.21 billion litres) of fuel over 20 years, or about 2 million gallons (7.57 million litres) a year per aircraft. Those savings can certainly pay off over time. Of course, the aircraft themselves are not cheap. When it debuted, a 767 cost $46–$52 million, while the 757 cost $36–$42 million. The last 727, delivered in April 1983, cost just under $20 million. By 1998, the sticker price on new 767s ranged from $83 million to $108 million; for 757s, between $62 million and $76 million.

Cutting weight from an aircraft is the most effective way to trim costs and ensure fuel efficiency. As the 757 was designed, Boeing created a weight improvement campaign, calling the 757 its 'Lean Machine'. In 1980 alone, the company's employees came up with 5,000lb (2,250kg) of reductions. To promote the campaign, Boeing created a logo showing a tan and black spotted cheetah and a silver, maroon and yellow 757 against a yellow sun. The 767 had a similar programme, aimed at delivering the lowest possible empty weight consistent with established design criteria. More than 500 proposals were approved for incorporation into the aircraft, leading to a weight reduction of more than 6,000lb (2,700kg), enabling the 767 to

stay at or below projected specification weights. This amounted to savings to airlines of more than $1.2 million per aircraft, in fuel alone.

Below are more details of how improved technology was able to give the 767 and 757 their revolutionary fuel efficiency:

1. Both planes were built using lighter materials. A relentless search for such materials is an important part of building an all-new aircraft. The goal is to carry the most people in the lightest aircraft, so a great deal of attention needs to be paid to structural concepts, techniques and materials. Boeing's biggest weight savings came through close attention to structural requirements, and diligent monitoring during the design process. For the 767 and 757, Boeing substituted metal with reinforced plastic or glass fibres, and used lighter alloys extensively. The 767 was the first Boeing aircraft to replace 3,500lb (1,716kg) of aluminium with 1,200lb (544kg) of graphite and graphite/Kevlar composites; these materials were lighter and stronger than the traditional aluminium or fibreglass, and fuel consumption was reduced through weight savings. On the 757, advanced graphite or hybrid composites were used in virtually all areas that were not primary structure, saving almost 1,140lb (513kg). An additional 650lb (292.5kg) were saved in the wing through the use of new, improved aluminium alloys. Carbon brakes save another 650lb (295kg) of weight, and have the added advantage of lasting longer than conventional steel brakes. On the 757 alone, state-of-the-art composite materials and improved alloys produced a weight saving of 2,000lb (900kg) over an identically sized aircraft of the previous generation, saving about 30,000 gallons of fuel (113,550 litres) a year for an aircraft making 1,400 trips of 1,150 miles (1,840km). On both aircraft, advanced composites such as graphite/epoxy are used in control surfaces (including rudder, elevators and ailerons), aerodynamic fairings, engine cowlings and landing-gear doors. This was the most extensive use of composites ever on a commercial aircraft.

2. The new electronics in the glass cockpit contributed to fuel efficiency. Computer-guided avionics are able to control fuel burn by plotting the most efficient flight plan. Estimated fuel-burn savings derived from the fully automatic flight

management system may be as high as 6 per cent.

3. Both planes had new, more fuel-efficient powerplants.

4. Both models had improved aerodynamics, combined with new wings.

The efficiency of the new airliners, combined with their seating capacity, gave airlines the ability to turn money-losing routes, previously served with larger aircraft, into profitable ventures. The 767's fuel efficiency – and lower long-term operating cost – was its greatest appeal, and a major factor in United's decision to be the launch customer for the type. Next to other wide-bodies, the 767-200 has a 5 per cent lower seat-mile cost advantage over the Airbus A300, and is 3 to 4 per cent better than the DC-10 or L-1011. (The seat-mile cost is the standard industry measure for an aircraft's efficiency, representing the cost of transporting one aircraft seat one mile.) Deciding on the 767 helped United to increase profits, as the modern, more cost-efficient aircraft replaced their fifteen- to twenty-year-old DC-8s.

The Magic of Flight

When a plane barrels down a runway, looking as if it is straining to get off the ground, the opposite is actually happening – at take-off speed, the plane can only leave the ground. The strain is the force of gravity pulling the weight of the plane towards the ground, as it rises in response to the upward pressure from the flow of air around the wings.

Providing an aircraft has wings, flying it is simply a matter of pushing it along the ground until it is going fast enough; this is always the case, no matter what its size. The groundspeed necessary is determined by the weight of the plane, and the area and shape of its wings. As speed increases, an upward force is generated on the wings, which should eventually overcome the weight and lift the plane off the ground.

A successful wing, like that of the 767 and 757, is one on which the top surface is longer than the bottom, looking at the wing in cross-section. As the wing is pushed along, the front edge slices through the air, forcing the air flow to be split in half. The flow over the top of the wing meets up again with the flow underneath at the back of a wing. The top flow travels farther and faster than the bottom flow, and this difference in speed generates negative pressure, or suction, over the top of the wing.

The result is a force that lifts the whole aircraft symmetrically into the air. Both of these forces are proportional to speed, so, when the plane reaches the speed at which the upward forces are greater than the weight of the plane, the plane begins to lift off the ground.

CHAPTER FIVE

Individuality and Similarities

A Closer Look at the 767

The 767 is not a 'flashy' plane. It is not as distinctive as the 747, nor does it stand out like the 777. It may even be confused with an Airbus model. However, it is a proven performer, and a valuable addition to any airline's fleet.

The 767 makes use of new-generation technology to provide maximum efficiency in the face of rising operational costs, while extending twin-aisle cabins to routes never before served by wide-body airliners. Its cabin follows the tradition of spaciousness established by the 747, the first wide-bodied airliner. In addition, thanks to the identical flight decks, airlines that operate both the 767 and the 757 can save in training time and costs by having their cockpit crews qualified to fly both.

The first 767, the -200 model, was completed and rolled out of the Everett plant on 4 August 1981, just three years after United ordered thirty. It made its initial flight on 26 September of that year. That first 767 is still owned by Boeing.

Following the company's tradition of stretching existing models to provide more capacity and range, the company launched the 767-300 programme on 29 September 1983. The 767-200's fuselage was extended by 21ft 1in (6.43m), increasing capacity by 22 per cent (an extra forty passengers), and cargo volume by 31 per cent, with just 10 per cent in additional costs. A freighter version followed in 1995.

Early 767s were hampered by their lack of range. Large US carriers, including Delta and American, convinced Boeing to take advantage of the 767's growth potential. Even Boeing's marketing people urged the company to give the model extra legs, so that it could fly the lucrative West Coast-Hawaii route. This resulted in the development of the 767-200ER ('extended range') and, later, the stretched 767-300ER. These versions gave airlines a wide-body with intercontinental range, generous cargo space and twin-engine economy in a plane carrying more than

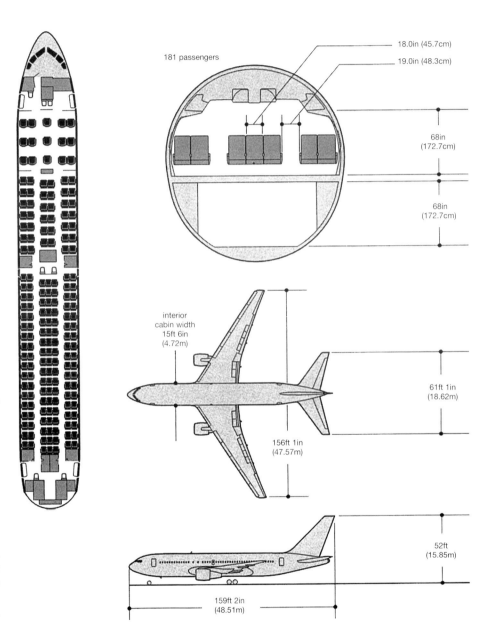

767-200 aircraft characteristics. Boeing

200 people. Some at Boeing felt that a long-range 767 would cut into 747 sales, but, as it turned out, the ER was ideal for overseas routes with an amount of traffic

that did not justify the services of a 747.

The extended-range versions made it possible for the model to fly the same routes employed by larger, more expensive aircraft such as the DC-10 and L-1011. To allow for long, over-water flights, new features were added. These included an advanced propulsion system, an auxiliary power unit with high-altitude start capability, a fourth generator driven by a hydraulic motor, increased cargo compartment fire-suppression capability, and cooling sensors for the electronic flight instruments.

Boeing's investment paid off: since February 1994, the 767 has crossed the Atlantic Ocean more often than any other type of aircraft.

The basic 767-200, at a maximum gross weight of 300,000lb (136,080kg), can take off with just 5,600ft (1,707m) of runway. Even the highest gross-weight version, the 767-200ER model, with a maximum take-off weight of 395,000lb (179,172kg), can take off in about 9,400ft (2,865m). It can reach up to 7,660 miles (12,330km), making non-stop flights such as New York–Beirut, London–Bombay and Tokyo–Sydney possible, with 181 passengers in a three-class configuration.

The basic 767-300 has a maximum take-off weight of 345,000lb (156,492kg) and can carry a two-class load of 269 passengers for 4,560 miles (7,340km). The highest gross-weight 767-300ER, at 412,000lb (186,883kg) maximum take-off weight, can carry 218 passengers in a three-class configuration for 7,080 miles (11,400km).

The -200 cabin, more than 4ft (1.2m) wider than that of a single-aisle jetliner, seats about 224 passengers in a typical mixed-class configuration (six abreast in first class in a two-by-two-by-two set-up), and seven abreast (two-by-three-by-two) in economy class. Other arrangements are possible, including up to 325 passengers in eight-abreast seating for charter flights in the 767-300.

The extended-range models typically have three-class seating of 181 to 218 passengers, using five-abreast, 747-sized first-class seats, six-abreast business-class seats, and seven abreast in the economy section. Boeing says that seven-abreast seating is preferred because it means that 87 per cent of the seats are next to a window or the aisle, and centre seats are only one seat from an aisle. Passenger studies conducted by Boeing also rate the 767 equal to the 747 in passenger comfort.

This seating arrangement had the effect of opening up the cabin, resulting in more usable overhead storage – 2.6 cubic ft (72 cubic cm) of bin space per passenger,

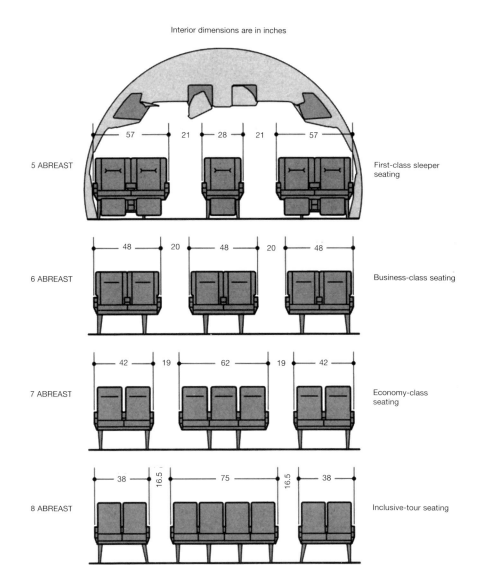

Interior dimensions are in inches

5 ABREAST — 57 — 21 — 28 — 21 — 57 — First-class sleeper seating

6 ABREAST — 48 — 20 — 48 — 20 — 48 — Business-class seating

7 ABREAST — 42 — 19 — 62 — 19 — 42 — Economy-class seating

8 ABREAST — 38 — 16.5 — 75 — 16.5 — 38 — Inclusive-tour seating

Interior view of the 767. Boeing

compared with 2 cubic ft (56 cubic cm) for the DC-10 and L-1011. This, along with the shape of the pressure bulkhead, resulted in another key selling point – a large, U-shaped galley at the aft of the cabin. This galley provides a large amount of work space for the flight attendants, removes the work area from passengers, and allows maximum use of the constant section of seat rows.

Boeing's objective was to design an aircraft with low operating costs that would be attractive and comfortable for passengers, in order to stimulate high load factors (in other words, the percentage of seats filled on a flight). The passenger cabin was the starting point, and the aircraft was designed around it, rather than squeezing

passengers into the available space after the aerodynamicists had finished shaping the body. That is why the 767 has a rectangular passenger cabin with straight aisles. The flexibility of this design was learned from the successful 727. It is also the reason why there is adequate width for the U-shaped galley at the aft pressure bulkhead. In the initial configuration development, the aft body geometry was designed around the space requirements of an efficient and spacious galley, which minimizes the use of valuable passenger-generating floor space.

One interesting feature in the 767 is the technical advance of its main entry door. The overhead door is mechanically counterbalanced, so that it can be raised using just the slightest pressure. Pressure forces the door to conform to the body shape, doing away with the adjustments required for conventional doors.

Lower-deck volume available for baggage and cargo on the aircraft totals 3,070 cubic ft (85.9 cubic m) for the -200, and 4,030 cubic ft (112.8 cubic m) for the -300. This capacity is more than 45 per cent greater than the lower-deck capacity of a Boeing 707, and greater than any other commercial transport in its class.

The 767 was the first plane with a sewer system; in it, an electrically driven pump provides the suction that is needed to keep the system moving. The system, also installed in later-generation 747s, was the first major improvement in lavatories since commercial jets first took to the skies. The 767 was also the first aircraft equipped with lavatories that were accessible by wheelchair users.

The 767 has a cruising speed of 542 miles per hour (873km) or 0.88 Mach at 35,000ft (10,668m). Its take-off speed is 192 miles (310km) per hour, and its landing speed is 178 miles (287km) per hour.

Two engine models are available for all versions of the 767, ranging in thrust ratings from 50,000–62,000lb of thrust (222.4–274kN) – the Pratt & Whitney PW4056 and General Electric's CF6-80C2. Early 767s were powered by Pratt & Whitney's JT9D-7R4 engine or GE's CF6-80A. All three major engine manufacturers provide engines for the 767-300 – the choice is between Pratt & Whitney's PW4056, GE's CF6-80C2, and the Rolls-Royce RB211-524G/H.

A Closer Look at the 757

At 155ft 3in (47.32m), the 757-200 is the longest single-aisle aircraft Boeing has ever produced (although its stretched version, the 757-300, has beaten that record). The 757-200 shares the same fuselage width (11ft 7in, or 3.5m) as the 707, 727 and 737, but any similarity to previous Boeing narrow-bodies ends there.

Soon after its introduction, the 757 achieved a reputation as the most fuel-efficient plane the company had ever built. Engineers had set two goals for the plane – 40 per cent more seat-miles per gallon than the 727-200, and a range of 2,500 miles (4,000km). As it turned out, the plane was 76 per cent more fuel-efficient than the 727-200, with a range of 4,000 miles (6,400km).

Although the 757-200 is just slightly longer than the 727-200, it can carry more passengers (178 instead of 143), because of the extra 26ft (7.92m) in cabin space. This extra space is made available by moving the engines from the tail and alongside the fuselage to the under-wing position. The extra capacity provided carriers with added value on growing routes previously served by 727s and 737s.

The 757-200 has a maximum gross weight of 255,500lb (115,900kg). Its initial gross weight, derived by analysis, was 220,000lb (99,000kg), but after stress tests, Boeing increased the weight on the wing centre section and landing gear. Along with more powerful engines and weight savings, this change increased the aircraft's range.

Designed to carry 194 passengers in a typical six-abreast layout, the 757-200 can carry up to 239 passengers in charter service, putting its capacity between that of a 737-400 and a 767. Like the 767, the 757 is also available in an extended-range, package and freighter version.

201 passengers

17.0in (43.2cm)
20.0in (50.8cm)
66.4in (168.7cm)
53.9in (136.9cm)

interior cabin width 11ft 7in (3.53m)

49ft 11in (15.21m)
124ft 10in (38.05m)
44ft 6in (13.56m)
155ft 3in (47.32m)

757-200 aircraft characteristics. Boeing

(Above) **A 757 interior. Unlike the wide-body 767, the 757 shares the same interior setup – two sets of three rows – as the narrowbody models that preceded it: the 707, 727 and 737.** Boeing

(Below) **The 757 in a cutaway view showing the interior makeup.** Boeing

Thanks to its versatility, the 757 is at home at just about any commercial airport in the world. It can fly on to the hottest plateaus, or into coldest valleys. It can fly long distances or short stages with equal aplomb. Whether as a transcontinental US aircraft, or as a quick-hop shuttle, the aircraft offers unmatched fuel efficiency. It can climb faster and higher than any other single-aisle twin-jet – from sea level to 35,000ft (11,000m) in 19 minutes. The fact that the 757 can get into the air so quickly is one reason why it has been approved for operation at some of the most noise-sensitive airports in the world.

High bypass-ratio engines give the plane its quiet, fuel-efficient reputation. The engines have large-diameter fans that move more air outside and around the hot core, boosting efficiency, while reducing noise. Noise containment is further aided by acoustic linings in the engine nacelles. Engines for the 757 are available from Rolls-Royce (RB211-535) or Pratt & Whitney (PW2000), in thrust ratings from 37,000–43,000lb (164.7–191.3kN).

The wing on the 757 is less swept and thicker through the centre than those on earlier Boeing aircraft, permitting a longer span. The lower wing surface is slightly flatter, and the leading edge somewhat sharper. This improves lift and reduces drag, leading to improved aerodynamic efficiency and low fuel consumption. With its efficient wing design, the 757 needs less engine power for take-off and landing. Even with full passenger payload, the 757-200 can operate from runways as short as those used by the much smaller 737-200 – about 5,500ft (1,675m) for trips up to 2,000 miles (3,220km). The versatile 757 can use airports limited by runway length, high altitude, hot weather and weight restrictions. In bad weather, it is capable of landing with runway visibility of just 300ft (100m).

Boeing offers a virtually unlimited array of interior features, and every plane is customized to the needs of each airline.

The first 757-200 rolled out of the Renton plant on 13 January 1982, and made its first flight on 19 February 1982. First delivery was made, on 22 December 1982, to launch customer Eastern Airlines; the aircraft proudly carried the designation '757' on its silvery tail. Eastern put the aircraft into service on 1 January 1983. On 14 January, the British Civil Aviation Authority certified the 757 to fly in the United Kingdom, and British

Airways began to operate it on its high-density, intra-European routes.

Boeing had hoped that the 757 would become a profit-making workhorse. Although it has sold less well than expected over the years, it has, none the less, the enviable honour of being the world's most fuel-efficient airliner in the short- to medium-range market.

Similarities Abound

In addition to the Boeing name, the 767 and 757 have a number of features in common. Both models retain what Phil Condit, the chief 757 engineer who became chairman of Boeing in 1995, calls the 'three inviolate rules', as described in the book about Boeing, *Legend and Legacy*:

> Rule number one was tameness: when a pilot loses an engine on any Boeing airplane, he must be able to control the aircraft with his feet on the floor, not with the rudder pedals – no rudder application should be necessary, and he can maintain stability with just the yoke [steering column]. Rule number two involved stall recovery. No Boeing airplane should be put in a position in which elevator control is lost because the air flow to the tail is blocked out. Rule three: every Boeing airplane must be able to recover from a vertical or near-vertical dive.

Since the 767 and 757 were developed concurrently, they are very similar to each other.

Both aircraft are powered by two engines and both were designed with fuel-efficiency as a priority. Both boast the same electronic flight deck, so that a pilot who learns to fly one type is also qualified to fly the other. Within the cockpit, the advanced flight-management system, including the inertial reference system, caution and warning system, thrust management system and electronic displays, and, where equipped, the windshear warning system, are the same. The hydraulic system, electrical system components, fuel system, air-conditioning packs, auxiliary power unit, and anti-skid/auto-braking systems of the 757 and 767 are also all essentially identical. The same fasteners are even used in their construction. Both planes share similar handling characteristics, checklists, and visual alerts, and have the same crew procedures, oral warnings, windshield, panel location and controls.

Of 1,066 non-engine replaceable units used on the 757, 63 per cent use the same part number as the 767. Seventy-five per cent of the most expensive items on the planes are identical, and the rest are similar. Considering that the two planes are still very different in size and capabilities, this commonality is quite remarkable.

Cost savings can obviously be made from operating both the 757 and the 767. The common cockpit and systems permit training and qualification of pilots for both aircraft. (The fact that pilots may fly and remain current on both planes also allows flexibility in crew assignments.) The interchangeability of parts for both aircraft also saves money, as does commonality in training and in procedures for maintenance.

Flying six 757s and six 767s in one fleet results in initial savings to an airline of $2.4 million per aircraft; these are achieved through reducing amounts of flight-crew training, ground support equipment, airframe spares and flight and maintenance simulators. Airlines also can achieve recurring savings of $2.7 million a year per aircraft; this is achieved through reducing flight-crew training, maintenance overheads, spares overheads, and flight-crew salaries and expenses. In addition, operational costs are reduced because a single flight-crew roster gives airlines the worry-free ability to interchange 757s and 767s within route structures, and they may even make last-minute equipment changes at the gate. This flexibility also increases revenue opportunities, since airlines operating both aircraft can serve a wider variety of markets, and can more closely adjust capacity to demand in the markets they already serve.

Below is a closer look at the commonality found in the dynamic duo.

The Flight Deck

Technology may dominate the 767/757 cockpit, but Boeing did not forget about the people.

Development of the cockpit made use of human evaluations that considered legibility of equipment, consistency of procedures and logic of control and switching applications. Colours for use in caution, warning and advisory messages were standardized. Placement of cockpit items had to be compatible with acceptable procedures for normal and abnormal conditions during various phases of flight. In addition

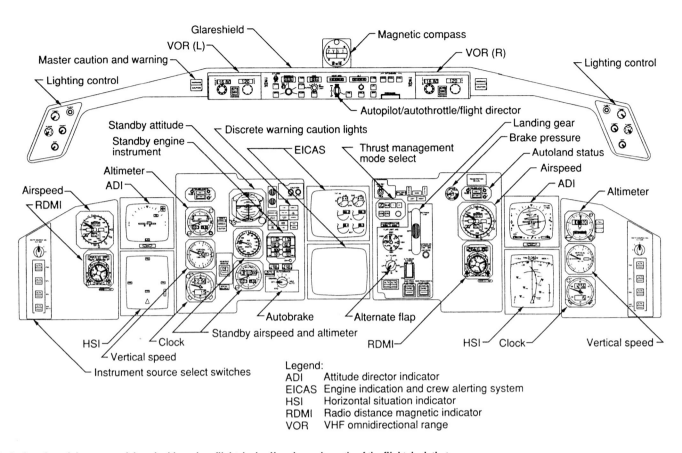

Glareshield
VOR (L)
Magnetic compass
Master caution and warning
VOR (R)
Lighting control
Lighting control
Autopilot/autothrottle/flight director
Standby attitude
Discrete warning caution lights
Landing gear
Standby engine instrument
Brake pressure
EICAS
Thrust management mode select
Autoland status
Altimeter
Airspeed
ADI
ADI
Airspeed
Altimeter
RDMI
Autobrake
Alternate flap
HSI
Clock
Standby airspeed and altimeter
RDMI
HSI
Clock
Vertical speed
Vertical speed
Instrument source select switches

Legend:
ADI   Attitude director indicator
EICAS   Engine indication and crew alerting system
HSI   Horizontal situation indicator
RDMI   Radio distance magnetic indicator
VOR   VHF omnidirectional range

Both aircraft models were envisioned with modern flight decks. Here is a schematic of the flight deck that would be used in both the 767 and 757. Boeing

Boeing was able to prove that the new cockpits led to lighter crew workloads; studies on flight-crew hand-eye motion showed that the 767/757 required less work than previous jetliners. This was done partly by leaving as many systems as possible in the 'on' position, so that control panels do not have to be scanned repeatedly before and after engine start. As a result, the pre-flight checklist is relatively short. The 767/757 flight deck offers increased reliability and advanced features, compared with older electro-mechanical instruments.

The flight deck has a low-profile control column, designed to give pilots a full view of the instrument panel. Pilots also enjoy excellent visibility, with a front wind-shield that is considerably larger than that on previous Boeing aircraft, allowing for good downward vision. This gives the flight crew a better view of runway lights on approach in poor weather.

All of the flight deck's systems controls are also within reach of either pilot. The optimum design and positioning of all controls and instruments were finalized following human-engineering studies.

Adjustable seats, lower noise levels, more efficient air-conditioning, better visibility, simplified procedures and accessibility of all controls to either pilot are just some of the ways in which the cockpit caters to crew comfort. The cockpit itself is more spacious than that of any earlier Boeing jetliner. The cockpit's inward-opening door is offset to the left, so that a pilot can enter or leave the flight deck without disturbing the observer on the left side behind the captain, or the occupant of the observer seat on the right. Inside, the cockpit is wider than the 747's at the pilot's shoulders. The windshield is flat and the side windows are curved, using a design that has been shown to decrease aerodynamic noise in the cockpit. Even at top cruising speed, noise levels in the cockpit and passenger cabin are low. Boeing's own measurement of flight-deck sound levels, taken in order to ensure that customer guarantees have been met, indicates that air-conditioning and aerodynamic sound levels are lower than those of older aircraft.

Pilots are required to sit for long periods in a relatively small space, so the cockpit seats can be raised or lowered to the correct eye level for pilots. Sheared-lambskin seat covers are standard, as a result of a Boeing seat-comfort evaluation. In the tests, instrumented seats of various types of coverings were used during simulated flights; levels of fatigue were measured by recording pilot movement. Lambskin proved to be the least tiring seat surface, and also allowed for better air circulation. Studies using crew members of a variety of sizes and heights allowed Boeing to ensure that controls, instruments and warning lights were within the reach and vision of everyone.

The glare shield over the forward instrument panel provides a clear view of the instruments for pilots and for those in observer seats. The pilots' control columns and wheels were designed and situated so as not to interfere with the pilots' view of the flight instruments. Even standard push-buttons were changed in an attempt to help the pilots. When a control is switched on, the 'on' light is visible even with bright sunshine filtering into the flight deck. The 'on' indication operates separately from the light that indicates an abnormal condition.

The six cathode ray tube video displays are the dominant feature in the cockpit, easily recognized by passengers peeking into the flight deck. Each pilot has three CRTs, which display the electronic altitude director indicator, electronic horizontal situation indicator and flight-management system control unit.

To make sure that all gauges and switches are within the reach of both the captain's and first officer's seats, Boeing automated the operation and monitoring of many of the aircraft's systems. A typical example is the auxiliary power unit – used to start the engines and provide power in the plane – which consists of one three-position knob above the captain. Turning the knob to 'start' initiates the start process; the rest is automatic. The system monitors itself and automatically shuts down if any operating parameters are exceeded.

Previous Boeing models used electro-mechanical indicators, which required constant monitoring by the flight crew. The many dials and gauges also used up considerable space on the flight deck. These systems did not offer the versatility of modern digital technology.

The 767/757 provides full-time monitoring of engine and aircraft systems, through the use of a computer and display system known as the Engine Indication and Crew Alerting System (EICAS). EICAS, found on the centre instrument panel, improves cockpit management by reducing the amount of panel space required for engine instrument displays. It reduces crew workload by effectively monitoring engine parameters, and displaying system status messages through all phases of flight, from engine start to post-flight maintenance. EICAS also displays colour-coded alert messages that communicate both the type of failure and the urgency of that failure. Only the parameters required to set and monitor engine thrust are displayed all the time.

With EICAS, pilots are alerted to any problems with the engines or the plane, from before take-off, through the flight, to after the landing. The system makes available pre-flight data, which is helpful in dispatching the aircraft, and maintenance data for ground personnel. EICAS is not just a tool for pilots. It provides an improved level of data for maintenance crews, who can tell immediately what needs fixing. During flight, pilots can create a recording of subsystem parameters through the use of a single push-button, eliminating the need for extensive hand-recording of malfunctions and performance data. These features increase the quality and accuracy of maintenance, improve communications between flight and ground crews, and reduce the flight-crew workload.

The 767/757 flight deck is designed to be quiet. Indicators are reserved for conditions that require such action as an evasive manoeuvre, to avoid a collision. The caution and warning system decreases the number of sound warnings – bells, horns and tones – by up to 75 per cent compared with previous aircraft. Sound alerts are categorized according to the level of crew action and awareness required – warning, caution and advisory. The reason for an alert is immediately posted on the screens. In general, flight-deck instrumentation is designed to present information to the crew in the best way, in order to achieve accurate and rapid interpretation. This reduces the chance of a misdiagnosis of a problem.

One key to the improvements in flight instrumentation is an inertial reference system, which makes use of laser gyroscopes rigidly fixed to the airliner's structure, rather than gimballed gyros, as on previous airliners. This system provides more accurate data – related to vertical speed and fuel quantity, for example – to other flight-deck systems.

A fully integrated flight-management computer system (FMCS) provides automatic guidance and control of both the 757 and 767, from immediately after take-off to final approach and landing. Along with digital processors, which control navigation, guidance and engine thrust, the flight-management system ensures that the aircraft flies the most efficient – or 'least time' – flight path, to achieve reduced fuel consumption, flight time and crew workload. The system is able to predict speeds and altitudes, resulting in the best fuel efficiency. The flight-management system tracks the aircraft's position at all times. Position, heading, track, flight-plan route, location of navigational aids, and distance and time to destination are continuously displayed. The computer also automatically tunes the aircraft's navigational receivers to the appropriate frequency as the flight progresses. The flight-management computer can store data on flight plans, checklists, routes, navigation aids, aircraft performance, performance optimization and flight guidance. This information may easily be displayed at any time during the flight.

One time-saver is the computer's ability to compute top-of-climb and bottom-of-descent points. It does this automatically during altitude changes, and displays a green arc on the monitors to indicate where the aircraft will reach a new altitude at its current groundspeed and rate of climb or descent. If the arc falls beyond where the new altitude must be reached, a thrust or pitch adjustment can be made to increase the climb or steepen the descent. Adjustments are reflected almost immediately on the screens with the movement of the green arc representing the target altitude. Also, with a vertical navigation mode, the computer is able to determine the best point to start the descent and the rate of descent from cruise altitude, initial approach altitude or any other altitude selected in advance.

The autopilot system in the 767 and 757 is known as the autopilot flight director system (AFDS). It provides flight-path control selected by the flight crew. Its operation is controlled from the mode control panel, and its status is displayed on the electronic airborne data indicators (EADI). Each aircraft has three flight-control computers, controlling pitch, roll and directional control. Autopilot operating modes are selected on the autoflight control system (AFCS) mode control panel. The flight-control computers use selected mode, navigation sensor inputs, and flight-management computer inputs to generate output signals. These signals can be used for flight director display only, or may be used actively to control the aircraft. The autopilot flight director system provides automatic control of the aircraft in all phases of flight.

Autopilot systems on the 757 and 767 are fundamentally identical; both use the same flight-management computer, with software specifically tailored to each configuration. Both aircraft feature the same CAT IIIb autoland system as basic equipment. With this advanced function, the planes can land in visibility as low as 150ft (45.7m).

The captain and first officer each has a pair of displays for primary flight instrumentation: the electronic attitude director indicator (EADI), and electronic horizontal situation indicator. The 767/757 EADI provides a multicoloured display of information previously found on attitude director indicators. This gives attitude information using an artificial horizon, and flight-path information showing the aircraft's position relative to the Instrument Landing System. In addition, the EADI indicates the mode in which the automatic pilot flight control system is operating and presents a digital read-out from the radio altimeter. Groundspeed is displayed digitally at all times near the airspeed indicator.

The electronic horizontal situation indicator (EHSI) provides an integrated multicoloured map display of the plane's position, plus a colour weather radar. The scale for the radar and map can be selected by the pilots. Wind direction and velocity for the airliner's present position and altitude, provided by the Inertial Reference System, is shown at all times. Both the horizontal situation of the aircraft and its deviation from the planned vertical path are also provided, making the EHSI a three-dimensional situation indicator. In poor weather, the colour weather radar can be displayed on the EHSI. Route, airport and other information can be superimposed over the weather imagery to enable crews to avoid severe weather, while staying relatively on course. This also helps flight crews steer clear of turbulence; by inserting the relevant coordinates, pilots can outline the area of turbulence on the route map displays, and that outline can be seen in relation to the route the aircraft is taking. (The crew in an aircraft without a glass cockpit is provided with a tear-off paper map, and required to plot turbulence manually.)

The 757 and 767 are available with a windshear-detection system. Caused by a violent downburst of air that changes speed and direction as it strikes the ground, windshear can interfere with a normal take-off or landing, and lead to deadly accidents. The detection system alerts flight crews, and provides flight-path guidance so that windshear may be avoided.

The communications system allows for contact between the ground and the aircraft, as well as from the flight deck to the passengers. A voice recorder records the last thirty minutes of flight-crew communications and conversations, and this is retrieved in the event of an accident. Communications systems on the 757 and 767 are virtually the same, with both using the same line-replaceable units and communication controls. Both planes have dual Very High Frequency (VHF) radios as basic equipment.

Boeing models that debuted after the dynamic duo, including the 737-300/400/500, 747-400, 777 and the new generation of 737s, sport digital flight decks similar to that found on the 767/757, integrating hundreds of software upgrades from the earliest 757s and 767s. Software in older models is constantly updated, so that a ten-year-old aircraft will carry the latest technology. Likewise, newer 757s and 767s feature the most up-to-date configurations.

The two aircraft share similar fuselage windows, located in three distinct areas: the flight deck, the passenger cabin, and service and emergency doors. Both offer access to various compartments and service areas through different-sized entry, service, emergency, cargo and access doors. These include passenger doors, emergency exits, cargo doors, landing-gear doors, external ground power receptacles, a toilet service door, water service door, hydraulic access doors, APU access door, elevator controls access door and aft body access door.

On the 757, the passenger doors open on hinges in the usual way; on the 767, the

Both the 767 and 757 have flexible cabins to allow for different classes of service or a one-class charter configuration. Bulkheads such as this one in a 757 serve to break up the long fuselage. Bill Dellinges

The Passenger Cabin

Cabin systems provide for the comfort and convenience of passengers and crew members, for the handling and stowing of cargo, and for passenger and crew safety in an emergency. The systems include furnishings, lighting, oxygen, galleys and lavatories. The 757 and 767 share many of the same elements in the passenger cabin, including seats, stowage bins, carpeting, seat racks, flotation devices, and dozens of other items. When the aircraft debuted, both featured a new interior design with pleasing lines and more efficient stowage bins.

doors slide into the ceiling. The overwing exits on both planes are similar to those used on the 707, 727 and 737 models.

The 757 and 767 passenger accommodation and cargo systems are essentially the same, except that the 767 has vacuum lavatories – a feature incorporated on the newer 757-300. Minor systems differences, such as plumbing and compartmental quantities, are required to accommodate differences in fuselage size (single as opposed to two aisles), and passenger counts.

The 757 has twelve exits: six cabin doors, four overwing emergency exits and two cockpit window hatches. The 767, although

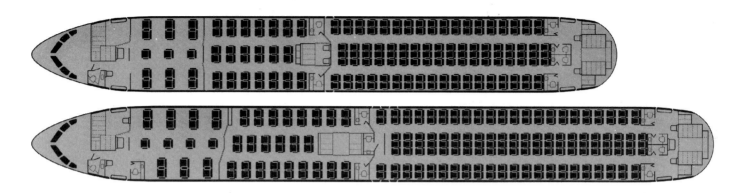

767 seating diagrams. Boeing

● Inclusive tour

● Two class

○ |Three class

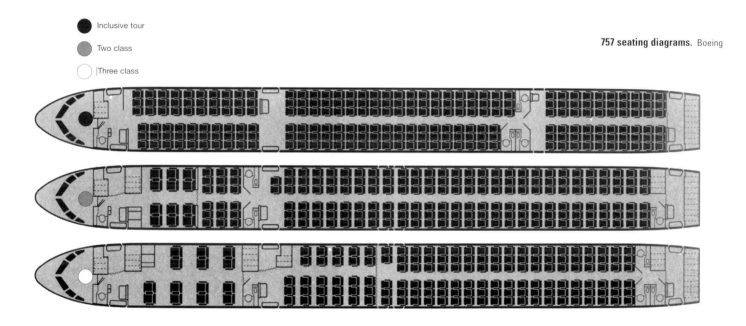

larger in capacity, has ten: four cabin doors, four emergency exits and the cockpit windows. Interior and exterior lights are almost identical on the 757 and 767.

Flight Controls

The 767 and 757 share the same flight controls: ailerons, which control the longitudinal axis (roll); the elevators, which control the lateral axis (pitch), and the rudder, which controls the vertical axis (yaw). The secondary flight controls are the spoilers and speedbrakes, horizontal stabilizer, leading-edge slats and trailing-edge flaps. All are controlled by electrical and hydraulic cables and wires with triple

redundancy – if one fails, two more are ready to take over.

The horizontal stabilizer is driven by an electrically controlled, hydraulically powered ballscrew actuator. Leading-edge flaps are mechanically controlled and hydraulically powered, using torque tubes and rotary actuators. Alternate operation is by electric control and an electric motor through the same torque tubes and rotary actuators. Trailing-edge and leading-edge flaps are mechanically controlled and hydraulically powered, using torque tubes and transmissions. Alternate operation is by electric control and an electric motor through the same torque tubes and transmissions.

All primary flight controls are hydraulically powered. The elevators and rudder are powered by three hydraulic systems, and each aileron is powered by two hydraulic systems. Each spoiler is powered by a single hydraulic system and is electrically commanded.

Flight-deck indications and controls for both aircraft are almost identical, but differences in aircraft size, aerodynamics and mission requirements produce some differences in flight controls. For example, the 757 actuators have pressure-reducers, and each elevator is commanded by a single load path linkage with centring springs; the 767 uses a linkage backed up by a sleeve cable.

The main landing gear of the 757 has two sets of four braked wheels.
Bill Dellinges

The 757 and 767 have two unbraked nosegear wheels. Shown here is a 757.
Bill Dellinges

The 767 employs both inboard and outboard ailerons with boost actuators for the control cables. The outboard ailerons are locked out for high-speed flight, and the inboard ailerons are drooped, to supplement the flaps. The 757 has one aileron on each wing and no cable boost. The 767 uses all twelve spoilers in flight. The 757 has ten spoilers, and spoilers number 4 and 9 are used only on the ground. The 767 has twelve slats, while the 757 has ten. The 757 has double-slotted inboard and outboard flaps; the 767 outboard flaps are single-slotted.

Landing Gear

Landing gear on both aircraft is retracted by the left hydraulic system, which consists of the left engine-driven pump and one electric pump. If the engine-driven pump is inoperative, the right hydraulic system operates a power transfer unit to retract the gear.

The nosewheel steering systems provide rudder-pedal steering and steering via the tiller. Hydraulic control consists of the steering metering valve and steering actuators. A single-loop cable system provides

inputs to the steering metering valve. A broken cable compensator is installed, to prevent a sustained steering input if the cable fails. The 757 incorporates the same concept used on the 727, 737 and 747 to prevent rudder-pedal steering when the aircraft is flying. Nosegear for the 757 and 767 is similar to that on the 737 but is larger.

Both the 767 and 757 have two unbraked wheels for the nosegear and four braked wheels for each main gear, for a total of eight. The 767 and 757 brakes, main wheels, nosewheels and tyres are different, but certified the same. Maintenance

The 767's landing gear and tyres are larger than a 757's to reflect its heavier weight.
Boeing

Fuel Systems

Fuel systems on the 757 and 767 operate in a similar manner, and maintenance is virtually the same. Both aircraft have the same fuel-system controls and display read-outs on the flight deck, follow the same basic layouts and have many common parts, but there are differences in tank geometry and tubing sizes, and they have completely different boost pumps. Although both aircraft have three separate fuel tanks, the 757 wing centre section is an active part of the centre fuel tank. On the 767, the centre section is used for fuel on the extended-range models only.

The fuelling panel for the 757 is located on the right wing; on the 767, the panel is on the left wing. Fuel capacity of the 767-200 and -300 is 16,700 gallons (63,216 litres). Extended-range models have an additional 7,440 gallons (28,163 litres) in a second centre tank. The 757's fuel capacity is 11,276 gallons (42,684 litres); ER versions carry slightly more.

Wings

The wings on both the 767 and 757 store fuel, house the fuel-system equipment, support the engines and contain the flaps, spoilers and ailerons. The primary structures are aluminium, and they consist of the front and rear spars, upper and lower spar chords, webs, skin panels and stringers, and ribs. The upper and lower spar chord extrusions attach to the front and rear spar webs. Chords, stiffeners and webs make up the ribs. Conventional ribs are spaced through the entire wing. Shear tie ribs distribute specific loads to the wing frame. The landing gear is supported by the landing-gear support beam and rear spar.

The secondary structures consist of the leading edge, trailing edge and wing tip. The leading edge is cantilevered forward from the front spar, and is made of aluminium ribs and skin panels. The leading-edge slats attach to the leading edge. The trailing edge is cantilevered aft from the rear spar, and supports the flaps, aileron and spoilers. The wing tip is an aerodynamic fairing covering the outboard ends of the wing. Navigation lights attach to each wing tip.

Auxiliary Power Unit (APU)

The auxiliary power unit supplies electrical and pneumatic power for the aircraft.

procedures for each landing-gear system, however, are almost identical.

Hydraulic Systems

Three functionally independent, full-time systems provide hydraulic power for fully powered flight controls, landing gear, thrust reversers, high-lift and braking systems. Hydraulic system reservoirs are pressurized with bleed air from either engine, the auxiliary power system or ground air carts. Hydraulic systems for the 767 and 757 are basically identical; with only the size differing. The hydraulic systems for both aircraft are designed to operate in the same manner with full redundancy.

The 767 and 757 use identical engine-driven and electric motor-driven pumps to generate hydraulic power, and similar ram air turbines provide back-up hydraulic power to the centre system for primary flight control actuation. Hydraulic system servicing is very similar because both models have parts in common, including fill service selector valves and ground connections.

Distribution system components, such as fittings, valves and tubing, are identical for almost all installations. Titanium tubing is used for pressurized lines. The filtration system is similar for both planes, with pressure and case drain filters for each pump and return filters for each system.

Hydraulic system flight-deck indications and controls for both aircraft are almost identical. Minor differences reflect the two distinct hydraulic power system architectures, which are based on subtleties in 757 and 767 control surface requirements. For example, the 757 uses only outboard ailerons, whereas the 767 employs inboard and outboard ailerons. The landing gear and high-lift devices are hydraulically powered by the left hydraulic system on the 757, and by the centre hydraulic system on the 767. Power for the left hydraulic system is supplied by an engine-motor pump, an electric-motor pump, and a power transfer unit that is driven from the right hydraulic system if power is lost on the left one. Power for the 767 centre hydraulic system is provided by two electric pumps and an air-driven pump.

On the ground, the APU makes the plane independent of support equipment. The Garrett-made APU is controlled by an electronic control unit located in the back of the plane. The electrical control unit co-ordinates the starting sequence, monitors the operation and pneumatic output of the APU, and ensures proper shutdown. The Engine Indication and Crew Alerting System (EICAS) shows the flight crew the APU exhaust gas temperature, revolutions per minute and oil status. The APU is warranted to start up to an altitude of 35,000ft (10,670m).

The APU supplies all the power needed for air-conditioning on the ground. Each of the three cabin zones in the aircraft has a separate automatic temperature control. Conditioned air is mixed by air-conditioning packs with recirculated and filtered air from two recirculation fans. Flight-deck air distribution is through ducting to various floor, shoulder and windshield outlets. Passenger-compartment air is distributed through sidewall risers and overhead ducts to the passenger areas, lavatories and galleys. Exhaust air from the lavatories and galleys is routed through a network of ducts, valves and fans, and is discharged overboard.

Air Systems

The 767 and 757 use basically the same heating, cooling, pressurization and air-conditioning packs. Components for the cabin-pressure control system are identical. Because of aircraft performance differences, the climb schedules for the two aircraft vary and are selectable for each model. The 767/757 electrical and electronic cooling systems are functionally and operationally similar. Both systems use similar fans, ducting, valves and avionics installations, and both have similar warning and indication systems.

Pressure inside the cabin is controlled by regulating the discharge of air from the aircraft. Manual and automatic controls for this system are located on the pilots' overhead panel.

Composite Materials

Both the 757 and 767 were among the first to take advantage of new-technology composites that are lighter and stronger than aluminium, and this is a key factor in their fuel efficiency. Significant weight savings were made by substituting carbon and aramid advanced fibre composite materials for conventional metal and fibreglass construction. These materials also provide improved resistance to fatigue, corrosion and sonic effects, and superior aerodynamic surfaces.

Carbon fibre is used for the primary movable surfaces, such as the ailerons, elevators, rudder, spoilers and aft flaps. Carbon-reinforced aramid-fibreglass hybrids are used for secondary fairing structures. High-strength cure carbon-epoxy raw material is used for the majority of the components. Large surface panels use honeycomb sandwich construction, with solid laminate edge bands for attachment to supporting structures. Each aluminium component is anodized, primed and enamelled individually. An isolating sealant is applied to all contact surfaces at assembly, and on all fasteners. Corrosion-resistant steel or titanium fasteners are used exclusively with carbon components.

The use of titanium has greatly increased in both aircraft. Titanium alloy forgings are used in the main landing-gear support structure, and for various fuselage and nacelle strut fittings. Titanium is also used for high-pressure tubing and ducting, and for firewalls, door thresholds and scuff plates. The primary fuselage bulkheads are the forward pressure nose and main-gear wheel wells, and the front spar and rear spar, main landing gear, aft pressure and horizontal stabilizer pivot bulkheads.

The passenger floor structure is a built-up grid system consisting of floorbeams, stabilizing straps, seat or freight tie-down tracks, and floor panels. Seat tracks are made of aluminium extrusions, and designed to allow placement of seats anywhere along the floor. Galleys and lavatories are attached to the floor structure using special fittings. Tracks made from stainless steel may be used when quick removal and replacement of the galley is required. Floor panels are lightweight laminations composed of fibreglass skins with an aluminium honeycomb core.

Fire Protection

Both aircraft share the same potent fire-protection system. Two fire-extinguisher bottles can be directed to either engine. The auxiliary power unit also has two fire detectors, but only one extinguisher. The lower cargo compartments have dual smoke detectors, as do all lavatories, which activate the fire-warning system if

smoke is detected. There are two extinguishing bottles located forward of the aft cargo compartment, and either one or both can be discharged into either compartment. Halon is used to extinguish fires in the cargo hold, because the substance will not damage sensitive equipment.

In freighters, the main-deck cargo compartment has a continuous air-sampling system for smoke detection, and the lower cargo compartments have the same systems as the passenger aircraft. There are no fire extinguishers for either the main deck or lower cargo deck. Fire is extinguished by depressurizing the aircraft, which reduces the oxygen needed for combustion.

The 767 and 757 fire-detection and extinguishing systems are very similar in indication and operation. Wheel well detectors and engine-fire protection systems differ only in the routing and positioning of sensing elements. Although three different manufacturers supply fire-protection equipment, all operate in the same manner and trigger the same indicators on the flight deck.

Ice and Rain Protection

To keep the wing free of ice during flight, engine-bleed air is directed to outboard leading-edge slats on each wing. Engine-bleed air is also directed to the engine-cowl inlet lip to prevent ice formation. Flight-deck windshields are electrically heated to keep fog and ice from building. The flight deck's side windows are electrically heated for anti-fogging only. Electric heating is used in the water and waste systems to prevent freezing during flight. Rain repellent is used with the windshield wipers to improve visibility during heavy precipitation. The ice- and rain-protection systems on the 767 and 757 work the same, but differ in size.

computer-aided design and manufacturing to design and build the 767 and 757. More than a dozen years later, this technology made possible the 777, which was designed entirely by computers.

New planes were traditionally designed in two dimensions, by making drawings on paper. However, the 767 and 757 were partly designed by computers, so that engineers could see how those drawings would fit together on a three-dimensional aircraft. In this way, unpleasant discoveries

the need for customized hydraulics was called TUBEND, a computer-aided design and manufacturing system developed for the 757. The programme moved hydraulics design from the drawing board and aircraft mock-up to a computerized model of the hydraulic system. It allowed engineers to see what would happen everywhere in the hydraulic system when a change was made in any one place.

On the 757 alone, engineers designed nearly 11,000 packages of drawings and

A full-scale 757 mock-up, used prior to assembly. Today, computers are used to design new planes, eliminating this time-consuming step. Boeing

Computer Design

Boeing did not just put computers in the cockpit of its new planes. In 1978, the company started using a computer design system to design some parts for some aircraft, and it made extensive use of

later in the manufacturing process – such as finding a particular part impossible to install because a designer had failed to leave enough space – are avoided.

In one example, Boeing introduced computers to streamline the manufacturing process. One programme to eliminate

data to build the plane, and almost half of them were made with the use of computer-aided design. When a wing strut was designed for the 767 using the computer design system, Boeing found it cut in half the number of changes that it might expect to have to make during manufacture.

CHAPTER SIX

Powerplants

There is a saying among those who work for engine-maker Pratt & Whitney: 'Without engines, aircraft are just flying Winnebagos.'

How do engines propel the aircraft? Think of it this way: an engine performs four tasks with air – it sucks, squeezes, burns and blows. Air is sucked in by a large rotating fan and compressed in several stages until it enters a combustion chamber under pressure. Here, heated by jet fuel, the air, bursting to expand, rushes out through turbine blades, which are rotated at high speeds by the rush of hot air. Huge fan blades on the front of the engine – 87–94in (2.41–2.61m) in diameter for the 767 and 78in (2.16m) for the 757 – generate the thrust an aircraft needs in order to take off. The fans are essentially giant propellers that pull the plane through the air.

Requirements, Reliability and Safety

The fact is, the contribution of an engine manufacturer is greater than that of any other supplier, and many aspects of engine technology are even more daunting than the design of the airframe itself. Some areas in the engine must withstand temperatures of 3,000 degrees centigrade during several hours of flight. Some parts travel at supersonic speeds, while others must survive hours of high-frequency vibration.

Powerplants for twin-engined aircraft face the additional demands of having to achieve flawless reliability; this is achieved through high-quality design and impeccable maintenance. The amazing thing about aircraft engines is that, generally, they manage to run hour upon hour, at various atmospheric pressures and temperatures, and at extreme rotational speeds, without a single problem.

The reliability of today's high bypass-ratio engines has made long-range, twin-engine flights possible. Bypass ratio measures the air ducted around the core of a turbofan to the air that passes through the core of the engine. For example, in a 6-to-

1 bypass-ratio engine, six parts of air pass around the core compared with one part that passes through it. In a high bypass-ratio engine, the fan at the front of the engine develops the bulk of the engine's total thrust. The air that passes through the core is called primary air flow. The air that bypasses the core is called secondary air flow. Bypass ratio, simply, is the ratio between secondary and primary air flow, and, the higher the ratio, the more efficient the engine. It is more efficient to accelerate a large mass of air moderately through the fan to develop thrust than to greatly accelerate a smaller mass of air through the core to develop equivalent thrust.

Jet engines made today are ten times more reliable than those produced a decade or two ago. This has commercial ramifications for engine-makers – greater reliability means that the engines must produce profits from their sale rather than from spare parts.

As engines have become more reliable, twin-engine flights have become safer over time. The 767, for example, had experienced just twenty-five in-flight shutdowns after one million hours of engine service – a rate of .025 per thousand hours. By 10 million engine hours, that rate had dropped below .02 per thousand hours. This is a huge improvement on pre-1981 airliners, when the engines had in-flight shutdown rates of .33 per thousand hours, or 333 times per thousand hours.

More than half of the in-flight engine shutdowns on commercial airliners have nothing to do with the core of the engine. They are more likely to be related to pneumatic systems or electrical systems, or to fire-detection systems vibrating. For example, an engine might be shut down because of a simple faulty warning light.

Engines and Engine Manufacturers

The airline, not the airframe manufacturer, selects the engines to be put into their

aircraft. Boeing specifies the thrust required, the engine size and position on the plane, then the major engine manufacturers – Pratt & Whitney and General Electric in the United States and Britain's Rolls-Royce – offer the engines. The dynamic duo required new or improved engines. The 767 was the first twin-jet to offer all three engine choices, while only Pratt and Rolls make engines for the 757.

The decision to pick one engine-maker over another is determined by many factors. Often, an airline chooses to go with a manufacturer that has already supplied engines for other planes in the fleet, giving the airline's mechanics an advantage in that they will be familiar with the equipment. Sometimes, the decision will follow a highly competitive bidding process as the airline tries to get the best cost and conditions. (Often, new engines are sold essentially at cost, so that a deal may be achieved, and engine-makers hope to make up the loss through long-term maintenance and spare-parts contracts.) Airlines will also take into consideration the fuel economy and the maintenance track record of an engine.

Engines for the 767

Alternative engines on the 767 are General Electric's CF6-80C2, Pratt & Whitney's PW4000 and the Rolls-Royce RB211-524/H (on the -300 only), all rated at between 50,000 and 62,000lb of thrust (222–276kN). The 767-200, -200ER and -300 are available with Pratt & Whitney PW4050 engines rated at 50,000lb of thrust (222kN), the PW4052, rated at 52,000lb of thrust (231kN), and the GE CF6-80C2B2F, rated at 57,900lb of thrust (258kN). The CF6-80C2B4F is available on the -200ER, -300 and -300ER. The PW4056, rated at 56,750lb (252kN), and the PW4060 and GE CF6-80C2B6, rated at 60,000lb of thrust (267kN), are available only on extended-range versions. The Rolls-Royce RB211-524G, rated at 60,600lb of thrust (270kN), has been available since 1990 on the -300.

Engine installation on a 767-300. Boeing

The first production 767s, and the first to enter service, were powered by Pratt & Whitney's JT9D-7R4 engine, an upgraded version of the type that was first certified in 1969 and debuted on the 747 in 1970 to power first-generation widebodied aircraft. When the engine was selected to power the 767, it had already proven itself on the DC-

10 and Airbus A300, in addition to the 747. Its track record largely contributed to its selection as the powerplant of the first of Boeing's new twins. Although not originally conceived for twin-engine aircraft, the JT9D was a natural choice as widebody twins grew in popularity. Major technological advances, including a wide-chord, single-shroud fan blade, single-crystal turbine blades and an electronic engine control, provided substantial fuel savings over earlier JT9D models.

Many 767s built in 1987 and later, including 767-300s, are powered by the PW4000, a new-technology JT9D replacement begun in 1984 and certified in 1986. The model is also found on such widebodies as the 747-400, A310 and MD-11. Larger versions of the PW4000 power the 777 and the Airbus A330. The model first powered a 767 in May 1986, and it entered revenue service in June

1987. Fewer parts and a simpler design made it cheaper to operate than the JT9D. The PW4000 is also 7 per cent more fuel-efficient than its predecessor. The PW4000 offers more power – 52,000–62,000lb of thrust (231–276kN), compared with 43,000–56,000lb (191–249kN) – than the JT9D-7R4; production of the latter ended in 1990.

Engine Specification – 767 General Electric CF6-80C2	
Thrust:	60,690–61,348lb (270–273kN)
Diameter:	93in (236cm)
Length:	160.9in (408cm)
Weight:	9,135lb (4,144kg)
Air flow:	1,769lb (802kg) per second

Engine Specification – 767 Pratt & Whitney JT9D-7R4 Engine	
Thrust:	48,000lb (213kN)
Diameter:	96.98in (246cm)
Length:	132.7in (337cm)
Weight:	8,885lb (4,029kg)
Air flow:	1,585lb (719kg) per second

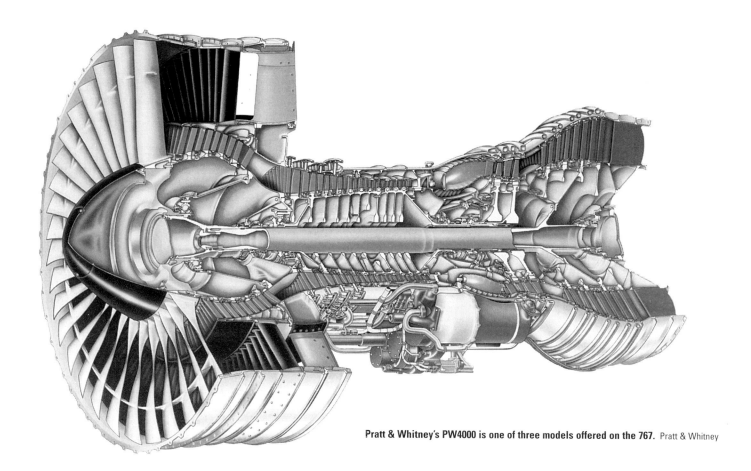

Pratt & Whitney's PW4000 is one of three models offered on the 767. Pratt & Whitney

Engine Specification – 767 Pratt & Whitney PW4000 Engine	
Thrust:	50,000–60,000lb (222.4–270kN)
Diameter:	96.98in (246.3cm)
Length:	132.7in (337cm)
Weight:	9,400lb (4,264kg)
Air flow:	1,705lb (773kg) per second

GE's CF6-80C2 engines, with 52,500–61,500lb of thrust (233–273kN), also power the 767. The engine family, like the PW4000, is found on other widebodies, including the 747-400, Airbus A300-600, A310 and A330, and MD-11. The CF6-80C2 provides a 7 per cent fuel consumption advantage over an earlier version of the engine, the CF6-80A. The first 767 powered by 48,000lb-thrust (213kN) CF6-80A engines took off for the first time in February 1982; it was the fifth 767 built. Certification followed on 30 September, with the first delivery to Delta Air Lines. While United Airlines chose Pratt for its order of 767s, both Delta and American selected GE for their 1978 order of fifty of the planes. When the 767 debuted, Pratt signed ten customers with orders and options for 158 aircraft, while GE had seven customers for 153 planes. An important advantage of both the JT9D-7R4 and the CF6-80A was that both had already flown the 747, and were therefore battle-tested. Neither was a totally new powerplant, unlike the engines of the 757. GE initially offered the CF6-45, a derivative of the engine powering the DC-10. But it was quickly realized the engine would not grow into enough thrust for a widebody twin. So GE developed the CF6-80A, which featured a new fan generating more thrust.

Although Pratt and GE got off to a quick start in engine orders, Rolls-Royce did not become a player on the 767 until February 1990, when the RB211-524H, a 58,000–60,000lb-thrust (258–267kN) variant of the engine that also powers the 747-400, was reconfigured for the 767-300ER. The engine is found on only about thirty 767-300ERs, almost all in the British Airways fleet. Their commonality with the RB211 that powers 747s benefits airlines operating both aircraft. In the three-way race, GE has 62 per cent of the 767 share, Pratt 32 per cent, and Rolls just 6 per cent.

The new 767-400 will initially be powered by an upgraded CF6, the CF6-80C2B7F1 model. This version features a 'boltless turbine' that improves performance, and reduces part count, weight and cost. The engine was selected by the -400's launch customer, Delta Air Lines. Pratt & Whitney is now working on an improved PW4000 to meet the higher-thrust needs of the newest 767.

Engine Specification – 767 Rolls-Royce RB211-524H Engine	
Thrust:	59,326lb (264kN)
Diameter:	86.3in (219cm)
Length:	125in (318cm)
Weight:	9,874lb (4,479kg)
Air flow:	1,604lb (728kg) per second

The General Electric CF6-80C2 is offered on 767s. GE Aircraft Engines.

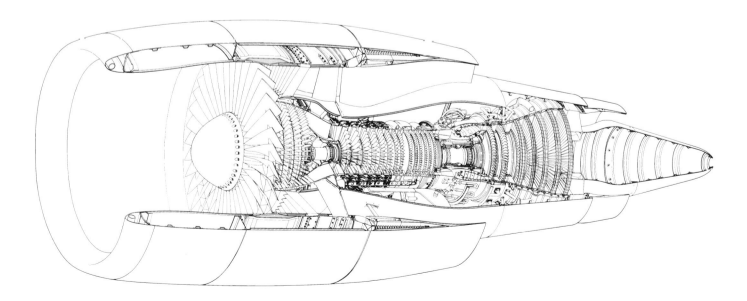

Although Pratt & Whitney and GE got off to a quick start on the 767, Rolls-Royce did not become a player on the model until 1990, when the RB211-524 was reconfigured for the 767-300. Rolls-Royce

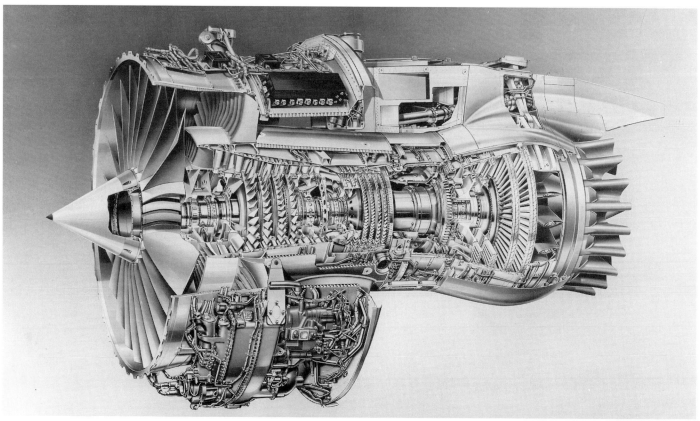

Engines for the 757

The 757 required a larger engine than the 737 or 727, but a smaller one than the 767. It was the first narrow-body plane designed with all-new high bypass-ratio engines, and it became the target of a spirited powerplant competition between Rolls-Royce and Pratt & Whitney. The first engine to enter service, Rolls-Royce's RB211-535, with 36,600lb of thrust (163 kN), was a reduced-thrust version of the already proven RB211 used on other widebodies, including the 747. Since it was a smaller derivative engine, the Rolls programme had an advantage over Pratt. The engine's track record was a big factor in Eastern Airlines choosing Rolls-Royce for the first-ever fleet of 757s. Frank Borman, the airline's former chairman, explains: 'We had had terrible experiences with Rolls in the past. But this was a derivative engine, and Rolls assured us it had fixed any problems. It's a wonderful engine. It made a lot of sense for Eastern.'

The 757 became the first new Boeing airliner to make its debut with foreign powerplants.

The 757 was originally offered with GE's CF6-32C1 engines. However, GE

Rolls-Royce RB211-535E4. This was the launch engine for the 757 – The first non-US made engine on a new Boeing. Rolls-Royce

Engine Specification – 757 Rolls-Royce RB211-535E4 Engine	
Thrust:	43,100lb (191.7kN)
Diameter:	74.5in (189.2cm)
Length:	117.9in (299cm)
Weight:	7,189lb (3,261kg)
Air flow:	1,150lb (522kg) per second

later withdrew as a contender to power the 757 when Pratt & Whitney designed a new engine, the PW2000, which was selected by Delta Air Lines. Delta took delivery of the first Pratt-powered 757 in October 1984. GE's engine was deemed to have a larger core than the aircraft needed. Following Pratt's entry into the fray with its PW2000, GE decided that the advantages of developing an engine for the 757 were minimal, and focused its efforts elsewhere. The 757 programme was 25 per cent complete when the CF6 pulled out, forcing Boeing engineers to make some quick adjustments. In April 1980, Hawaiian carrier Aloha Airlines was the only airline to order 757s with CF6-32 engines. However, Aloha never took delivery of 757s, and GE never powered the aircraft.

The highly fuel-efficient PW2000, featuring low noise and emissions, spans a take-off thrust of 30,000–44,000lb (133–196kN). The PW2037 – the '37' indicating the number of pounds of thrust in thousands – was the first in the series, and received FAA certification in December 1983, four years after the programme's launch. Development of the engine, as with the planes it powers, was a collaborative effort, with MTU of Germany sharing 11 per cent of the engine work, and Italy's Fiat 4 per cent. A higher-rated PW2000 model, the PW2040, offering 41,700lb of thrust (185kN) for all 757 models, was certified in 1987, and introduced into service that year by United Parcel Service on its 757 Package Freighter.

The PW2000's compressor and turbine disks are made of a powder metal alloy. This technology allows operation at higher rotor speeds and temperatures than engines operating with disks made by conventional methods. The model also introduced commercial aviation to electronic fuel controls; this was an uncertain development that raised many questions. 'It was a gutsy decision to make,' recalls Doug

Miller. 'We all put a game face on to make sure an electronic fuel control would work. But I said, "Show me a way to put a hydro-mechanical device on here if we have to".' As a result of this suggestion, the plane did include the electronic fuel control, but there was also room for an alternative if necessary.

Both 757 engine manufacturers improved their product over the years. An upgraded Rolls version, the RB211-535E4, has proven to be 6.5 per cent more fuel-efficient than the -535C. It was built on to later 757s, or even retrofitted in some cases. Improvements included a high-efficiency, wide-blade fan, a better high-pressure module, and a single-nozzle exhaust system. The first 757 to fly with the improved engine was delivered to Eastern on 10 October 1984. Further improvements to the -E4 included the introduction in 1999 of a scaled combustor from Rolls-Royce's Trent engine series, leading to lower emissions. Pratt improved its PW2000 in 1994 with the PW2000 RTC (reduced-temperature configuration), which offers better fuel economy, lower operating temperatures and lower maintenance cost than previous models.

The new 757-300 is available with Rolls RB211-535E4 and Pratt's PW2043 engines.

Boeing has given credit to both engine manufacturers for their role in making the 757 so fuel-efficient. According to Pratt & Whitney, a fully loaded 757 flying from Frankfurt to New York can carry 11,200lb (5,080kg) – or 55 passengers – more than an RB211-powered 757. This offers a yearly revenue potential of up to $7.5 million per aircraft.

Initially, five customers with firm orders for 55 planes ordered 757s with Rolls engines, while Pratt signed three airlines for 81 firm orders. The initial batch destined for Eastern, British Airways, Monarch Airlines and Air Florida were powered by the Rolls engines. Another early customer, Transbrasil, opted for three Rolls-powered 757s and six Pratt-powered planes, giving the engines a side-by-side trial from 1984–7.

Rolls leads Pratt in engines installed in 757s (about 500 planes against 400, and thirty-eight customers against fifteen), although Pratt was selected by Delta, United and Northwest Airlines, three of the largest 757 customers.

Although the engines were developed for the 757, both companies have found

additional applications for them. The PW2000 also powers the Ilyushin IL-96, a four-engined Russian passenger aircraft similar to the Airbus A340, along with the four-engined C-17 military cargo jet. The RB211 powers the Tupolev 204, a Russian 757 lookalike.

The PW2000 Programme

Pratt's decision to develop an all-new engine for the 757 was a pivotal moment in the engine business. Over the years, the company has made more than 14,000 venerable JT8D engines to power 727s, 737-100s and -200s, DC-9s and MD-80s, most of which are still flying today. In the early 1980s, Pratt decided not to design an engine for newer 737s – this proved to be a poor decision, considering that the 737 would go on to become the most popular model ever made. Boeing advised Pratt that the new 757 would be an even bigger programme, so Pratt dropped plans to build a new engine for the 737 (the JT10D), and focused instead on the PW2000 as its future hope. 'Boeing said the 757 would be a replacement to the 727, which was at the time the best-selling airplane in the world,' says Ed Crow, senior vice-president of engineering at Pratt & Whitney. 'We wanted to be on that airplane.'

Crow recalls how Pratt's parent company, United Technologies, was approached for the $1 billion needed to develop the PW2000, an engine that would decrease fuel burn in comparison with the 727. 'We told Harry Gray [United Technologies' chairman] that when this engine would go into service, fuel prices would be $3 a gallon,' Crow says. 'So fuel efficiency was the name of the game. Unfortunately, the world changed. When it went into service, fuel prices were not $3 a gallon, but 50 cents a gallon; consequently, airlines made a decision to keep flying their 727s.

Engine Specification – 757 Pratt & Whitney PW2000 Engine	
Thrust:	37,000–43,000lb (164.7–191.3kN)
Diameter:	84.8in (215.4cm)
Length:	146.8in (372.9cm)
Weight:	7,300lb (3,311kg)
Air flow:	1,340lb (608kg) per second

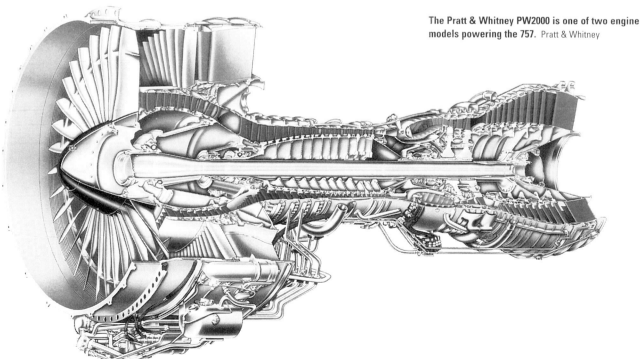

The Pratt & Whitney PW2000 is one of two engine models powering the 757. Pratt & Whitney

A Rolls-Royce RB211-535C is prepared for assembly onto a 757. Boeing

The 757 did not sell the way we expected it to. However, today, when you look at it, every major US airline has 757s as a replacement for their 727 fleet. So by and large, the PW2000 has succeeded.'

Crow, who was responsible for the PW2000 programme, recalls that one major problem almost kept the engine from flying on time – fan-containment failure. Fan blades rotate at near-supersonic speeds inside the engine. In case the blades come loose, or are damaged by an outside source, such as a bird or stone, the engine must contain the broken blades; otherwise, they could slice through the passenger cabin. Until the PW2000, every engine used a steel casing to contain the blades in the event of fan disintegration during engine failure. The PW2000 was the first Pratt engine to use Kevlar, a light but strong synthetic material, to do the job. With the first Pratt-powered 757s coming off the production lines in November 1983, the PW2000's Kevlar casing was failing the fan-containment tests. As a back-up, engineers decided to use standard steel instead. This last-

minute move led to the engine's certification on time. (Despite its unsuccessful start, Kevlar protection did succeed on later engines.)

Crow confirms that Pratt is pleased to have played a role in the development of both the 767 and 757. 'These are truly great transportation systems. World class,' he says. 'The 767 has revolutionized travel over the north Atlantic. Both of these planes are very fuel-efficient transporta-

tion systems. Either one of these airplanes with our engines on them will move one passenger a distance of 100 miles [160km] at a speed of 500 miles an hour [800km/h] on a single gallon [3.75 litres] of gas. They largely introduced the world to flying. Look at flying now compared with the time when they entered service, and at the number of people who fly today. It is way, way up. These airplanes have largely contributed to that.'

Testing the Engines

An engine is shipped to Boeing from the manufacturer's – Pratt & Whitney in East Hartford, Connecticut, GE in Evendale, Ohio, and Rolls in Derby, England – having been fully tested and certified. Once mounted on to the wings of the 767 or 757, these massive powerplants are put through additional testing before a plane may receive the green light to fly. About 300 control and indication wires link the engines to the flight deck.

Like the flight-control test system, engines are tested with computer-controlled simulators. The computer is programmed to simulate engine response to the flight-deck controls and instruments in a test sequence according to engineering requirements.

Once installed, engines have to be 'trimmed'. This means verifying that the engines are adjusted and operate properly so that they can achieve their rated thrust for take-off and in flight. Engines are adjusted at the factories, but they must be checked again after they are installed. During the engine trim, the engine is run up and throttles are set at certain power settings. Flight-test engineers then read the instrumentation. If the primary thrust rates are not to specification, adjustments are made to fuel controls, air inlet and bleed valve, and between the engine compressors, to bleed excess air.

CHAPTER SEVEN

Rollout

Worldwide Partners on the 767

Just one month after United's order for the first 767s, Boeing began to organize an international team of risk-sharing participants and subcontractors. It was the beginning of a long partnership, through which Boeing selected companies from all over the world to furnish parts for the new airplanes. The 767 was the first Boeing plane to involve the efforts of overseas partners.

The Italian firm Aeritalia, a partner on the original 7X7, became the first risk-sharing participant in the 767 development and production programme. A contract was signed on 14 August 1978, with Aeritalia agreeing to manufacture the wing control surface areas, wing trailing-edge flaps and leading-edge struts, wing tips, elevators, vertical tail, rudder and radome. A month later, on 22 September 1978, Civil Transport Development Corp. of Japan (now Commercial Airplane Co., or CAC) also became a risk-sharing participant. About fifty Japanese engineers became involved in the design process, and Japanese subcontractors were subsequently to play a significant role in the manufacturing. Three Japanese companies – Mitsubishi, Kawasaki and Fuji – manufacture the entire 767 fuselage, with the exception of the cockpit, known as Section 41, which is built at Boeing's facilities in Witchita, Kansas. Fuji produces lightweight, aluminium and composite outboard trailing-edge flaps, located on the rear of each wing. They serve as flight-control devices, which, when extended by the pilot, create extra lift during take-off and lower the plane's speed when landing. Civil Transport Development Corp. also produces body panels and doors, fairing assemblies and main landing-gear doors.

To allay the fears of its local employees about foreign work on the plane, Boeing explained that, at the time, 60 per cent of its sales were going abroad, and that other countries wanted to play a role in the production process. Boeing also told its workers how difficult it was to compete with Airbus, which at the time was subsidized by the four European nations making up the consortium – France, Germany, Britain and Spain.

The 767 Rollout

With partners in place and orders in hand – United's launch, along with Delta and American's $1.9 billion order in November 1978 – the manufacturing of parts for the first 767 began, on 6 July 1979, at Boeing's Central Fabrication Division in Auburn, Washington. Final assembly of the first 767 began on 8 April 1981, in Everett. Once completed, the aircraft quickly achieved a series of major steps, which included standing on its own wheels for the first time, and being moved for the first time.

When the 767 first rolled out of the Everett factory on schedule, on 4 August 1981, Boeing said it was better prepared for the programme than for any other effort in its history. The 767-200 was the first all-new Boeing aircraft in twelve years, since the 747 had ushered in the widebody era, on 30 September 1968. The 767 represented the first increment of new planes that included the 757 and 737-300, a re-engined and stretched version of the 737. For months before the rollout, workers celebrated the impending event with a special motto: 'Day by Day We Make it Happen'.

The rollout ceremony was slightly marred by an air-traffic controllers' strike in the United States, which reduced the number of invited dignitaries, including the scheduled keynote speaker, US Transportation Secretary Drew Lewis. It also came at a time when the financial prospects of the airlines were cloudy, despite signs of recovery from a recent downturn, and strong forecasts for aircraft orders in the new decade. Airlines were particularly excited about Boeing's promise that the 767 would produce a 35 per cent improvement in fuel burned per seat, saving an airline with ten of the

---

767 Fun Facts

- The 767 has 800 suppliers world-wide.
- The paint used on a typical 767 weighs 400lb (182kg).
- In a three-class configuration, the 767 has one of the largest overhead baggage stowage volumes – 3 cubic ft per passenger, matched only by the 777-200.
- The 767 was the first Boeing aircraft to replace 3,500lb (1,575kg) of aluminium with 1,200lb (540kg) of graphite and graphite/Kevlar composites, which are lighter and stronger. The weight savings contribute to the plane's operating efficiency.
- The 767 has about 3.14 million parts.
- Each 767 has 56 miles (90km) of wiring and 3,800ft (1.5km) of tubing for the hydraulic system.
- The 767 is the first twin-jet to offer three engine choices.
- Eighty-seven per cent of the seats on the 767 are next to a window or aisle. No seat is more than one seat away from a window or aisle.
- The plane has carried more than 740 million passengers.
- The airframe was service-life tested for two lifetimes (40 years of airline service). It was cycled through 19 months of tests consisting of 10,000 simulated flights over 100,000 hours.
- Punta Arenas, Chile, near the Antarctic, is the farthest south a 767 has ever flown.
- The 767 can cruise at an altitude of 43,000ft (13,100m).
- The 767 was the first plane to earn an extended-range twin-engine operations (ETOPS) rating in May 1985. Because of its reliable and redundant systems, it may fly up to three hours from the nearest airport.
- The 767 is the most popular plane on transatlantic routes. More than 30 airlines fly it across the north and mid-Atlantic.
- The 767 is 54 per cent more fuel-efficient than a 727-100 and 29 per cent more fuel-efficient than the 727-200.
- Each 767 with a full passenger load equals two 727s plus half a 707 freighter, all for 2 per cent less fuel burn than a 727.
- The 767 flies automatically, from take-off climb to landing, with the help of 140 microprocessors and computers.
- The sound of a 767 taking off from a 1½-mile (3,000-m) runway is about the same as the average street-corner noise.

Thousands gathered to watch the rollout of the first 767 on 4 August 1981. The 767-200 was the first all-new Boeing aircraft in 12 years, since the 747 ushered in the widebody era on 30 September 1968. Boeing

planes up to $25 million per year in fuel costs, in 1981 dollars.

The 767 was rolled out with a backlog of 173 firm orders and 138 options – more than any other airplane in Boeing's history at that point. All milestones for the 767 programme were met on or ahead of schedule, and rollout came on the exact day that had been chosen three years earlier.

On rollout day, the first-ever 767 was moved from the final assembly bay of the 40-24 Building on to the apron, as 15,000 employees, special guests and reporters looked on. Eighteen other 767s, at various stages of production, were inside the building. By 1983, four planes were being made each month.

During the 45-minute ceremony, Boeing employees heard from Washington Senator Henry M. Jackson, Boeing chairman 'T' Wilson, Boeing Commercial Airplane Company president Tex Boullioun and United Airlines Chairman Richard Ferris, who spoke on behalf of the seventeen initial customers that had ordered the 767.

'What I remember most about the rollout was the nostalgia,' Ferris says today. 'It marked the coming together again of the three original companies [Boeing, United Airlines and Pratt & Whitney] of United Aircraft.'

During the ceremony, Boeing's Dean Thornton acknowledged 'outstanding support' from programme partners Aeritalia and Japan's Civil Transport Development Corporation, along with 800 other subcontractors and suppliers. These partners had helped the 767 division meet every major production milestone on or ahead of schedule.

The inaugural 767, registered N767BA, was dedicated by Grace Wilson, the wife of the company chairman, assisted by 10-year-old Rogers Summers, the son of two 767 employees, who represented future travellers. With typical American bravado, music at the rollout was provided by the 126-piece Seattle All-City High School Marching Band. Under blue summer skies, the first 767 rolled out of the final assembly building shortly before noon, to the strains of Richard Strauss's 'Thus Spake Zarathustra', the music used in the film *2001: A Space Odyssey*.

The 767 'advanced the frontiers of technology', United's Richard Ferris told the crowd. 'The terrifically complex machine you've built does things no other machine can do. This machine performs its mission better than anything else humankind has

767 Chronology

14 July 1978 – Production of the 767 begins when United Airlines places a $1.2 billion order for thirty of the new aircraft equipped with Pratt & Whitney JT9D-7R4 engines.

14 August 1978 – Boeing and Aeritalia, Italy's largest aircraft firm, sign a contract; the Italian firm became a risk-sharing major participant of the plane's development and production programme.

22 September 1978 – Civil Transport Development Corp. of Japan becomes a risk-sharing partner.

15 November 1978 – American Airlines and Delta Air Lines announce total firm orders for fifty 767s. The value at the time, $1.9 billion, makes it the largest single sales day in Boeing history. American orders thirty and Delta twenty, all with General Electric CF6-80A engines.

6 July 1979 – Fabrication of the first 767 parts begins.

8 April 1981 – Final assembly of the first 767 begins.

4 August 1981 – The first 767 is completed and rolled from the 767 final assembly bay at Everett.

26 September 1981 – The first 767 completes an initial flight lasting 2 hours and 4 minutes, four days ahead of the first flight date scheduled in 1978.

27 May 1982 – The first 767 fitted with a two-crew member flight deck makes its initial flight, and begins the test programme leading to FAA certification of the configuration.

July 1982 – The first 767 international demonstration flight takes the new plane to cities in Europe, the Middle East and North Africa.

30 July 1982 – Certification for the 767 is awarded by the Federal Aviation Administration.

19 August 1982 – The first 767 is delivered to United Airlines.

8 September 1982 – The first commercial 767 flight is made, from Chicago to Denver.

January 1983 – Boeing announces the 767ER.

6 June 1983 – FAA certifies the 767 for a maximum take-off gross weight of 315,000lb (142,880kg), 15,000lb (6,800kg) heavier than the 767s delivered at that time. The increased weight permits up to 760 miles (1,125km) added range and greater payload.

22 July 1983 – The FAA clears the way for pilots to fly both the 767 and 757 after passing a type-rating test for either of the airliners. This is made possible by the similarity of the 757 and 767 flight decks.

29 September 1983 – Japan Airlines orders the 767-300.

27 March 1984 – The first 767ER with optional 335,000lb (151,950kg) gross weight makes the first 767 commercial non-stop transatlantic flight the day after being delivered to El Al Israel Airlines.

1 June 1984 – The first 767ER for Ethiopian Airlines sets a twin-jet airliner distance record, flying 7,500 miles (12,082km) from Washington, DC, to Addis Ababa in 13 hours and 17 minutes.

14 January 1986 – The first 767-300 is completed and rolled out from Everett.

25 September 1986 – The first 767-300 is delivered to Japan Airlines.

22 December 1986 – Extensive flight test of 767-300ER begins for certification with GE engines.

31 December 1986 – ETOPS-equipped (Extended Twin-Engine Operations) 767s log more than 60,000 flights, since May 1985, with 99.8 per cent successfully reaching their destination without turnback or diversion.

25 March 1987 – Rolls-Royce provides the third engine choice, RB211-524H, for the 767 family. Commonality with RB211-powered 747s benefits airlines operating both aircraft.

18 April 1988 – An Air Mauritius 767-200ER sets a new distance record for commercial twin-jets, flying from Halifax, Nova Scotia, Canada, to Mauritius – 8,727 miles (14,042km) – in 16 hours, 27 minutes.

27 July 1989 – An Air Seychelles 767-200ER sets a new distance record for a commercial twin-jet, flying 8,893 miles (14,309km) from Grand Rapids, Michigan, to the Seychelles, in 16 hours, 49 minutes.

8 February 1990 – The first 767 powered by Rolls-Royce is delivered to British Airways.

10 June 1990 – A Royal Brunei 767-200ER sets a new distance record for twin-jet airliners, flying 9,253 miles (14,890km) from Seattle to Nairobi, Kenya, in 17 hours 51 minutes.

15 January 1993 – United Parcel Service launches the 767 freighter with an order for thirty aircraft and thirty options.

February 1994 – The 767 becomes the most widely used aircraft across the Atlantic, with more flights than any other aircraft.

20 May 1993 – The 500th 767 rolls off the line at Everett.

12 May 1995 – The first 767 freighter rolls out.

18 May 1995 – EVA Air begins the first regularly scheduled 767-300ER twin-jet operations across the North Pacific.

21 June 1995 – The first 767 freighter makes its initial flight from Paine Field in Everett.

16 October 1995 – The first 767 freighter begins revenue service.

28 April 1997 – Boeing officially launches the 767-400ER, with an order for twenty-one aircraft from Delta.

31 October 1997 – Air New Zealand sets a new speed record with the 767-300ER. The aircraft flew from Everett to Christchurch, New Zealand, a distance of 12,272km, in 14 hours, 54 minutes.

11 March 1998 – Boeing delivers the first two of four 767 AWACS aircraft to the Japanese government.

yet devised. You've enabled us all to take our next step forward in the history of human flight. You've advanced the frontiers of technology. The 767 you've built is everything that is right with new technology. The 767 will bring consumers better air service more efficiently than the planes the 767 will replace.'

Ferris pointed out that the 767 would bring widebody comfort to travellers from cities that have never had widebody service. 'The plane you've built will let us help airlines give better service – and let us hold back the rise in fares at the same time. The 767 will help us compete effectively by giving our customers good service at a good price.'

Boeing's Thornton began his remarks by commenting on the splendid, sunny weather. 'Even God likes the 767,' he said. 'I look at this plane as my baby, though 40,000 other people do too,' he went on, referring to employees, partners, subcontractors and engine-makers. 'The 767 is a long-term commitment with the underlying goal of producing a plane that will burn less fuel and better serve the travelling public of the world.'

In his speech, 'T' Wilson told the crowd, 'The 727 is a tough act to follow, but we believe the 767 will measure up in all respects. It was developed to meet the new equipment needs of the aviation industry, which is experiencing steadily increasing fuel and operating costs. The 767 was designed with the co-operation of our airline customers, who helped verify our concepts in size, payload, range and other important areas.'

The first 767 carried red, white and blue markings, which ran the length of the fuselage and swept upwards along the vertical stabilizer, which was emblazoned with a blue '767' on a white background. The lower fuselage was blue and the upper white, bearing the words 'Boeing 767' in blue. The engine nacelles were similarly decorated. The fuselage bore the logos of the seventeen customers that had ordered the plane.

The first 767 differed significantly from the first 747. It was missing only about a dozen parts out of 3.1 million at rollout, compared with the several thousand that the first 747 lacked. The missing 767 parts, mostly related to the flight-management system, did not affect the schedule. The first 767, used on a vigorous static and flight-test schedule, never entered commercial service, and it is still owned by Boeing today. It was the second 767 that joined United's fleet.

The 757 Rollout

More than 1,300 companies in thirty-one US states and eight nations contributed to the 757 assembly process. The launch costs of the 767 were absorbed by Boeing, but other companies were directly involved in the development of the 757.

For the 757, Boeing contracted with Short Brothers of Belfast, Northern Ireland, for inboard trailing-edge flaps, with Hawker de Havilland of Australia for wing in-spar ribs, and with CASA of Spain for outboard wing trailing-edge flaps. These partnerships led to dozens of Boeing employees and their families being sent abroad to supervise the progress of foreign supply chains.

Boeing typically awards 50 per cent of a plane's value to contractors. This was highlighted on 11 October 1979, when Boeing signed contracts for $1 billion relating to the 757; this was the largest single-day award of supplier contracts in civil aircraft manufacturing history. Up to five billion dollars' worth of work on the 757 programmes went to non-Boeing manufacturers.

From the official programme go-ahead, on 23 March 1979, Boeing had just 45 months to design, build, test, certify and deliver the first 757. A decision was made to

757 Fun Facts

- More than fifty operators from more than twenty countries have ordered more than 900 757s.
- 757 has carried more than 825 million passengers.
- The fleet has flown the equivalent of 14,000 round-trips to the moon.
- The fleet has produced more than 13.5 million hours of revenue service, equivalent to 1,541 years of continuous service.
- The 757 freighter can hold more than 6 million golf balls.
- At 225,000lb (102,060kg), the 757 weighs as much as a diesel train locomotive.
- The surface area of a pair of 757 wings is 1,951 square ft (181 square m).
- There are 626,000 parts in a 757. About 600,000 bolts and rivets fasten those parts together.
- The length of wires in the plane is about 60 miles (96km).
- Airlines fly the 757 on a variety of routes. The twin-jet serves routes as long as 4,133 miles (6,612km), or as short as 68 miles (109km).
- The common cockpit type rating permits flight crews trained on the 757 also to fly the 767.
- A typical 757 uses more than 1,800 fibreglass blankets to help insulate passengers and cargo from sub-freezing temperatures at high altitudes.

build the plane at Renton, where Boeing could take advantage of a labour pool trained in building narrow-bodies – the 707, 727 and 737 – and used to turning out high numbers. An area was carved out of the facility to accommodate the 757. Because Boeing was not hiring any more employees, its key suppliers lent engineers to design the plane. The same people then returned to their firms to build parts and sections.

Parts fabrication for the 757 began on 10 December 1979. Assembly started on 5 January 1981, when the front spar of the wing was loaded into its major assembly tool. Eight days later, wing assembly began as the lower wing panel was loaded into a wing jig. It was the first totally new aircraft to be built at Renton since 1966, when the first sections of the 737 started coming together on the production line. The first 757 was completed on the same day in September 1981 when the first 767 for United Airlines received its paint job.

The 757 was rolled out of the factory on 13 January 1982, representing Boeing's second weapon in a double-barrelled assault on commercial aviation in the early 1980s. It was the company's second new plane in five months, and it arrived amid anxiety resulting from the financial squeeze in the airline industry. The 757 had a solid order base of 136 firm orders and 71 options from seven airlines, exceeding (by nine) the number of firm orders for Boeing's 727 when it rolled out of the Renton plant in 1963. Still, some carriers warned of delays or cancellations due to the uncertain economy. The world's aviation industry looked to be in trouble, as a result of a soft economy, poor traffic, constraints on airline schedules and a fuel outlook that created a poor market for new planes. While buying decisions were delayed, and airlines negotiated with manufacturers to alter delivery schedules, other carriers proceeded with long-term plans to capitalize on the competitive advantage of new aircraft.

The 757's debut – an hour-long ceremony witnessed by more than 12,000 employees, airline representatives and reporters – resembled a Hollywood production. The ceremony was held indoors, with the aircraft hidden behind a huge curtain. Festivities included a disco-like light show and slides projected on to a huge screen. The lights formed a gigantic '757' on the curtain. The curtain lifted, revealing the plane in a cloud of artificial smoke, while the 'Music for the Royal Fireworks' filled Building 4-82 in Renton.

The 757 was rolled out on 13 January 1982. Boeing

757 Chronology

31 August 1978 – Eastern Airlines and British Airways announce their intention to order 757s.

23 March 1979 – The 757 programme is authorized.

15 May 1979 – The 767 nose incorporated into the 757.

11 October 1979 – Boeing signs $1 billion in contracts for work on the 757, the largest single-day award of supplier contracts in civil aircraft manufacturing history.

10 December 1979 – Fabrication begins.

12 November 1980 – Delta Air Lines announces order of first 757s with Pratt & Whitney engines.

5 January 1981 – Fabrication of the first 757 begins.

13 January 1982 – The 757 is rolled out.

19 February 1982 – First flight of the 757.

21 December 1982 – Federal Aviation Administration certifies the 757.

22 December 1982 – The first 757 is delivered to Eastern Airlines.

8 July 1987 – The first 757ER is rolled out.

14 August 1987 – First flight of 757 freighter/package freighter.

1 May 1988 – First 757 ETOPS flight.

15 June 1988 – The first 757 Combi is rolled out.

18 July 1988 – The first 757 Combi conducts its first flight.

31 July 1990 – The FAA grants 180-minute ETOPS certification for 757s equipped with Rolls-Royce engines.

2 September 1996 – Boeing launches 757-300 programme at Farnborough Air Show.

9 September 1997 – Assembly begins on 757-300.

31 May 1998 – The 757-300 is rolled out of the factory.

2 August 1998 – The first 757-300 completes its first flight.

22 January 1999 – 757-300 certified by FAA.

The 757's debut resembled a Hollywood production during an hour-long ceremony witnessed by more than 12,000 employees, airline representatives and reporters. Boeing

Jane Boullioun, wife of Boeing Commercial Aircraft Group president Tex Boullioun, christened the gleaming aircraft, saying, 'May this great airplane, and the hundreds to follow, serve us well.' More curtains rose, the hangar doors parted and the aircraft was towed outside, under threatening skies. Like the first 767, the 757 carried Boeing's red, white and blue colour scheme, and was festooned with the logos of the first seven customers – Eastern Airlines, British Airways, American Airlines, Delta Air Lines, Air Florida, Monarch Airlines and Transbrasil. Its tail number read N757A.

'The 757 should be a money-making machine for our airline customers,' 'T' Wilson told the crowd. Some of the customers on hand saw the 757 as a bold step into the future. '[The decision to buy the plane was] probably the most important single purchase decision ever taken by a British airline,' said Roy Watts, at the time deputy chairman and chief executive of British Airways. 'The more the shape of European air travel changes, the more apparent it becomes that the 757 is the right size for British Airways.' The airline needed the 757 to

fill the capacity gap between the 737 and the L-1011.

Fortunately for Boeing, both the 767 and 757 made it into service within budget and right on schedule. Both aircraft boasted performance figures ahead of the minimum guarantees offered to the airlines, the first time this had happened since the 727. This was crucial; if a plane does not meet a performance target, such as weight, the supplier is obliged to compensate the airline, since the airline will certainly see reduced revenues if an aircraft weighs more than guaranteed.

CHAPTER EIGHT

How the Birds are Born

The Factories

Metropolitan Seattle is an aviation enthusiast's dream. The area is ringed with airports. Float planes take off from the city's waterfront for nearby islands. Airliners align themselves for arrival at Seattle-Tacoma International Airport. And a steady stream of brand-new, gleaming Boeing aircraft – in vibrant colours, representing airlines throughout the world – roar above downtown on their way to Boeing Field after a flight test. Visitors to the Museum of Flight even can spot aircraft ready for delivery.

Just to the north and south of the city are Boeing's two commercial aircraft assembly plants, where the long road to rollout comes together with lots of brains, plenty of brawn and a healthy dose of good management. The task of constructing large commercial aircraft is among the most complex in the world. Yet, to a visitor, the process can seem as smooth as making a household item.

Everett

The building where 767s are built is the largest on earth, by volume. The aircraft are assembled in the same cavernous structure

The 767 is assembled in Boeing's Everett plant, the largest building, by volume, in the world. Boeing

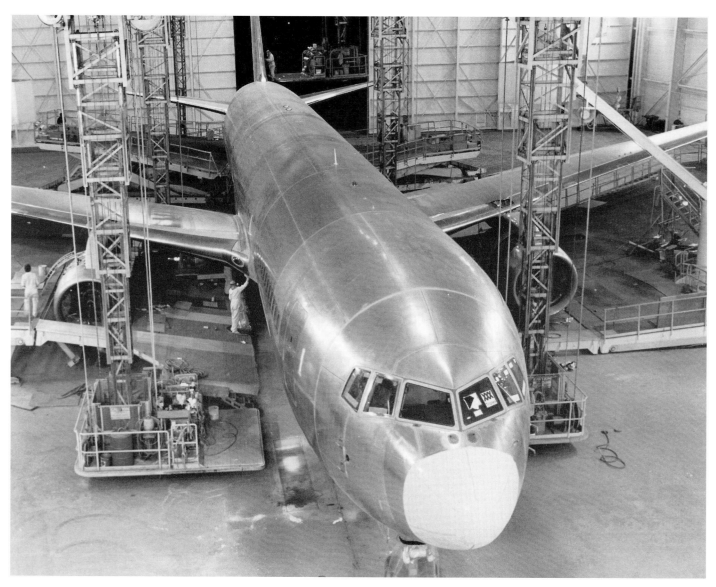

One of the first 767s is assembled in Everett. Boeing

as the 747s and 777s in Everett, 35 miles (56km) north of Seattle. Just south of the city, in Renton, 757s are built alongside 737s. Both airliners are built in virtually the same way, with large and small pieces – from tiny rivets to railroad car-sized fuselage panels – shipped to the factories by plane, train and truck from all over the world.

Viewed from a platform set up to accommodate 140,000 annual visitors, the scene in Everett is surprisingly calm. Thousands of workers, scattered throughout the building, prepare rows of glinting aircraft fuselages for their dramatic rollout from the factory. The muted sounds of riveting and drilling echo through the building. Employees on golf carts and bicycles navigate seemingly

endless passageways. One million piercing white lights glow from the ceiling.

The facility was built in 1966–67 to produce the 747. When the 767 received the go-ahead, in 1978, there was one very big logistical problem – no room to build the new widebodies. Instead of investing in a new facility, the Everett plant was enlarged by 285 million cubic feet (7.98 million cubic m); the main structure had originally covered about 200 million cubic feet (5.6 million cubic m), and was already much larger than the Vertical Assembly Building at Kennedy Space Center in Florida, which until then had been the world's largest building. In all, Boeing built four factory buildings and three office buildings, with a

total area of more than 1 million square feet (92,900 square m). Since then, the factory has been expanded again, in 1993, to make room for the 777, and now covers 1.5 million square feet (139,350 square m).

The factory in Everett stands eleven storeys tall, offering 472 million cubic ft (13.3 million cubic m) of space – 98.3 acres (39.8 hectares) in all. The factory is so large that Disneyland would fit inside the building, along with parking for every visitor. The main section of the 115-foot (38-m) building consists of six massive bay doors, big enough to drive an aircraft through, or roughly the size of an American football field. Each door is 273ft (91m) wide and 79.5ft (26.5m) tall.

More than 2,000 widebody planes have rolled off the Everett assembly line since 30 September 1968, when the first 747 made its debut. On average, four 767-300s are produced every month. (Boeing will only build a -200 extended-range model when a previous customer orders one. Although the -200 programme has not been closed, it is rare when airlines will order the -200ER because of the -300's added capacity and savings per seat. The last 767-200 was completed in 1997 for Japan's AWACS defence force. However,

customer for the new -400 model, and will receive the -400's interior in the new -200s when they enter service in the year 2000.)

On its own, the Everett plant is among the largest single export sites in the United States. Besides carrying out the final assembly of widebodies, the plant produces the interior decorative sidewalls, ceiling panels, carpet and stowage bins for all Boeing jetliners, providing enough work for 28,000 people.

The 767 is one of Boeing's steadiest models, less affected by the ebb and flow of

and 777 have two production lines each, but only one of each is used.

High above the assembly floor are eighteen overhead cranes – on 31 miles (49.6km) of track – that make an average of 250 lifts per day from a height nearly nine storeys above the floor. The cranes are used to transport large aircraft pieces, such as entire fuselages or tails, into the required manufacturing positions.

Outside the cavernous building lies the 9,000ft (2,740m) runway of Snohomish County's Paine Field. Adjacent to this are

767-300s in final assembly. Boeing

Continental Airlines surprised the aviation community in November 1998 when it ordered 10 new 767-200ERs to replace older widebodies for European and South American routes. Although previously not a -200 customer, Continental is a launch

international aircraft sales than its larger Everett cousins. It has its own dedicated assembly line, although the model is often overshadowed by the crowd-pleasing 747-400 and the 777 and its derivative, the 777-300, the longest plane in the world. The 747

three gigantic paint hangars and a flight line fuelling system that can fuel three aircraft at the same time. Aircraft assembled in Everett take off from Paine Field and return there to have any problems fixed. Finished 767s are then delivered to customers from

Everett. (In June 1998, a Renton-built 757 was the first Boeing narrow-body to be delivered from Everett as part of a temporary plan to take some strain off Boeing Field, where 757 and 737 deliveries normally take place.)

Renton

While not as large as at Everett, the scene is equally impressive 35 miles (56km) away in Renton, at the south end of Lake Washington. Here, the smaller 757s are assembled next to 737s, the world's most popular commercial aircraft. The factory, about one-third the size of the Everett site, began in the 1940s to build B-29s for the Second World War. Following the war, Renton was home to Boeing's commercial

aircraft, growing steadily with the expanding product line. It was at Renton that Boeing ushered in the jet age with the 707, and, later, built all 727s and 737s. To accommodate the new 757 programme, factory space was expanded by 2 million square ft (185,800 square m).

The 757s are assembled in one production line, 1,000ft (305m) long, in Building 4-81, opposite a line of 737s. As in the Everett plant, giant cranes 114ft (35m) above the floor manoeuvre huge chunks of airliner. An average of four 757s roll out of the factory every month. In the early 1990s, when 757 production peaked at eight aircraft a month, two production lines were needed. This was later cut back to one. A second assembly floor in an adjacent building houses two more 737 lines.

It takes about four and a half months to build the 757, from the time the first wing spar comes into the factory until rollout.

About 15,000 employees work at Renton. Other sub-assembly and major sub-assembly operations at the plant are located in the balcony of the 4-21 Building, where struts, skin panels, bulkheads and slates are produced; in the 4-20 building, where the wings are produced; and in the 10-50 building, where three major 757 body sections are built.

The 757s take off from the relatively short 5,300ft (1,615m) runway at Renton Airport and head out over Lake Washington. Most 757s make their first landings at Boeing's commercial delivery centre at Boeing Field in Seattle, less than 8 miles (13km) away.

The first 757 for Eastern Airlines takes shape in Renton. The model was rolled out on 13 January 1982. Boeing

The Production Line
The 757 is assembled at Boeing's Renton factory in one production line 1,000ft (305m) long in Building 4-81, opposite a line of 737s.

1. Like in the Everett plant, giant cranes 114ft (35m) above the floor manoeuvre huge chunks of airliners.
2. In the final join position, fuselage sections are joined with the centre section, which is attached to the wing.

3.

4.

3. After final join, the aircraft move into final assembly.
4. Insulation is placed into the fuselage. A 757 uses more than 1,800 fibreglass blankets to help insulate passengers and cargo from sub-freezing temperatures at high altitude.
5. 757s nearing completion.
6. In Everett, the 767's fuselage sections are joined together.

7.

7. As one 767 is assembled, another one, with its centre section, awaits other fuselage sections.

8. A 767-300 in final join position.

8.

757 production in the first few years required two production lines. Today, only one line is used in Renton.
Boeing

From Millions of Parts to Delivery

Assembling a modern airliner requires a combination of miraculous technology and good, old-fashioned perspiration. At one end of the spectrum is the daily manufacture of thousands of separate components, some of which are made up of even smaller elements. At the other is the bringing together of a series of sub-assemblies to construct an aircraft that will, a year later, stand on its own three undercarriages, roll out and take to the skies.

Building the 767 and 757 involves thousands of people from hundreds of different organizations. Boeing puts it thus in its booklet entitled *How to Build*

an Airliner: 'It's a high-technology tale filled with financial and political forces, the complexities and subtleties of the industrial process, and a dash of continuous quality improvement.' With every aircraft that leaves Boeing, the company learns more about how to do things better; as a result, the planes that follow benefit from constant refinements and improvements.

Millions of Parts

While the planes themselves are assembled in the Seattle area, manufacturing is spread around the world. A 767 has 3.14 million parts, held together by an additional 600,000 titanium and cadmium

fasteners and rivets, plus 60 miles, or 96km, of wiring. It can take months to purchase materials and to manufacture all the parts needed for final assembly, but the pieces are merged into an airliner in just a few shifts. Final assembly is followed by painting, flight testing, delivery and follow-up customer service.

Each year, Boeing buys tons of raw material and tens of thousands of parts – from main landing gear and electronic flight instruments, to raw sheet-metal stock and rivets. Billions of dollars are paid to thousands of suppliers for items that must be at hundreds of different locations at just the right time in the production process. Boeing buys from companies in nearly every state in the United States and from subcontractors in Canada, South America, Europe, the Middle East, Asia and Australia.

To maximize its buying leverage, Boeing's Commercial Airplane Group purchases basic items on an order base outlined by top management. This maintains a smooth flow of parts into the company's receiving area.

About 30 to 36 months before the delivery of an aircraft, Boeing begins purchasing basic parts for each plane, including forgings and landing gear. About 11 to 18 months before delivery, the company begins buying the unique parts needed for a customer's specific configuration. At this point – when customers make their orders, and delivery dates are locked in – subcontractors missing delivery deadlines can lead to delays and excess cost.

The purchase of parts and materials can begin only after the engineering organizations have given their approval. Engineers play a key role, from the analysis of the need for a new aircraft, through design and manufacturing, to testing and after-delivery support. Early on, they consider the changing requirements of the airline industry relating to range and payload, and speed and safety. During product definition, engineers decide what the aircraft is going to look like. Datasets and parts lists are developed, including such details as the finish needed on parts and suggested heat treatments.

The Manufacturing Plan

After the aircraft is fully defined, a manufacturing plan is drawn up. This plan instructs everyone involved in the manufacture of the aircraft how to turn the raw materials into an aircraft. Each manufacturing task is broken down into a more detailed, step-by-step plan. While that plan is being put together, tooling engineers design the various complex and unique tools necessary to build the plane, such as jigs, assembly tools and holding fixtures. Then parts begin to flow into the assembly plants. As assembly begins, manufacturing, design and analysis engineers roam the factories to ensure that each part is installed according to specifications.

Sub-Assembly

Sub-assembly is the vital step that occurs after parts are fabricated, but before major body sections are joined during what is called the final assembly. Sub-assembly

767 front sections and horizontal stabilizers are prepared for assembly. Boeing

A 767 centre section and wing are lowered into place. Boeing

involves compiling parts and assemblies into larger and more complex components until those components are ready for final installation. These parts include frames, floor beams, spars, bulkheads, struts, doors, landing gear, flaps and horizontal stabilizers. Before parts are shipped to the plants, all exterior surfaces are coated with a thin layer of green vinyl, to guard against scratches.

In parallel, a Boeing shop assembles smaller, more detailed parts shipped in from the company's fabrication division in Auburn, Washington, and outside suppliers. These include small latches, frames, tubes, pulley brackets and similar items.

The fabrication division turns raw materials into many important items for assembly lines; it produces those parts that are difficult to make, or are critical to keeping aircraft on delivery schedules. The division produces 350,000 parts every week.

It takes about 18 months to build the parts and assemblies that go into each plane, and a month more to assemble the pieces into an airliner ready for its first flight. The 767 and 757 are manufactured in a series of operations; some operations are huge, such as hoisting tons of metal by crane, and some are tiny, such as aligning body sections to within thousandths of an inch.

Towards the Final Assembly

The parts that begin the assembly process are the wing spars, the internal beams that run the length of the wing. Wing spars and skins, machined in Auburn, arrive in a unique truck. It is so long that its rear wheels must be steered by a driver sitting in a cab beneath the back of the trailer. Panel assemblies and spars are joined together with titanium rivets on a series of large tool jigs. Some of the rivets are cooled to minus 40 degrees Fahrenheit before installation, providing a tight fit as they expand as they warm to room

During final body join, the 767's centre section and wings are lowered into position by huge overhead cranes, which manoeuvre the section so it can be joined with other fuselage sections. Notice the wires coming from where the engines will hang. Boeing

Each fuselage is held together by hundreds of thousands of rivets. Boeing

The forward section of a 767 is inched toward the waiting fuselage in the Everett factory. Much of the movement of large components is done overnight. Boeing

(Below) 767-200s in final assembly in the early days of the programme. Finished planes exit the cavernous factory through the giant doors in the background. Boeing

temperature. The wings are moved adjacent to the final assembly line, where flaps, slats and other sub-assemblies are joined. Although manufactured separately, the right and left wings are joined together to form a single unit before other aircraft sections are attached. Altogether, this cavernous unit serves as the main fuel tank of an aircraft, and it is tested for leaks before final assembly.

The 767 and 757 begin to come together when their wing assemblies are joined with a centre section, then attached to a short, hollow section of fuselage known as Section 44. The entire assembly is then attached to cables and hoisted into the air by two ceiling cranes that can lift as much as 34 tons (31 tonnes). In a procedure normally done at night, crane operators slowly bring the section into place over an array of steel scaffolds, beams, braces and ramps. The scaffolding contains hydraulic jacks to level the fuselage.

The next section lowered into place is the aft body section, Section 46, which extends from just behind the wings to the back end of the aircraft. The vertical tail and the horizontal stabilizer are attached later. Finally, huge doors open to allow a tractor to bring in the forward body section (43), which includes the attached nose section (41), with the flight-deck equipment already installed and the lavatories and galleys in place. One crane hooks on to the front of the nose section and another hooks to the rear. The hollow shell is hoisted and set in alignment.

Although the three individual sections are still more than a foot (30cm) apart, the plane has broadly taken shape. Over the next several hours, workers will inch the body sections together, measuring and levelling them until they fit. At this point, electrical and plumbing systems are installed, flaps and slats are installed and rigged, and cargo liners and cockpit panels are put in. The landing gear is then installed and the plane is ready for final assembly.

Final Assembly

Both models spend about five days in their final join position before moving to the final assembly area. The placement of fuselages and aircraft changes dramatically every day in final assembly. Major moves are conducted on night-time shifts, when fewer workers are in the factories. In the final assembly area, an aircraft's position changes every four days.

There are usually six final-assembly positions. In the first and second positions, lavatories and galleys are installed, the fuselage pressure, electrical and hydraulic systems are tested, and fuel tanks are closed. In the third and fourth final-assembly positions, the

engines are attached, major functional testing begins, interior panels and carpeting are installed and seats are put in. In the fifth and sixth positions of final assembly, the plane undergoes a shakedown, or top-to-bottom test, and the engine cowlings are installed.

Six Boeing 767s are shown in the 767 final assembly area during the early days of the programme. In this photo are (from front), a United Airlines model, one for TWA, another United, a Delta model and two additional Uniteds. Boeing

767s in final assembly, while other sections wait for assembly in the background. Boeing

Painting

Finally – usually during the dark of night, for safety reasons – the giant doors open to release a gigantic new hulk, sporting a light green/silvery metallic finish. The completed aircraft is then tugged into the paint hangars, where, over the course of four days, it is painted, and given an identity.

After a plane is rolled into the paint shop, its composite panels are sanded and it is sprayed with soap to begin to remove the temporary protective coating on the aluminium skins. Painters, moving about on large cranes and scaffolding, scrub the entire plane with solvents. Abrasive pads are used to remove grease and other unwanted residue, and to prepare the surface for paint adhesion. The painters also use air-pressure hoses to shoot dry, filtered air into all of the aircraft's seams and cavities, to blow out dust and water. After a protective solution is sprayed on, all of the windows – and other surfaces that are not painted – are masked with paper and tape.

A yellow priming paint and white topcoat are applied to all painted surfaces. The paint is flexible enough to expand every time the passenger cabin is pressurized. The paint is then cured, with two large steam boilers heating the entire building to 120 degrees Fahrenheit (49 degrees centigrade) during the curing process, usually on the overnight shift. On the second day in the paint hangar, painters use templates and stencils to lay out all of the major lettering and decorative markings of airlines from around the world. Many of the templates are computer-generated to ensure exact reproduction. Each colour is then sprayed on in a predetermined sequence. This is followed by more curing at the end of the day. A painted 757 uses 100 gallons (455 litres) of paint. The heavier 767 can use up to four times that amount.

Some airlines need as many as nine separate colours on their aircraft, although most use only a few. White is the most popular colour, and it is available in dozens of

A 767 is prepared for painting. Water is used to clean the surface before the process begins. Boeing

initial fuelling, the aircraft's fuel-storage tanks and systems are tested. Fuel tanks are filled completely. The tanks are then emptied, to test the fuel-feed and fuel-pump systems, and then filled again with slightly more than a full flight load of fuel, to allow the engines to run completely without additional fuelling.

At the same time, mechanics and electricians start to prepare the engines for initial run and operational checks. Engine-testing usually takes two to three days. First, the engines are opened to make sure that everything is attached properly. Then the aircraft is moved into the engine-run position, facing the wind. Air-bleed and starting systems are tested while the engine is motored without ignition. Oil-system pressure, the auxiliary power unit, hydraulic pumps and the generator are checked. Once the engine is ignited for the first time, engine performance is monitored and adjusted under both manual and automatic controls. Thrust reversers are then fine-tuned and the air-conditioning system, which is powered by the engines, is adjusted. Cabin pressurization is also checked.

After the engine tests, the flight controls are studied, and the aircraft shakedown continues. The goal is to make sure that the aircraft is safe to fly, with no loose connections, no defects and no uncompleted adjustments. Tests are also conducted on the safety systems.

On the day before the first flight, everything is checked again: flight-control systems, lighting and warning systems, cockpit and avionics systems, radar, autopilot, autothrottle, flight-management computers, and flight and voice recorders. Finally, the engines are readied for take-off, after the tyres have been kicked just one more time.

shades. Any special decals are applied on the third day of painting. On the same day, masking is removed, small markings are painted for identification and maintenance, and small decals are applied. Until this process is completed, every plane is just another aircraft. With an airline's livery, it takes on its own identity.

Quality is vital in the paint shop, particularly on aircraft which rely on their fuel-efficiency for their popularity. If an area the size of two doors is poorly painted, with rough surfaces, on ten planes, this

could result in 777 unnecessary gallons (2,941 litres) of fuel burned a year. That equates to 25 passengers and their luggage left behind on a typical journey.

Testing and Final Installation

First flight is closer when the engines and instruments come to life. This happens during pre-flight activities. Each plane undergoes about two weeks of testing and final installation work before it is ready to take off for the first time. During the

Delivery

New 767s are handed to airlines at Paine Field in Everett; Boeing Field in Seattle is the final location for 757s before they are turned over to their owners. During its ten to fourteen days there, each plane undergoes more flight testing, sometimes by customer, Boeing or FAA pilots. Last-minute installations, adjustments and fixes are made. Bills and receipts are then signed, and the aircraft is flown away by airline pilots to its new home base around the world.

Each aircraft is also weighed before delivery. Boeing may pay penalty fees to the customer if the aircraft is heavier than specified in the contract, since a heavier plane will burn more fuel, increasing operating costs. Each aircraft is weighed at Boeing Field on three 8 by 10ft (2.4 by 3m) scales, one under each landing gear, inside the flight-test hangar. The aircraft is backed into a stall, with the stabilizer in the neutral position and flaps up. While fuel,

The hangar doors are closed and blowers turned off, to eliminate any possible disturbance of the aircraft's wings. When the digital readings of the three scales settle, the weight is compared to the calculated expected empty weight. An empty 767-200 weighs 177,500–186,000lb (80,510–84,370kg); the -300 model weighs more, at 192,100–199,600lb (87,135–90,535kg).

call is arranged with the customers' and Boeing's bankers, so that funds can be transferred without delay. Typically, an airline representative will call his banker to transfer the money. A banker for Boeing then acknowledges that the millions have been transferred to Boeing's account, and ownership is then transferred. The plane is then ready to be flown

Completed aircraft are normally moved out during night-time hours to avoid traffic congestion. Boeing

drinking water and toilets are drained, to make the plane empty, flight-test crews scour the aircraft to remove every item that does not belong – tools, fire extinguishers, left-over lunches. A tractor moves the aircraft to the hangar and carefully backs it up on to the electronic scales. An engineer then signals when the wheels are centred on the scales, and the tractor pulls away.

The 757-200 weighs in at 127,810lb (57,975kg). As new items are added over time, an aircraft's empty weight can increase by up to 1 per cent each year.

On the day an aircraft is scheduled for delivery, representatives of the airline, Boeing and others gather to sign the papers in a conference room. Because millions of dollars are involved, a conference

away, just as a new car is driven away by its happy owner.

Naturally, the work does not end when planes are flown away by customers. Boeing's customer-service division provides manuals and CD-ROMs telling customers how to operate and maintain members of their dynamic duo. The division also offers training and spare parts.

After flight testing, most new Boeing jets take off for their delivery flights from Boeing Field in Seattle.
Here, a new British Airways 757 leaves for home. Ed Davies

This Finnair 757 awaits modifications prior to delivery at Renton. Ed Davies

CHAPTER NINE

Flight Testing

Static Tests

Soon after first rollout, the 767 and 757 underwent a static test programme as part of their certification. In such a test, the entire airframe is subjected to increasingly severe loads until it fails, and this provides precise knowledge of the plane's structural capability. Every new plane, without its engines or avionics, is twisted, turned and pulled in various ways, to ensure the design can cope with the worst battering that wind, weather and poor piloting could inflict upon it.

During the final static test of the 767 airframe, a load test was conducted that pulled the wing tips up 15.5ft (4.7m) over the top of the fuselage, at a pressure of 1.2 million pounds (544,300kg). The wing did not break, but the aft fuselage below the cargo floor did. As a result, that area was later strengthened. The wings proved to be 150 per cent stronger than the engineers had anticipated. Static testing showed that higher gross-weight versions could be offered earlier, and that this could be achieved with fewer changes than expected.

Static tests on the 757 were completed on 16 July 1982, when both wings failed at the same predicted location at 112 per cent of ultimate load, allowing the 757's gross weight to be increased to 240,000lb (108,900kg) from 220,000lb (99,800kg).

The 767 Early Testing Programme

The objective of the flight-testing programme is to identify any problems and work out the kinks prior to certification.

The 767's first flight occurred on schedule on 26 September 1981. The maiden journey of the world's newest airliner began on Paine Field, less than twenty-four hours after the aircraft had moved under its own power for the first time. It was an extraordinary achievement, showing how demanding the company's

Static testing is as important as flight testing. Here, a 767 is prepared to test the airframe's ability to withstand both the forces of nature and pilot error. Boeing

flight-test programme was, during its unprecedented effort to produce two new planes less than five months apart. Usually, with a new-model aircraft, taxi tests are followed by a few days of debugging.

The first 767 was cleared for flight at 8.07 am that morning, after the replacement of some troublesome hydraulic pumps, which had delayed the start of initial taxi tests for several hours.

The aircraft had not moved under its own power until 12.20 pm the day before,

However, within about 90 minutes, half the time allotted, the aircraft had completed eight runs up and down the runway and achieved its test objectives. These included achieving a speed of 130 knots, 180-degree turns, S-turns, nose-wheel lift-off, rudder steering, and full thrust reverser and shimmy checks. Following the success of the taxi tests, the decision was made to fly on 26 September. Programme officials were anxious to get in the air ahead of the approaching storm front.

seat, with John Brit in the soon-to-be-extinct flight-engineer's station.

The maiden flight encountered a problem 40 minutes after take-off. Edmonds tried to retract the landing gear, but the central hydraulic system failed as a result of a fluid leak, which was spotted by the pilot of the chase plane. As a result, the gear would not come up, and all photos taken from the chase plane showed the 767 with gears down. Wallick confirmed that the instruments showed a loss of hydraulic fluid.

The first 767 during its first flight on 26 September 1981. The landing gear did not retract because of a hydraulic failure during the flight. Note the stickers of the seventeen original customers on the forward fuselage. Boeing

25 September, when two Pratt & Whitney JT9D-7R4 engines powered it from the flight line to the runway. At the time, flight-test officials were sceptical that the three-hour taxi test programme could be accomplished, the resulting data absorbed and analysed, and the aircraft checked out in time for a flight the following day. With forecasters predicting deteriorating weather conditions, starting from midday on 26 September, the first flight date of 30 September – chosen three years earlier – appeared to be in jeopardy.

The 767's First Flight

Project pilot Thomas Edmonds sent Boeing's biggest twin screaming down the runway at 11.54 am. After a 3,600ft (1,097m) take-off roll and a speed of 120 knots (222km/h), the 767 lifted smoothly into the air, heading north. Edmonds then made a gradual turn to the west, over the Olympic Peninsula, where the 767 was joined by a Boeing-owned North American F-86 fighter, serving as the chase plane. Lew Wallick was in the co-pilot

It was the only sour note in an otherwise flawless first flight, which lasted two hours and four minutes. It was not a serious problem, since the 767 has three hydraulic systems. 'The aircraft is designed to fly on one engine and to fly on a single hydraulic system. We have three,' Edmonds told Aviation Week & Space Technology after the flight. 'It is going to be operated in airline service, and at some time in its life it will have a hydraulic failure. For me this was another way of saying that the aircraft operated as designed.' An inspection after the flight showed the leak was due to a broken hydraulic line in the nose-gear area. The broken line drained nearly all the fluid from one system. It was unrelated to the hydraulic pump problem that had delayed the taxi tests.

There was one other problem during the first flight. When Edmonds flushed one of the toilets, there was a boom like a gun going off. The noise came from a valve in the vacuum flushing system – a problem that was later quickly fixed.

Nearly all the initial first-flight objectives were met. The aircraft flew at altitudes of between 17,000 and 18,000ft (5,180–5,500m). Cruising south over an area just south of the Juan de Fuca Strait between Port Townsend and Port Angeles, Washington, the crew investigated the handling characteristics, and performed some initial buffet checks at flap settings of

25 degrees and 30 degrees. The new transport met up with a photo aircraft for about 30 minutes, then returned to Paine Field for a fly-by at 800ft (244m). It then made an approach at 125 knots (231km) and a smooth, uneventful landing at 1.58 pm – just as the oncoming front began to darken the skies.

The big jet then taxied across to the adjacent flight line, where hundreds of employees and guests applauded the flight crew. 'I don't think we've ever had a cleaner airplane on a first flight,' 'T' Wilson told the crowd. Edmonds described it as a 'very marvellous' first flight, and confirmed that the aircraft had performed very close to expectation, following the simulator tests. He noted the plane's hallmarks – fuel efficiency and quietness. 'It looked like we had more fuel when we came back than when we left,' he said at the time. While

engine noise and fuel efficiency would be carefully noted in future test flights, observers near the runway also said that the take-off seemed remarkably quiet.

Edmonds was pleased with the colour displays of the electronic attitude director indicator and the map display on the horizontal situation indicator. 'It's like holding a map on a TV screen,' he said. 'You can see where you are all the time.'

The 757's First Flight

Test runs of the 757's Rolls-Royce RB211-535C engines began on 23 January 1982, on the pre-flight line at Renton. Power was restricted to idle that day, due to high crosswinds. Full take-off power was achieved the next day. On 17 February, Boeing rolled the aircraft under its own power, to

757 test pilots John Armstrong *(left)* and Lew Wallick prior to the aircraft's first flight on 19 February 1982. Boeing

conduct taxi tests. The 757 returned to the flight line after only three runs.

At this point, all was ready for a 10 am flight the following day, but persistent heavy rains – common in the Puget Sound area at that time of year – caused a series of postponements and, finally, a midday decision to abandon flight plans for the day.

On 19 February, the weather was still threatening, but now concern centred on the wind. Because it was a first flight, the FAA required that the 757 take off to the north over Lake Washington, rather than south into the wind – a path that would have taken the aircraft over populated areas. A weather station near the runway was recording tail winds of about 16 knots (30km/h), unacceptable for a downwind take-off from the 5,300ft (1,615m) runway. However, conditions swiftly improved, enabling the red, white and blue twin-jet to taxi to the south end of the field. When the wind speed dipped to 10 knots (18.5km/h), it was time to go.

The crew brought the engines up to power and carried out a short taxi test by moving the plane down the runway a short distance before braking. The 757 then

returned to the end of the runway and started its take-off roll.

The aircraft rotated at 125 knots (231km/h) and lifted off smoothly over Lake Washington. Like the 767, it was joined by an F-86 chase plane. Later, after achieving all first-flight objectives, the plane met up with a 727 photo aircraft for a 40-minute photo session over the Straits of Juan de Fuca. The plane flew between 16,000 and 18,000ft (4,900–5,500m), flying at speeds below 250 knots (462km/h).

The landing gear was intentionally retracted for most of the first flight, and did not suffer the hydraulic problems that had been faced by the 767 five months earlier. Objectives of the maiden flight included checking the aircraft at all flap settings and all speeds below 250 knots, and initial buffet at each flap setting. Trailing cones were deployed during the flight, to check the calibration of the airspeed recorded on board.

A plan to perform a ceremonial fly-by before landing at Paine Field in Everett was scratched because of impending rain clouds, but the 757 touched down smoothly. It landed at Everett, because the area is less populated. The first 757 operated from there

for ten hours of flight time, in order to prove to the FAA a level of airworthiness that would allow it to operate over populated areas. It then moved to Boeing Field, headquarters for the 757/767 flight-test effort.

The 767 had experienced some problems on its first flight, and the maiden voyage of the 757 was not quite without any flaws, either.

Towards the end of the 757's first flight, one of its engines stalled, because of an inadvertent blast of high-pressure air while at flight idle. The No. 2 engine intentionally had been brought down to idle, while the other engine remained at full power, as part of the control checks. A valve was left open in the interconnect system between the engines, allowing higher-pressure bleed air to flow from the engine operating at flight power to the idle engine. That created a stall condition. The engine was shut down for a few minutes and re-started. The first flight, which had lasted for two hours and thirty-one minutes, ended with a normal landing.

The problem with the Rolls engine came about twenty minutes before the plane landed, and the issue never came up

The first 757 conducts flight testing at Edwards Air Force Base in California. The base's long runways, desert climate and a lack of population is an ideal place to test new aircraft. Boeing

Northwest Airlines flies more than seventy 757s, many flying coast-to-coast routes in the US. Ed Davies

US Airways is among the major US carriers flying the 757. Ed Davies

A 767 AWACS, one of four built for Japan, is shown at Boeing Field. Ed Davies

Delta Air Lines, the third-largest carrier in the world, operates 110 757s, the most of any airline. Ed Davies

(Above) American Airlines uses its 767-300s on domestic and international routes. Ed Davies

(Below) German charter carrier Condor gets in the spirit of holiday travel with this Rizzi Bird livery on a 757-200. Stefan Roesch

American Airlines is the second-largest operator of 757s, with 102 in service. Darren Anderson

(Above) One of America West's 757s is painted in the team colours of the Arizona Diamond Backs, a baseball team in the airline's hub city, Phoenix. Darren Anderson

(Below) Germany's Condor Flugdienst is the launch customer for the 757-300, a stretched model that rolled out in May 1998. Condor Flugdienst

Air China operates four 767-300s. Michael Pellaton/Flying Images Worldwide

(Above) **Transbrasil uses both 767-300s, shown here, and -200 models.** Michael Pellaton/Flying Images Worldwide

(Below) **It doesn't take special liveries to make America West's 757s look beautiful.** Ralph Olson/Flying Images Worldwide

(Opposite) **The 757 Freighter was rolled out on 8 July 1987 for United Parcel Service.** Boeing

Asiana's 767-300s are used on both trans-Pacific and Asian routes. Michael Pellaton/Flying Images Worldwide

This LTU Süd 757 is among many flying for European charter carriers to warmer climates. Peter Sweeten/Aviation Images Worldwide

All Nippon Airways operates forty 767-300s. Peter Sweeten/Aviation Images Worldwide

Vietnam Airlines unveiled its new colours in 1998 on one of its 767-300ERs. Peter Sweeten/Aviation Photography Worldwide

Eastern Airlines was the launch customer for the 757-200. Andrew Abshier

United Parcel Service is the largest operator of 767 freighters. Terry Hale

This United Parcel Service 767-300 is painted in special Olympic colours in honour of the company's Olympic sponsorship. Terry Hale

This KLM 767-300 lands at Vancouver following a long flight from Amsterdam. Robert Rindt

The C-32A, the military version of the 757, entered service in 1998 to transport US government officials. Boeing *(Below)* **757 assembly in Renton.** Boeing

in the press. Only several days later, one newspaper reported that the 757 had lost engine power on the flight. Although not damaged, the engine was replaced for the second flight. No one takes any chances during flight testing.

As the pilots went to stride proudly out of the plane, there was a little incident – they could not get the 757's door open. Due to a relief-valve failure, the pressurization system had broken – in effect, the plane was still pressurized. Test pilot John Armstrong simply went back to the cockpit and opened a window to let air out.

The first 757 was a more complete aircraft at rollout than any other Boeing model that had been produced before. 'We achieved everything we intended to do on the first flight, and everything worked just as advertised,' says Armstrong, who was joined in the cockpit by Lew Wallick, who had also flown on the 767.

'It was a thrill to get the sucker in the air,' Armstrong recalls today. 'It performed just like they said it would.'

Pilot Profiles

Thomas Edmonds

Edmonds was the 767's project test pilot. Working with engineers, he represented the pilot viewpoint in cockpit and aircraft-systems design.

Edmonds began flying while he was an aeronautical engineering student and joined the US Navy flight programme in 1951. In 1956, after graduating from the US Air Force Test Pilot School, he joined Boeing as a flight-test engineer on the KC-135 military jet tanker programme. He was the project pilot of the 707 programme and also took part in the 727, 737 and 747 programmes. At the time of the 767, Edmonds offered 31 years of flight experience. Both Edmonds and his co-pilot on the 767, S. L. 'Lew' Wallick, had flown every type of Boeing jetliner produced.

S. L. 'Lew' Wallick

A former Second World War naval pilot, Wallick joined Boeing in 1951. He was Boeing's director of flight test and chief test pilot at the time of the 767 launch. He was involved in five initial flights of new Boeing aircraft, and three maiden flights of derivative models. He was co-pilot on the 767 and 757, and the chief test pilot for

An Employee's Perspective

Seeing the new planes leaving the assembly line and flying away can be an emotional experience for the Boeing employees who help to design and build them. One worker, Jack J. Joseph, shared his feelings in a 1982 issue of *Boeing News*, the company newspaper:

'We went to Renton Field to watch the first flight of the 757. Waiting there for a few minutes in excited anticipation, which I think we all felt, the clouds dissipated almost suddenly as if by some magic to expose a great expanse of sunshine and blue sky – a portent of future greatness for the 757.

'It occurred to me that this great airplane that was about to be launched into service was a total manifestation of the creative energies and abilities of many men and women working in harmony to produce the very finest that their cooperative talents and efforts could conceive. Having had a part in this effort and seeing it evolve into this beautiful machine caused a feeling of pride and exhilaration, which I felt compelled to express in some way:

"She sits on the runway in the morning sunlight.
Silver wings spread for flight; sensing, testing, tasting the wind.
Poised, gleaming and with a great bellowing lurch, projected on her run.
Straight as an arrow sprung from ten thousand bows, she goes, ever faster.
Mighty engines burning, pulsing, thrusting, singing their song.
Up she goes toward the great heights; up where the angels play.
Born of a breed whose playground is the stars
Launched by a million careful hands who came to see her fly."'

Armstrong *(left)* and Wallick disembark following successful first flight of the 757. Boeing

the 727 and 737, and also co-piloted the 720, 707-300 and 747SP derivatives. Wallick was named co-pilot for the initial flight of the 767 in September 1980.

John Armstrong

John Armstrong worked with the 757 designers right from the aircraft's inception, representing the pilot's point of view during the design process.

A graduate of Washington State University, with a Bachelor of Science degree in mechanical engineering, Armstrong joined Boeing in 1959 as a flight-test engineer. He returned to Boeing in 1965 after five years in the US Air Force, and served as a production test pilot and an engineering test

could arise – but in 1982 Boeing was faced with testing two new aircraft at the same time. On top of that, the all-new digital flight decks had to pass muster.

The Programme

The test-flight programme was the most demanding yet for Boeing. The company met this challenge, which was complicated by a tight time schedule and stringent federal requirements, by doubling its flight-test organization from 524 employees to more than 900, redeveloping its flight data management system, and conducting an intensive training programme to make efficient use of people and equipment.

Flight testing was especially critical for the new jets, since both planes were technically very different from previous Boeing models. Airframes and engines were not the only items under the microscope. 'A lot of the systems were totally new,' Wygle says. 'The glass cockpit was a novel concept, and the industry was watching very closely.'

Overall, the 767 and 757 performed well, both aerodynamically and structurally. 'Both were relatively trouble-free and they met or exceeded take-off and cruise performance,' Wygle says. 'These were two of the best-behaving models we had ever built, certified and delivered on time. That is a success story.'

With every successive test flight, the performance envelope on both planes was

The 767 during flight testing. The model underwent 1,648 hours of flight testing in ten months. Boeing

pilot on 707s, 727s, 737s, and 747s. He had been the project test pilot for the 727 and 737 when he was named for the 757 programme in 1978.

Flight Testing

With the dynamic duo's first flights successfully completed, Boeing embarked on a strenuous and ambitious flight-test programme. Flight testing is always an anxious time – just when engineers are hoping to have thought of everything, a new problem

The company's seven-day-a-week flight-test workload peaked in 1982 at seventeen aircraft, nine more than the maximum used during the 747 flight-test programme. At the same time, new regulatory requirements forced Boeing to produce more data to a greater degree of accuracy in less time.

Brien Wygle, vice-president of flight operations, who oversaw the 767 and 757 flight-testing programmes, says now that gearing up for two test programme was not easy. 'That was no small task,' he recalls. 'Our facilities and manpower were stretched real thin.'

constantly enlarged. The second flight of the 757, for instance, reached speeds of 460 knots (851km/h) and an altitude of 35,000ft (10,700m) instead of 250 knots (463km/h) and 18,000ft (5,500m) on the first flight. (Armstrong and Wallick, though, reported an engine throttle slightly out of adjustment, and minor trouble with electronic indicators – the type of problems common to brand-new aircraft.)

The 767 underwent 1,648 hours of flight testing in ten months; the 757 completed 1,380 hours in ten months. Each went through similar trials to test capabilities, performance and safety both in the air and on the ground. The tests focused on cruise performance, low-speed stability and control, engine-cooling, noise, flutter, and landing and take-off performance, including the dramatic tail-drag test. The aircraft also underwent a series of aborted take-offs, to show that they are able to stop when losing an engine at a critical moment, in conditions that destroy brakes, tyres and wheels.

The later 757 programme did use certification data from 767 flight tests, but the two planes are sufficiently different to warrant their own extensive test programmes. On the 757, for example, equipment is installed in different locations and in different proximity to other equipment in the two models, and these differences affect operating temperatures, electromagnetic interference and other characteristics, all of which needed to be checked out in flight. Still, the commonality of the 767 and 757 reduced testing from what would have been required for two completely new aircraft.

Hundreds of landings were conducted on each plane under a variety of wind conditions, weights, centre-of-gravity locations, flap settings, and other variables. Many of these were done at Boeing Field in Seattle or at Moses Lake, Washington, at a former air base in Glasgow, Montana, and in the high desert of Palmdale, California.

Much of the testing focused on the glass cockpit and accompanying electronics. The first 767 did not have the glass cockpit at all, and the 757's, although further along, was incomplete. In fact, the digital decks were not fully ready until just before the aircraft were certified, giving engineers enough time to demonstrate that all the new gadgets on board would not interfere with communications or cause electronic problems. Engine Indicating and Crew Alerting System (EICAS) testing was done on the 757 before the system was used on the 767.

The Test Fleets

The first five 767s used in flight testing were outfitted with three-member crew decks, since they were built after Boeing was allowed to offer two-crew cockpits. Four 767s – the Boeing-owned first one and three in United Airlines colours – equipped with Pratt & Whitney engines were used for the basic flight test programme. The first 767 was used to perform

initial airworthiness tests, high-speed structural tests and testing of stability and control and aerodynamic performance.

The second aircraft began tests in October 1981. It was used to test controls, digital avionics and the flight-management and electrical systems, and also to certify the engines. The third 767 joined the programme in November to concentrate on

brake development, flight loads and tests of the pneumatic system, automatic flight controls, and stall and buffet loads. The fourth aircraft, fitted with a complete interior in the front half of the passenger cabin, began work in December 1981 to perform airline-type flying and reliability checks.

A fifth aircraft equipped with GE CF6-80A engines was used to certify the aircraft

Test equipment on board the 767 measures aircraft performance. The barrels *(top)* are used to simulate flight loads. Boeing

with that engine. It first flew in February 1982. A sixth 767, outfitted with a two-person flight deck, began operating in the spring of 1982. This one was used for final certification of the aircraft, including evacuation testing.

The 757 test fleet comprised six aircraft, used for the same tasks. One aircraft, for Eastern Airlines, offered a rearranged electronics bay, to allow for more baggage. Another 757 was in the Delta Air Lines configuration, which differed from other 757s in the division of electrical and electronic equipment between the fore and aft compartments. Delta also chose to eliminate a door, opting instead for an overwing exit.

Dramatic Tests

The dramatic rejected take-off braking testing was conducted on the hot and dry desert floor at Edwards Air Force Base in California. For these tests, an aircraft was loaded to full take-off weight, brought up to take-off speed and then stopped abruptly, putting maximum energy into the brakes. The new airliners had to demonstrate that they could withstand the ensuing brake fire for five minutes.

Another scary manoeuvre was velocity minimum unstick testing, to determine the minimum speed at which the aircraft can lift off, and to demonstrate that it can remain stable during climb after such a

take-off. During these tests, the aircraft's tail, protected by a wooden tail skid, scraped the lakebed runway, sending a column of smoke and dust into the air. Data from such tests were used to calculate field length and take-off performance. Both the 757 and 767 performed these challenges somewhat better than expected, and the flight-test crew was pleased with both the handling characteristics and stability under such abusive conditions.

To simulate the rigours of flight, parts were judged on their ability to withstand the number of cycles in a normal service life, plus 50 per cent. 'Cycle' refers to the number of flights; one cycle is one take-off and landing. Both airframes were service-

Velocity minimum unstick testing, a scary flight-testing manoeuvre, is done to determine the minimum speed at which the aircraft can lift off, and to demonstrate that it can remain stable during climb after such a take-off. During these tests, the aircraft's tail, protected by a wooden tail skid, scrapes the lake-bed runway at Edwards Air Force Base. Boeing

Cold-Weather Certification

When Russia's Baikal Airlines ordered the 757 for service in Siberia, Boeing had to satisfy Russia's aviation authority, the Aviation Register, that the aircraft could withstand the world's coldest temperatures. To obtain cold-weather certification in Russia, in January 1995, about thirty Boeing employees flew a 757 to the city of Yakutsk, Siberia. The trip entailed a quick stopover in Fairbanks, Alaska, a flight across the Bering Sea and landing in the city, which is just south of the Arctic Circle. There, the plane was left 'cold-soaked' (sitting outside) for fourteen hours in temperatures down to −65°F (−54°C). Then the crew conducted several ground and flight tests, showing that the plane could operate at below −30°F (−34°C), the temperature to which the Russian authorities had limited the aircraft.

The Boeing team was anxious to find out how the bitterly cold weather would affect fuel and hydraulic systems, the auxiliary power unit, the Rolls-Royce engines, landing gear, tyres and doors. The cold-weather demonstration was a complete success; the aircraft performed almost flawlessly. As a result, Boeing was able to validate and develop minor revisions to the maintenance and flight-operations manuals.

The 757 arrived on 17 January 1995 in a dense cloud of frozen ground fog that obscured much of the area. The aircraft was immediately prepared for cold soak. The aircraft was powered down and all heat sources were removed. The cold soak began at a temperature of −50°F (−45.5°C). The temperature hit a low of −58°F (−50°C) during the test, driving temperatures in the interior cabin to −27°F (−33°C); it was −33°F (−36°C) in the flight deck.

Following the cold-soak test, the Boeing crew used two ground heating units to warm the air inside the 757. Four hours later, the cabin temperature was warm enough for systems to work. It took less than 45 minutes after that to bring the cab temperature up to 75°F (24°C). Engines were then started, and the plane flew a short demonstration flight. As a result, the 757 is certified for operation at temperatures as low as −65°F (−54°C) − cold enough to solidify fuel − and is, therefore, suitable for Russian operators in the winter.

The 757 was flown to Yakutsk, Russia, in January 1995 for cold-weather certification in Russia. Boeing

life tested over two lifetimes, or forty years of airline service. They endured 19 months of tests consisting of 100,000 simulated flights over 100,000 hours.

To test the real-life capabilities of the new jets, both the 767 and 757 flew in some odd places to ensure their durability and reliability, from the hot Arizona desert in the middle of the summer to the depths of a Siberian winter.

Meeting and Exceeding Expectations

In general, both planes performed close to design in flight tests, and Boeing experienced fewer testing problems on the 767/757 than on the 727. 'These were two of the best programmes we've ever produced coming out of our factory. It was quite a happy programme,' says Brien

when they ordered the plane. This was due largely to lower aerodynamic drag. The aircraft was also found to be 1,500lb (680kg) lighter, as the result of an aggressive weight-reduction programme. Flight testing found that each 767 with a full passenger load equals two 727s plus half a 707 freighter, all for 2 per cent less fuel burn than a 727.

'The 767 is a better airplane than [the one] we sold, and our airlines are going to

The 757 during a test flight. Both the 757 and 767 performed well during this critical phase. Boeing

Among the most significant tests was the test carried out in Lhasa, Nepal for high-altitude certification. To be flown in China, the 757 had to show that it could take off in the thin Himalayan air, even with one engine out, and maintain sufficient altitude, for long enough, to cross the mountains and fly back to Chengdu, China. For these tests, the pilots wore oxygen masks during descent and landing.

Wygle. 'Those two planes were beautiful. They were well engineered and met all expectations.'

The 767

Flight tests confirmed that both aircraft were as fuel-efficient as advertised. The 767's fuel burn was found to be 4.5 per cent less than the level the airlines had been told

get a better airplane than they bought,' Dean Thornton, vice-president and general manager of the 767 division, told reporters during a demonstration flight from Seattle to Chicago. 'That's not just engineering calculation, but hard, measurable data with the airplane in the sky.' Boeing knew about these better-than-expected results even before the first flight, but chose to wait until testing could confirm them.

(Above) **A 767-300ER about to touch down after a test flight over the Californian desert.** Boeing

(Below) **A 767 cruises on a test flight over Washington State's Olympic Mountains.** Boeing

The 767's exit chute, used in emergency evacuations, was among the aircraft's many features tested on the ground. Boeing

The 757

Continued 757 testing found that the wings' decreased sweep, greater length and thicker cross-section led to improved fuel efficiency. Improved low-speed performance and a higher lift-to-drag ratio resulted in lower engine thrust requirements during landing, helping to reduce noise. To test the wing's structural dynamics, Boeing used a flutter vane, extended from the wing tip, which activated in flight to induce flutter. Flutter tests on the 757 were completed in record time for a Boeing transport. In fact, testing of the 757 went so well that one of the five aircraft planned for the test fleet was retired early and prepared for delivery.

Armstrong, the 757 test pilot, now says that the smooth progress of the aircraft's testing programme was in part due to the experience derived from the earlier 767 programme. The 757, which was not intended to be a transcontinental aircraft, quickly received that reputation after the airlines saw its performance during flight testing. 'It became a longer-range airplane real quick,' says Armstrong.

Mock Flights

Long before the first flight of the 757, Boeing and launch customer Eastern Airlines decided to test the galley positions of the new plane. Boeing recruited 174 employees to act as 'passengers', to sit on an imaginary flight in a full-scale mock-up of the new jet. This time and motion test was aimed at determining the better of two methods a carrier might use to serve food. Cameras recorded the 'flight' for later analysis. In the study, flight attendants provided customers with beverage service, followed by lunch or dinner. In the 757 design, the galleys are located forward and aft, with lavatories bracketing the centre section of the aircraft.

The flight attendants used aisle carts in the morning test and distributed meals by hand in the afternoon test. Cart service was found to require a 40in (100cm) deep galley, compared with the hand-carry system, which needed a 30in (76cm) deep galley. Consequently, the type of food and beverage service selected by an airline will affect the seating arrangement.

During the tests, employees were given play money to buy drinks, and were told to walk to the lavatories at given times, in order to demonstrate the difficulty or ease of

Early test flights by members of the industry press gave the 767 high marks: 'Apart from its high level of automation, the 767 has retained the stability and handling qualities of earlier Boeing planes. Control forces are slightly on the heavy side, though responsiveness has been improved from previous aircraft such as the 707, especially at low speeds,' wrote *Aviation Week & Space Technology*'s reporter. 'The new aircraft also has very straightforward stall characteristics, with natural and artificial stall warning margins adequate enough to prevent inadvertent stalls. Spaciousness of the 767's cockpit is similar to that of other widebody transports currently in service, but the absence of a flight engineer's panel at the rear of the

flight deck makes the cockpit feel even roomier. Late adoption of the two-crew configuration in the evolution of the 767 design has resulted in a greater amount of space at the rear of the flight deck.'

The 767 flight-test programme resulted in a number of refinements in the software for digital avionics, and a change in the mounting arrangement of the wing's leading-edge slats. An inability to retract the slat on the third flight led Boeing to strengthen the slat-attach structure somewhat, and move it further forward.

The avionics systems for both new aircraft went through their paces in less time and with more thoroughness and precision than in any previous Boeing aircraft.

(*Above*) The 757 executes a water spray test during flight testing. This test measures how the aircraft and engines perform if standing water lines the runway. Boeing

(*Below*) Boeing employees were used to test the 757's comfort and speed of in-flight service. Boeing

A 757 embarks on another test flight. Note its silvery finish, unlike other Boeing test aircraft.
Boeing

(Below) The 757 returns to Boeing Field following a test flight. Boeing

A 757 takes off at Renton. Boeing

passenger movement during meal service. Employees who served as passengers were asked to complete a questionnaire stating how long they had to wait for a meal, whether it was hot enough, if they were allowed ample time to eat, and whether the cart in the aisle was a hindrance.

Similar tests were conducted on 767s at the Everett plant, when 446 'passengers' enjoyed mock flights during an American Airlines time and motion study. The two days of tests were recorded by five television cameras on fifty hours of videotape. American Airlines officials viewed the tape in order to determine the best configurations for passenger comfort.

Today, Boeing selects a group of employees to take test flights before any first new model is delivered. They check everything, from cushion comfort and cabin temperatures, to air circulation and whether they are able to read during take-off.

Data Analysis

When the dynamic duo was tested, Boeing had the advantage of a sophisticated onboard airborne data analysis and monitor system called Adams 2, as well as a ground-based flight-test computing system. These systems had not been available when previous aircraft were tested. Together, they enabled engineers on board to look at live flight-test data, so that they could evaluate whether completed tests were sufficient, or whether the tests needed to be repeated in the air. In older testing programmes, the aircraft would have to land first. Data tape would be run through a computer, and the results sent to the technical people, who would have to evaluate it before returning with a decision as to whether it was necessary to repeat the specific condition in flight. With the new systems, such decisions could be made with the plane still in the air.

The Fuel System

Tests are also conducted on the fuel system to certify and document its accuracy. At stake is safety (is there enough fuel in the tanks for the flight?) and reputation (how accurate is performance compared with promised performance?). Fuel for both the 767 and 757, as on almost all aircraft, is carried in the wings. Fuel quantity is measured by probes, which change in electrical capacitance as the fuel level around them changes. This is indicated by gauges beneath the wings and on the flight deck. A densitometer in each wing tank automatically determines the unit weight of the fuel, which the fuel-system computer multiplies by the quantity of fuel on board to determine fuel weight. This is important for calculating aircraft gross weight, to keep within structural weight limitations, and where take-off distance is weight-critical.

Wind-Tunnel Testing

How did Boeing know the 757 and 767 would be among the world's most fuel-efficient aircraft? One answer is wind-tunnel testing.

Boeing's wind-tunnel testing facility is the largest in the world, and the company conducts more wind testing than any other. Boeing operates the facility for three shifts every day. Scaled-down models of both the 767 and 757 airframes underwent thousands of hours of wind-tunnel tests.

The wind tunnel can blow winds of 600mph (965km/h) – the speed of aircraft flying at cruising altitude – to test force on an airframe. Data from sensors is sent to computers. When models are put through the tests, engineers can tell immediately if changes are needed to optimize an aircraft's performance. Those changes can then be made, even while the aircraft is still in production.

(Right) **The 767 model, still with a T-tail prior to final configuration, is prepared for wind-tunnel testing. The wind tunnel can blow winds of 600mph (965km/h) – the speed the aircraft flies at cruising altitude – to test the force on the airframe.** Boeing.

The 757 is prepared for wind-tunnel testing. Boeing

To test the accuracy of the system, a multicoloured pictorial display on the video control terminal shows the critical elements of the fuelling system, such as switch and valve position, pumping rates, system pressures, weight of fuel in the tanks, and the percentage difference between the amount pumped and the amount indicated by the aircraft's gauges. Each step of the test and the results are printed out by computer to document the accuracy of the fuel system. Abnormalities are noted and can then be fixed.

Touring the World

As part of the flight-test programme, both aircraft visited a variety of airports around the world. The 767 finished a world-wide promotional tour by setting a non-stop distance record for a twin-jet on 21 July 1982, flying non-stop from Oslo, Norway, to Seattle in the USA, a distance of 4,990 miles (7,984km), in 9 hours and 50 minutes. (This record was later easily broken.) The tour covered 29,000 miles (46,400km) in

seven countries in Europe, the Middle East and Africa. It featured many firsts for the new plane: the first transatlantic flight by a 767 (Boston, USA, to Turin, Italy); the first 767 landing in Europe; the first 767 landing

High-Tech Testing

An array of interconnected sensors, digital computers and touch-sensitive video terminals has revolutionized the testing of new aircraft. On the 767 and 757, automated test systems and components were used for the first time, both built into the aircraft and attached temporarily to obtain faster, more accurate and more consistent results. After all, introducing the first aircraft with digital flight avionics required sophisticated testing equipment.

Other testing, such as checking the landing gear, employs more old-fashioned methods. The landing gear is checked simply by cycling the landing gear after the aircraft is supported on tripods, and sections of the assembly floor are lowered beneath the landing gear. Avionics testing is done in a special facility and by a mobile test van on the flight line.

The flight-control surfaces on the twin-jets – the flaps, ailerons and spoilers on the wings, the elevators and rudders on the tail – have small transducers built

into them, which send electrical signals on their positions to the flight deck. Transducers convert energy from one system to energy in another system. In the 767 and 757, transducers convert the movement of actuators moving the elevators, for instance, into electrical energy. Transducer signals in the planes are used on the flight deck to indicate the position of the control surfaces. In the case of the spoilers, which are controlled by an electrical-hydraulic link, the signals provide feedback to the control loop. The signals are recorded for any malfunctions. The result is that testing is much more accurate, quicker, and can be repeated. For testing, microprocessors convert the transducer signals into digital form and send the signals to a computer mounted on a mobile console outside the aircraft. The computer compares the signals from the flight-deck controls and from the control surfaces with values from a test document based on engineering requirements.

Hundreds of Ethiopians line up at the Addis Ababa airport in March 1982 to view the world-touring 767. Ethiopia was one of eight African nations on the 23-nation tour of Boeing's new-generation aircraft. Ethiopian Airlines was the first African carrier to select the model. Boeing

in the Middle East, at Amman. Even the late King Hussein of Jordan, a registered pilot who often piloted his own L-1011, flew the 767.

The 757 also flew on several round-the-world tours, and it was enthusiastically received at smaller airports, where it demonstrated its ability to land on short, remote runways. One such trip to seven Asian nations was capped by a 9-hour, 7-minute flight from Tokyo to Seattle, on 28 August 1982, a 4,917 mile (7,867km) journey. It was the longest non-stop flight, and the longest time aloft for the 757.

Certification

Both planes breezed though FAA certification, although the 757 did suffer as a result of some last-minute red tape.

The 767 was certified on 30 July 1982, during a simple ceremony at Everett. The FAA said that this had been the most vigorous certification programme ever. The first 767 was certified with a two-person cockpit and Pratt & Whitney JT9D-7R4 engines, and delivered to United Airlines on 19 August. Certification of the first model powered by GE engines, destined for Delta Air Lines, occurred on 30 September 1982, with delivery to Delta on 25 Octo-

ber, and to American Airlines shortly after. The programme met a certification date that had been set three years earlier, despite a mid-programme switch from a three-member crew to two members, overlapping flight testing with the 757, more demanding FAA certification requirements, and the extra work involved in testing and approving the new glass cockpit.

At the time of certification, Boeing rolled out twenty 767s for six customers and forty-three planes for eight airlines by the end of 1982.

The 757 was to have received its type certificate, the licence needed to carry passengers, on 21 December 1982. That deadline had been set three years earlier, before production had even begun. However, just three hours before a ceremonial luncheon in Renton, the FAA notified Phil Condit, the 757's chief engineer and now Boeings Chief Executive Officer, that the certificate would not be issued, because one of the two cockpit jump seats failed to comply with regulations.

Boeing maintained that the jump seat had nothing to do with safety or technical matters, and thus was not covered by the certificate. After a flurry of coast-to-coast phone calls, the FAA agreed to grant a temporary, six-month certificate, pending resolution of the jump-seat issue. Condit

turned down that offer. While the luncheon proceeded – complete with flowers and a 757 model at each table – the mood was far from festive.

After lunch, Condit announced that he had given in – it was the only way Boeing could meet first delivery to Eastern. The airline had to take delivery of the plane in 1982, in order to receive millions of dollars in tax credits for that calendar year. Three months later, the 757 received its full certification, after resolution of the seat issue.

Like the 767, the 757 also completed a number of world tours, specifically to show its ability to land at high-altitude airports in hot climates. Children in Nairobi, Kenya, learned about the aircraft during a stop there in 1983. Boeing

---

Marketing

Marketing a Boeing aircraft is as important as making one. An airline in need of new planes usually approaches or is approached by both major airframe manufacturers, Boeing and Airbus. Apart from the 747-400, these two companies make aircraft of a similar size. The airline considers a host of factors – financing, price, cost of ownership, engine selection, commonality, passenger comfort, maintenance, and even political pressures – before making its selection. Throughout the process, Boeing is ready to supply information and answer hundreds of questions.

The 767 and 757 made their international marketing debut at the 1982 Farnborough Air Show in England. At the time, the 767 was competing vigorously against the Airbus Industrie A310, particularly in Europe, where early sales lagged behind those in other areas of the world. These leading commercial airframe manufacturers were displaying new products at a time when many airlines were opting to delay purchasing new technology in lieu of used equipment.

Boeing's new jets were the darlings of the show. They drew applause from the crowd with their quiet take-offs and landings. Both planes flew once a day, even performing fly-bys over the runway.

The show coincided with the first commercial service of the 767, which was scheduled to make its inaugural flight on 8 September. Farnborough was critical for stimulating a rather lacklustre sales situation: in the previous 13 months, Boeing had not received any new orders for the 767. Despite the gloomy outlook, the company continued to tout the fuel efficiency of its new jets. Tex Boullioun, the president of Boeing's commercial aircraft group, went so far as to guarantee that the 767 would beat the fuel efficiency of the Airbus A310 that Trans World Airlines was set to buy. Boullioun bet TWA that, if the plane did not match his fuel-efficiency guarantees, Boeing would pay the airline. If it did, the airline would have to pay Boeing. Sure enough, TWA had to pay up.

To help drum up 757 sales at Farnborough, Boeing revealed that flight testing had proved that the plane had performed better than promised, carrying 3,600lb (1,633kg) more payload, while burning 3.5 per cent less fuel. That amounts to carrying 18 more passengers and their baggage, and using just 58 per cent of the fuel used by the 727-200. When the plane was conceived, in 1978, Boeing had predicted a 30 per cent fuel saving over the 727-200.

CHAPTER TEN

The Family Grows

Boeing had considered stretching the 767 long before the aircraft had even carried its first revenue passenger. Soon after the airliner entered service, several airlines expressed an interest in a longer version, particularly in Asia, where dense passenger loads were, and are, more common.

The 767-300

Responding to requests from Japan Airlines, All Nippon Airways and Delta Air Lines to increase passenger capacity and improve seat-mile costs, Boeing decided, in September 1983 – only a year after the 767's debut – to continue its tradition of stretching existing models. The 767-300, as it became known, would feature a fuselage 21ft 1in (6.43m) longer than the 767-200. To achieve that stretch, Boeing extended the 767's fuselage with two 110in (2.79m) plugs fore and aft of the wing. This change increased seating capacity by 22 per cent (or about 45 passengers), and cargo volume by 31 per cent. Compared with the 767-200, the stretched aircraft would use 10 per cent more fuel, but 10 per cent less fuel *per seat*.

The -300 has a maximum take-off weight of 345,000lb (156,500kg) and can carry a two-class load of 269 passengers for 4,560 miles (7,340km). Most airlines opt for 250–260 seats in the plane. The -300 is also available in an extended-range version. The highest gross-weight 767-300ER, at 412,000lb (186,900kg) maximum take-off weight, can carry 218 passengers in three-class configuration for 7,080 miles (11,400km). Flying out of New York, the new version would be able to reach all of Europe and South America, and reach well into Africa and the Middle East. Out of London, it could reach all of the United States and Mexico City, and even Singapore.

The stretched model was rolled out of the Everett factory on 14 January 1986. Its first flight, with JT9D-7R4 engines, followed on 30 January. The first -300 model

was certified with that engine, and with GE's CF6-80A2 on 22 September 1986. British Airways ordered eleven in August 1987, later increasing that order to twenty-five, with Rolls-Royce RB211-524H

engines. It was the first time that the Rolls engine had flown on the 767, for delivery beginning in November 1989. At the time, the 767-300 was the longest twin-engine plane in the world, later supplanted by the

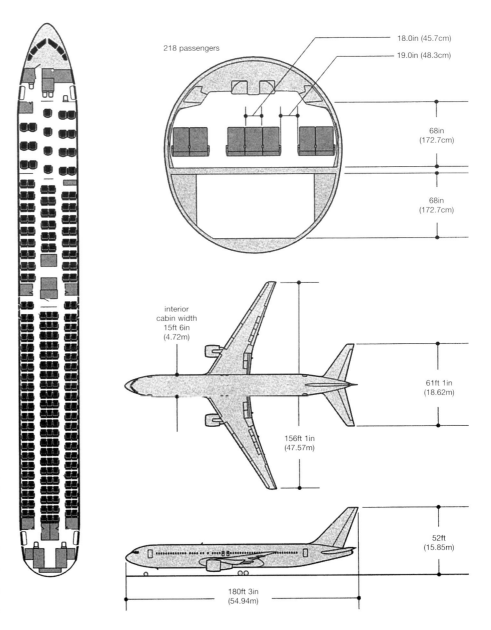

767-300 aircraft characteristics. Boeing

(Above) **Two 767-300s (foreground) being built alongside a -200 model.** Boeing

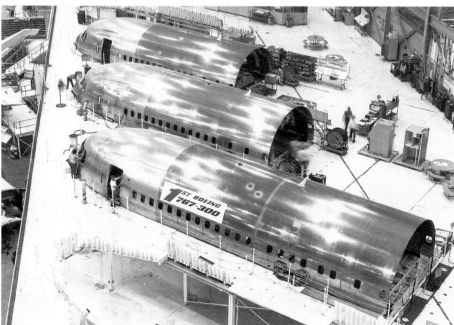

The forward section of the first 767-300. Note its length compared to the 767-200 forward sections next to it. Boeing

The 767-300 was rolled out on 14 January 1986. Its fuselage is 21ft 1in (6.43m) longer than the 767-200, increasing seat capacity by 22 per cent (about 45 passengers) and cargo volume by 31 per cent. Boeing

A 767-300 is parked next to a -200. Notice the difference in length. Boeing

777. Over time, the model has proven so popular that it has outsold the -200 by two to one.

The extended-range 767-300ER made its debut in late 1986, with higher-thrust versions reaching the market in 1987 and 1988. The -300ER can fly more than 6,660 miles (11,100km), farther than more than half the 747s flying today, thanks to a wing centre-section fuel tank, which carries an additional 24,050 gallons (91,029 litres) of fuel.

Stretching the 767 was easy, primarily because Boeing had planned for it, according to Joe Sutter. The 767-200's overly large wings ensured that the same wings could be used for a stretch.

Sutter was surprised that demand was so quick for the -300: 'Airlines wanted more

right away,' he recalls. 'It was stretched two to four years before it was supposed to. The success of the airplane, I believe, actually pushed the stretch earlier. It was a natural evolution.'

With the -300, Boeing was hoping to revitalize sales of the 767 and, in turn, develop further derivatives that would add range and capacity to challenge the widebody tri-jets. The shift toward smaller jets (stimulated by a deregulated US industry), and the unexpected levelling of fuel prices were major factors in limiting early 767-200 orders. With the -300, the goal was simply to remove range and capacity barriers that may have stalled sales. At the time, extending the range of the aircraft became more meaningful when restrictions on overwater operations of twin-jets

were relaxed. The -300 was aimed at operators of the A300-600, L-1011 and DC-10. It took a leisurely three years from go-ahead to first delivery, to Japan Air Lines on 25 September 1986. JAL ordered four of the models, powered by JT9D-7R4E engines. Delta Air Lines later ordered nine, powered by CF6-80A2 engines. All Nippon Airways was the third customer for the new model. The -300 was later powered by new Pratt & Whitney PW4000 and GE CF6-80C2 engines.

When it first came out, Boeing saw the -300 as a basic transcontinental aircraft. Although the aircraft would not have as many seats as the DC-10 and L1011, its economics were attractive.

Three versions of the 767-200 were offered prior to the decision to stretch the

Two sections of shiny skin show where this 767 engineering mock-up has been lengthened for use as a 767-300 development tool. The mock-up was separated to insert a 10ft 1in (3.38m) section forward of the wing and an 11ft (3.35m) section aft. Boeing

plane: the initial aircraft, one with higher-thrust engines, and the 767-200ER, offering a gross weight of 345,000lb (156,500kg) and a range of 5,290 miles (8,510km). The extra range of the 767-200ER was made possible by higher-thrust engines, and a centre fuel tank holding an additional 3,600 gallons (13,626 litres). Extended-range models featured heavier landing gear and tyres, and a stronger landing-gear support structure, wing leading edge and aft body. The first 767-200ER was delivered in the first quarter of 1984.

The 767-300 has the same take-off gross weight as the 767-200ER – 345,000lb (156,500kg) – as well as the same landing gear, wing structure and powerplants. In addition to the fuselage plugs, changes from the -200ER include a strengthened nose gear and wheel well, a stronger centre fuselage, a tail skid to keep the longer fuselage from striking the ground during take-off and landing, and a second overwing exit. Software was also changed in the flight-control computer. Other than that, all other systems remained the same, including the flight deck. The use of carbon brakes on the -300 and an aggressive weight-reduction programme helped to cut 4,000lb (1,815kg) from the empty weight originally specified.

The 767-300 on a test flight over Washington State in 1986. Boeing

767-300s take shape in Everett. Pictured is the first 767-300ER for Holland's Martinair. Boeing

The 767-300ER (Extended Range) was introduced in 1987 to increase the model's range. Boeing

The 767-300 during flight testing. Boeing

A 767-300 bound for Japan Airlines in the foreground, with -200s behind. Boeing

The first 767-300 was slightly different from the model that had originally been envisioned. The fuselage plug forward of the wing was increased by 11in (28cm), and the aft plug was extended by 22in (56cm), adding just one seat row, but also the capacity for four additional LD-2 cargo containers. This contributed a big boost to revenue potential.

Boeing offers two versions of the 767-300. The basic arrangement has two passenger doors and two emergency overwing exits on each side. This permits an emergency exit limit of 290 passengers. An alternate arrangement offers three doors on each side and no overwing exits. This configuration breaks up the forward cabin, so that first-class passengers can be loaded through the forward exit, with aft cabin passengers boarding through the second door, located just aft of the wing. In an all-economy configuration – common on high-density Asian routes – this arrangement speeds loading times. The emergency limit for this arrangement is 330 passengers, which charter operators can use in an eight-abreast configuration.

Boeing also offers 767-300 customers the option of using the same centre wing tank as in the 767-200ER; this increases fuel capacity up to 20,300 gallons (75,100 litres).

Anxious about the slow initial sales of the -300, Boeing briefly studied the possibility of modifying existing -200s to the -300's stretched configuration. Several airlines expressed an interest in such a retrofit, but soon enough airlines were ordering enough -300s to make the idea obsolete.

The 757-300

In Boeing's final assembly hangar in Renton, there is no mistaking the newest 757 – it's the one with its tail sticking out into the aisle. At 178ft 7in (54.5m) long, the 757-300 is the longest, largest and heaviest aircraft ever made in Renton; it is even longer than the 707-300, which measured 152ft 11in (46.6m). The 757-300, 23ft 4in (7.1m) longer than the 757-200, has the lowest seat-mile cost of any single-aisle jetliner on the market. It is also the largest single-aisle, twin-jet airliner in the world. The DC-8 was a longer single-aisle aircraft, but it had four engines.

While Boeing offered a stretched 767 just a year after the original 767 entered service, it would take 14 years for a longer 757 to debut. With the stretching of the 757, every Boeing jetliner since the 707 has now been extended. (The 747s stretch was limited to its upper deck.)

First Customers

At first, Boeing was not convinced that stretching the 757 would be worthwhile. After all, such a decision would mean millions of dollars in investments for no guarantee of returns. Customers of the 767 had demanded a version with increased capacity and range, but this was not the case with the 757. However, when Dietmar Kirchner, managing director of German charter carrier Condor Flugdienst, began to look around for new planes, he knew exactly what he wanted: a stretched version of the 757, which would enable his airline to carry more passengers at lower costs.

Unfortunately, Boeing had scrapped plans to build a stretched 757 in the early 1990s, so Kirchner had to switch roles and start pitching the idea of the plane to Boeing, as if he were the salesman and Boeing the customer.

Condor launched the 757-300 on 2 September 1996, at the Farnborough Air Show, with an $875 million order for twelve of the planes, with options for twelve more. Icelandair became the second customer, announcing an order for two aircraft at the Paris Air Show on 16 June 1997. The third customer for the new model was Arkia Airlines of Israel, which also ordered a pair. All three carriers selected Rolls-Royce engines.

Although the program is off to a slow start, sales of the 757-300 will likely pick up as airline markets around the world deregulate and costs per seat become more critical. The 757-300 has low seat-mile (kilometre) costs and good range.

Benefits

Like all other stretch developments, the aircraft has gained in operating efficiency. The 757-300's extra length allows it to carry 48 additional passengers (21 per cent more) than the 757-200, and 48 per cent more cargo volume. It can carry between 243 and 289 passengers, depending on configuration, between the capacity of the Boeing 757-200 and the 767-300. To accommodate the extra load, the 757-300's maximum take-off weight has increased to 270,000lb (122,500kg).

The derivative's extra seating and increased available cargo volume lowers operating costs. The 757-300's cost per available seat-mile is expected to be 9 per cent lower than on the -200. Boeing pegs the 757-300's costs at 10 per cent lower than a 767-200 and 19 per cent lower than an Airbus A310-300, both aircraft with a similar seating capacity.

In addition to flying more people more cheaply, the 757-300 offers 767 operators increased seating flexibility, gives airlines the ability to swap a 757-200 with a -300 at peak times and, despite a trend for smaller aircraft, will be able to perform well at airports where access is slot-constrained.

The 757-300 is designed to allow both chartered and scheduled airlines to fly economically on short-range, medium-range or long-haul routes. With a range of about 4,000 miles (6,440km), the 757-300 can fly transcontinental routes, complementing the 757-200, which has a somewhat longer range of 4,520 miles (7,240km). Typical routes for the 757-300 include New York to Los Angeles, Reykjavik to Baltimore, and Frankfurt to Tenerife. A charter-configured 757-300 with 289 passengers will be capable of flying from London to Bahrain and reach popular tourist destinations in the Atlantic islands and the Mediterranean. The -300 has a shorter range than the -200, because the two have the same engines and fuel capacity, but the -300 has a higher gross weight.

Engines available for the aircraft are the Rolls-Royce RB211-535E4 or Pratt & Whitney's PW2043 in thrust ratings of 43,100lb (192kN) and 43,850lb (195kN), respectively. Lower thrust is also offered.

With the new model, Boeing has repositioned the 757 into a higher seating category, and away from its closest competitor, the Airbus A321. In addition, the company is addressing and filling a gap in the middle market, between the largest narrow-bodies (757 and A321) and the smallest widebodies (767-200, A310 and A330-200). The 757-300 is an attractive economical alternative to ageing DC-10s and L1011s, even if it falls 50 seats short of those aircraft. It also can replace older 767-200s. However, given the declining ratio of available aircraft take-off and landing slots to number of passengers wishing to fly, aircraft need to grow in size. For this reason, the -300 also is a viable alternative to existing narrow-bodies.

The 757-300 is a 'fly more people' plane, which charter and tour operators

Specification – 757-300	
Engines (two):	Rolls-Royce RB211-535E4-B or Pratt & Whitney PW2043
Dimensions:	Overall length 178ft 7in (54.5m); height 4ft 6in (13.6m); wingspan 124ft 10in (38.05m); body width 12ft 4in (3.7m)
Passengers:	243 (two class), 258 (one class), 279 (inclusive tour)
Cargo volume:	Lower cargo hold volume 2,387 cubic ft (67.6 cubic m)
Fuel capacity:	11,490 gallons (43,490 litres)
Weights:	Plane weight 141,330lb (64,100kg); max. take-off weight: 270,000lb (122,500kg)
Performance:	Range (243 passengers) 4,000 miles (6,440km)
Take-off field length:	9,000ft (2,740m) (at sea level)

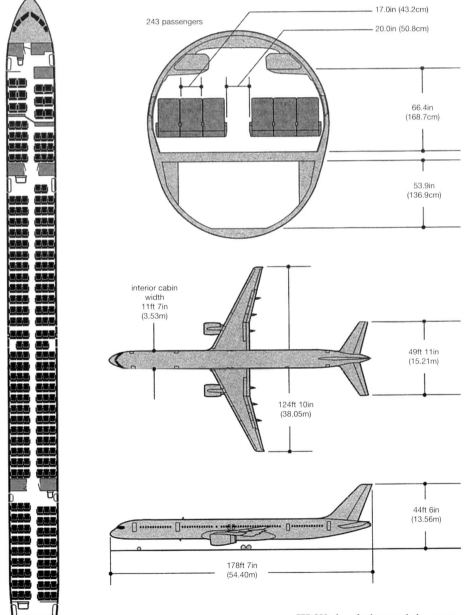

757-300 aircraft characteristics. Boeing

can appreciate. Passengers may prefer widebodies on longer flights, but passenger preference is not a big factor for charter airlines. With the -300, German charter carrier Condor Flugdienst is able to add 45 seats per aircraft, and fly 15 to 20 per cent more revenue-generating hours each day. The airline plans to replace its three DC-10s with the new model.

The Stretch

Boeing's Doug Miller, chief engineer of the 757 for seven years, says that he was thinking about a 757 stretch ten years earlier. Luckily, 757 pioneers had the foresight to make it stretchable. In the past, the 707's landing gear, for example, had been kept small because of concerns over weight, and that had hurt its ability to grow.

'Traditionally, airplanes that stretched made money for everyone. You could get a 20 per cent payload increase for just 10 per cent more cost, and the stretch was done around the cheapest part of the airplane – the middle of the fuselage,' says Miller. 'I was convinced the 757 could be stretched. I went through three different design studies to stretch the 707 to compete with the DC-8, which was stretched and outselling Boeing. That's why today there are so many more DC-8s still flying. But the reason we couldn't do it was simple: the landing gear. When I saw the 757, I noticed a long gear that can take a stretch. I think the guys who laid the airplane out had a view to stretch it.'

Dan Mooney, chief project engineer for the 757-300, says that the 757's high landing gear was, indeed, an important reason why the aircraft was easy to stretch. He also confirms that designs for a stretched model had floated around Boeing for five years before the -300 was actually launched.

Boeing set an aggressive goal of seeing the first 757-300 enter service just 27 months after firm configuration, which occurred in November 1996. The first deliveries of the $65-million aircraft to Condor took place in March 1999, giving the 757-300 the shortest design-to-production and delivery-cycle time of any Boeing derivative-aircraft programme.

To accomplish the quick turnaround, Boeing has kept the stretch as simple as possible, with very few customized features for the longer version to limit unnecessary design changes. In addition, a variety of design and production initiatives from several other programmes, including the 777 and the next-generation 737, are being used for the 757-300, to help reduce the complexity and cost of its development. At the same time, the -300 continues to share a common flight-crew rating with other models in the 757/767 series, making it an attractive addition to the family.

Other Revisions

Despite the simple stretch, the 757-300's length forced Boeing to make several revisions to the standard -200 model. The 757-300 shares the same wings as the -200, but the -300's has been structurally rein-

For the time being it is unlikely that narrow-body planes will grow much longer than the 757-300, largely because of the limitations imposed by ground clearance with the current undercarriage. At first glance, it looks like the stretched 757 will almost certainly hit the runway on take-

A 757-300 and 757-200 together in an animated drawing. The stretched -300 can carry 48 more passengers than the -200, giving it the lowest per-seat cost of any single-aisle aircraft. Boeing

To stretch the 757-200, Boeing extended both sides of the fuselage's centre of gravity, with a 13ft 4in (4.06m) fuselage extension of the forward fuselage at Section 43, and a 10ft (3.05m) extension at Section 46, aft of the wings. The 757-300 is just 16in (40cm) shorter than the 767-300.

forced to handle the increased load. The overwing section of the fuselage, Section 44, was strengthened, as were the horizontal stabilizer and landing gear. The -300 is also fitted with bigger tyres and stronger brakes, to cope with heavier landing weight and faster landing speed.

off. The 757-200 already stands fairly high off the ground, and the issue of tail scrapes was addressed on the -300 by increasing take-off and landing speeds, delaying spoiler deployment on landing and adding a new hydraulically activated retractable tail skid. The tail skid protects the aircraft from possible damage from tail strikes during take-off and landing, a problem that has affected even standard 757-200s. The tail skid is similar to that on the 767-300 and 777. It has a body-contact indicator that alerts the crew to more serious contact with the ground. The design is intended to make it harder for the crew to accidentally scrape the tail on landing, by linking the pitch-attitude sensor to the spoiler-deployment system.

'We don't expect the tail strike to be any bigger an issue than on the -200,' says Dan Mooney. To mitigate the chances for tail strikes, Boeing modified the aircraft's spoiler-deployment sequence. If a landing is too slow or the nose too high, the spoiler schedule is adjusted to bring the nose down, avoiding tail impact. The landing-flap position on the -300 has also been changed, to help bring the nose down.

Mooney says that the engineers had at first considered stretching the -300 20in (50.8cm) more than its eventual configuration, but that to do so would have increased the chance of tail strikes, challenged the performance of landing gear and engines, and reduced fuel efficiency, in addition to posing several structural implications.

The 757-300 aircraft has a higher-capacity environmental control system, to accommodate additional passengers and increased cargo volume. The air-conditioning packs the 757 shares with the 767 were not changed, but they provide increased flow rates without having to modify the air-conditioning packs, taking advantage of system commonality between the airplanes. An extra temperature-control zone has been added, along with a new, larger pre-cooler and higher-capacity re-circulating fans. Passengers in the -300 use a centrally plumbed vacuum-lavatory system. The lower cost and reduced service time of the new system make up for its additional weight.

Boeing has taken advantage of the -300's development to introduce the new cabin interior developed originally for the 777, and then tailored for Next-Generation 737s, based on airline feedback. The 757-300's new interior is designed to upgrade the overall look and aesthetics of the passenger cabin. Longer overhead stowage bins and the new sculptured ceiling, with indirect overhead lighting, have smoother curves, giving the cabin a more open, spacious feeling. A handrail that extends along the bottom of the stowage

bins and a moveable cabin class divider are also available. Eventually, this cabin configuration will be built into future 767-300s and 757-200s, beginning in the year 2000.

In the longer 757-300, Boeing has taken steps to alleviate the effect of the long, thin fuselage by dividing the cabin up into small sections with strategically positioned cabin bulkheads. One option is convertible seating that enables carriers to switch from six-abreast economy class to five-seat business class.

Despite a passenger load one-fifth greater than the -200, Boeing believes the charter-configured -300 will take only four extra minutes to load and two additional minutes to unload. Its overwing-exit body section and a strengthened four-door aft stretch section allow Boeing to meet evacuation requirements without having to redesign doors. To speed up baggage handling, Boeing offers a sliding-carpet baggage and cargo system, which offers a conveyor system and movable bulkhead pushed along the belly hold by a drive system.

The flight deck of the 757-300, like that of the 757-200, is designed for two-crew operation and furnished with the same digital electronic displays. Pilots can fly both types with little additional training. The 757-300 flight deck incorporates two improvements that have been built into new 757-200s: the Pegasus flight-management system, and an enhanced Engine Indication and Crew Alerting System (EICAS). With the Pegasus system, operators can choose software options that include elements of the Future Air Navigation System (FANS). FANS functions will provide operators with the ability to use advanced systems, such as GPS (global positioning system) sensors and satellite communications, to take full advantage of new communication, navigation and air-traffic management systems. The EICAS upgrade will replace existing computers with enhanced devices that are software-loadable. The enhanced EICAS has improved built-in test equipment (BITE) functions that will allow for improved self-diagnosis of faults in a more readable format. Onboard software loading will enable operators to use the same EICAS computer as a replacement on any 757 or 767, reducing spare-parts inventory.

In all, 90 per cent of the 757-300's parts are interchangeable with the -200 model, and 40 per cent fit 767 models.

The flight characteristics of the -200 and -300 are very similar. One difference for pilots, however, is that the increased length of the fuselage means the flight deck's relative position is higher off the ground during landing. Changes made to the flight-deck panels due to the 757-300's additional length and weight include a new EICAS message of tail-strike warning, additional notifications of door openings (since the -300 has two more doors than the -200), an enhanced ground-proximity warning system that is intended to reduce controlled flight into terrain (when pilots fly into mountains or hillsides because of navigational error), and a predictive wind-shear-warning system.

Building the Stretched 757

Building a longer -300 has posed many problems for Boeing. Because of the model's increased length, new tooling was needed to build the fuselage, wings and other parts of the plane. For this derivative, 750 new tools were needed and another 555 had to be modified to fit the longer aircraft. The tooling supporting the lengthened fuselage had to be extended so that crews could work on cabin doors, which are in different locations from those on the -200. The body-join process was also changed to reflect the use of a different sort of fastener. Rivets once used to join the huge sections of fuselage together have been replaced by fasteners, which are better able to support the additional weight of the -300's fuselage.

Many of the aircraft's parts, from panels and spars, to the fuselage itself, are the largest the Renton facility has ever seen. Some of the fuselage panels alone are as long as 400in (10m). Many parts do not fit into standard shipping containers, and new containers have had to be designed.

The new plane has also given Boeing a chance to try 'lean manufacturing', a term used to describe manufacturing with little waste or duplication. This has been applied to the new plane's skin panels, for example. In the past, employees shipped the skin panels lying flat and stacked on top of each other. When they arrived in Renton, the panels were hung up on racks and stored until they were needed. The -300's longer panels are now transported standing upright, like plates in a dishwasher. They are delivered directly to the factory and then pulled out of the box as needed, eliminating the need for storage

The first 757-300 in final assembly. Note its length compared to the -200 model. Boeing

space and reducing potential damage to the skins from too much handling.

As a cost-saving measure, the longer -300 will be built on the same production line and in the same building as the -200. To do this, Boeing has had to make a year's worth of changes to the factory, including extending assembly machines, lengthening trailers and pushing out walls to make room for the longer plane. Factory workers are now faced with assembling an aircraft with twelve skin panels, each more than 33ft (10m) long, something they have never done before at the Renton plant. The panels are 13ft (2.96m) longer than those of the -200 model, and help to form the

longer fuselage sections. Lengthening skin panels is a better option than inserting a traditional plug. The move also reduces weight and necessitates only small changes to the manufacturing process.

Much of the 757-300 has been designed digitally, including about 80 per cent of the aircraft's wings. Drawings have been digitized to feed information into a computerized spar-assembly system that is being used for the first time to manufacture 757 wings. Components designed using high-technology, computer-aided design software account for more than half of the aircraft, including the interior of the passenger cabin, the twelve extra-long

skin panels for the fuselage, and the air-conditioning system. Drawings for other parts of the aircraft that are identical to the -200 also have become digitized, to incorporate the changes the -200 has undergone since its introduction.

'The thrill of seeing [the 757-300] go from being designed on the computer to seeing the parts come together in the factory to seeing it fly is really something,' says Laura Sebesta, a flight-control systems engineer. 'It's just an amazing effort.'

Building of the first -300 began on 12 September 1997, as workers loaded a 63ft (19.2m) front left wing spar into a state-of-the-art automated spar-assembly tool that drills and installs more than 2,600 fasteners into the wing structure. On 21 August 1997, manufacturing of the first skin panel for the fuselage began in Witchita. Major assembly began in Renton on 9 September 1997, and assembly of the first fuselage got under way on 5 November. Final assembly of the first -300 began on 15 March 1998, when the wings were joined with the body.

The -300 will complement, rather than replace, the -200, and both will be in production at the same time. The model may also be offered as a freighter or combi plane. Together, the -200 and -300 will allow operators to add capacity to growing routes and developing markets. The 757-300, Miller says, 'is going to be a money-maker. It's slow to take off but it will fly when airlines realize it will be a money-maker. It's the perfect plane to bypass crowded hubs on more point-to-point services.'

Rollout

The first 757-300 rolled out at Renton on 31 May 1998, wearing Boeing red, white and blue livery. The rollout was highlighted by an announcement from Condor that the airline is ordering another 757-300.

'We are so convinced this airplane will be a money-maker for us that we've ordered another one before we've even seen it fly,' Dietmar Kirchner, managing director of Condor, told an audience of 10,000 Boeing employees, customers and suppliers on a brilliant sunny day. 'The 757-300 has the lowest seat-mile operating costs of any single-aisle airplane on the market – lower than many widebody airplanes. The 757-300 complements our strategy of providing a high-quality, high-service product to the charter market.'

The festive rollout celebration recognized the work of Boeing employees who,

The 757-300 was rolled out on 31 May 1998. Boeing employees tugged the new airliner into place for a ceremony. Boeing

in just 19 months, had brought the aircraft from concept to reality. The rollout date remained on schedule, despite production problems with the Renton-built 737s that backed up the entire factory. To introduce the derivative to the world, 100 Boeing employees, customers and suppliers, wearing white coveralls, tugged the first 757-300 into view of the crowd. Its great length compared with the -200 was so noticeable that it was immediately dubbed 'Long Tall Sally' by Kirchner.

The theme of the -300 among employees had been 'Bringing the Family Together'. The motto had several meanings. The 757-300 brings the 757/767 family together by adding an aircraft in the 240- to 289-seat niche. A family of suppliers from around the world worked together to produce the plane. Also, as Boeing puts it, the aircraft's low seat-mile costs will help make air travel more affordable, allowing people to bring more of their family along on trips.

Another family theme was the cadre of Boeing veterans who contributed to the design of the stretched 757. Such former company leaders as Everett Webb, Joe Sutter and Dick Taylor served on its configuration advisory board, no doubt bringing back memories of the days when they worked on the original 757-200.

Mooney credits Condor's Kirchner for seeing that the 757-300 could be used to build up routes that are not big enough for larger, more expensive aircraft. 'He saw very clearly what the benefits of the -300 would be – economics,' Mooney says. 'For an inclusive-tour operator with lower yield, that is important.' While Boeing researched the viability of the model for more than a year, its evolution came down to customer demand. Finally, by January 1996, six months before its official launch, serious development began.

'He's a great salesman,' Mooney says of Kirchner. 'He was telling us there really was a good market and business case for it. He's very excited about the model and convinced it will be a money-maker. We really wanted this to be a longer version of the 757, not a next-generation aircraft.'

First Flight and Testing

While the 757-200 was launched at the dawn of the computer era, the -300 debuted right in the middle of it. The 757-300's first flight, on 2 August 1998, was shown live on the Internet, bringing thousands of computer-users right to the Renton runway. It was the first live Internet broadcast of the first flight of any aircraft.

After heading north over Lake Washington, Leon Robert, the chief engineering test pilot, and Jerry Whites, senior engineering test pilot, flew the newest member of the 767/757 family – dubbed NU701 – west towards Port Angeles, Washington. The $72 million aircraft then headed south to Astoria, Oregon, and back and forth over Washington State's Olympic Peninsula before landing at Boeing Field. During the inaugural mission, which lasted for 2 hours and 25 minutes, Robert and Whites conducted a series of tests on the aircraft's systems and structures, including the wing flaps, main landing gear and flight controls. The pilots also evaluated the aircraft's handling qualities and performance. Behind them, in the passenger cabin, sat 14 flight-test instrumentation racks, which recorded data on engine performance, surface positions and flight-control inputs. The information was sent back to flight-test personnel sitting in a control room at Boeing Field, in a process called telemetry.

Also in the plane were 32 keg-shaped water barrels, which were used to change the aircraft's centre of gravity and simulate the weight of passengers and baggage. 'This airplane flies great; everything is normal,' Robert said during the flight. 'It flies like a 757-200, which is what we intended.' The flight reached an altitude of 15,000ft (4,570m).

The test programme was the shortest ever conducted by Boeing for a derivative – 5½ months. During that time, more flight-test hours were packed into a shorter amount of time than for any other major Boeing derivative. Tests specific to the -300 included evaluation of the retractable tail skid and slight changes to the flight controls. Alterations have been made to the control logic of the spoiler actuation system, which will prevent three spoiler panels deploying on each wing in case of a so-called 'abused landing'.

To obtain certification, Boeing used three 757-300s to conduct 1,286 hours of ground testing and 912 hours of flight testing. Certification requirements were a lot tougher for the -300 than for its parent; those requirements, including wiring, bird-strike, smoke detection and structural regulations, have become more stringent in the years since the 757's original launch.

While the -300 offers the advantage of lower seat-mile costs, it has been rather slow to sell after its launch. Airlines appear

Specification – 757-300 vs. 757-200		
	757-300	*757-200*
Engines (two):	Rolls-Royce RB211-535E4 or Pratt & Whitney PW2043	Rolls-Royce RB211-535E4 or Pratt & Whitney PW2043
Overall length:	178ft 7in (54.5m)	155ft 3in (47.32m)
Wingspan:	124ft 10in (38.05m)	124ft 10in (38.05m)
Tail height:	44ft 6in (13.6m)	44ft 6in (13.6m)
Body width:	12ft 4in (3.7m)	12ft 4in (3.7m)
Passengers:	243 (2-class), 258 (1-class), 279 (inclusive tour)	201 (2-class), 231 (inclusive tour)
Cargo volume:	2,387 cubic ft (67.6 cubic m)	1,790 cubic ft (50.7 cubic m)
Fuel capacity:	11,490 gallons (43,490 litres)	11,526 gallons (43,625 litres)
Max. take-off weight:	270,000lb (122,500kg)	255,000lb (115,700kg)

757-300 Facts

- There are about 70 miles (117km) of wire in a 757-300.
- There are about 700,000 parts in the plane, fastened with 690,000 bolts and rivets.
- An average of about 120 gallons (450 litres) of paint are used on the 757-300. That paint weighs about 720lb (325kg).
- More than 670 suppliers from 24 different countries make parts for the aircraft.

to be concerned about the practicalities of operating the aircraft. Its length and single aisle may result in long times required to load and unload passengers. This could result in a negative passenger appeal. Long turnaround times result in a reduction in aircraft productivity, while also possibly causing disruptions to the co-ordinated arrivals and departures at hub airports.

Although the initial response to the aircraft has been cautious, Boeing believes that the 757-300's outstanding economics will eventually sell big among European and Asian carriers. Indeed, just after rollout, Boeing acknowledged that it was discussing the aircraft with a large US airline; it may secure from this company the kind of order that will really kick-start the programme.

It remains to be seen how the newest 757 will perform, but Boeing projects a market for 400–600 models. It is likely, however, that the aircraft will be examined closely under the industry's microscope before orders really begin to flood in.

The 767-400

As arch rival Airbus was coming out with the A330-200, a shorter and longer-range version of the A330-300, on 6 January 1997 Boeing's board of directors authorized the marketing of a further stretch of the 767-300, the 767-400ER (Extended Range). According to Boeing, the upgraded model, scheduled to enter service in May 2000, will seat 15 per cent more passengers than the 767-300ER, while offering 4 to 7 per cent better direct operating costs compared with the similar-sized A330-200.

Boeing officially launched the 767-400ER on 28 April 1997, with an order for 21 aircraft from Delta. The first aircraft is scheduled to roll out of the factory in August 1999, to be delivered to Delta in May 2000. Continental Airlines has ordered 26 of the aircraft and International Lease Finance has added five to the order book. Boeing estimates a market for 900 of the aircraft after the turn of the century.

The 767-400ER was launched after Boeing decided it would not shrink the 777-200 to a proposed -100 series; the 767-400 is sized between the 767-300 and the 777-200. It will seat 245 passengers in three-class configuration, or 303 in a two-class layout, compared with 229 and 269, respectively, in the -300. The added seats will lead to operating costs even lower than the -300's, which are already the lowest in its class. The stretch will add 11ft (3.36m) fore and 10ft (3.07m) aft of the wing for a new fuselage length of 197ft (60m), or about 21ft (6.4m) longer than the -300ER.

The 767-400ER will be the first in the 757/767 family to offer wing tips, vertical extensions of the wing that help to boost performance. This enhancement increases the model's wingspan to 170ft 4in (52m), compared with 156ft 1in (47.6m) for the -300.

Although the wing tips will add range capability, the -400's range of 6,480 miles (10,430km) will still be somewhat less than the -300ER's. Still, the new model will be able to serve nearly all the same routes as the -300ER, including Chicago–Frankfurt, Seattle–Osaka, Atlanta–Honolulu and Los Angeles–London. Speed and other performance measures will remain the same as the existing 767s'.

The 767-400ER is designed to be the most efficient aircraft in its size category, making it an ideal replacement for the ageing L-1011, DC-10 and A300 models. In

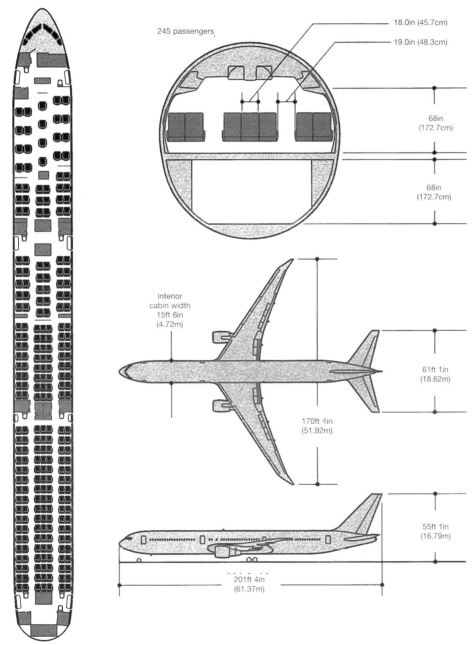

767-400 aircraft characteristics. Boeing

The 767-400ER, shown here in a computer-generated photo, is the first in the family to feature wing tips. It is due to enter service in May 2000.
Boeing

Specification – 767-400ER	
Engines (two):	Pratt & Whitney PW4062, General Electric CF6-80C2B7F-1 and CF6-80C2B8F-1 or Rolls-Royce RB211-524G/H
Dimensions:	Overall length 201ft 4in (61.4m); height 55ft 1in (18.79m); wingspan 170ft 4in (52m); body width 16ft 6in (5m)
Passengers:	245 (three class), 304 (two class), up to 375 (inclusive tour)
Cargo volume:	4,580 cubic ft (129.6 cubic m)
Fuel capacity:	24,140 gallons (91,370 litres)
Weights:	Plane weight 227,300lb (103,100kg); max. take-off weight 450,000lb (204,100kg)
Performance:	Max. range 6,480 miles (10,430km)

growing markets, it will be able to fly more passengers on routes served by existing 767s, A300-600s and A310s. Because of its commonality with the 767/757 family, as well as the 777 and new 737s, Boeing also hopes to capitalize on airlines already operating 767s for growing air routes. The 767/757 common type rating can, with the 757-300, extend to five aircraft types: the 767-200, -300 and -400, as well as the 757-200 and -300.

In addition to the stretched fuselage and wing tips, the 767-400 offers a gross take-off weight of 440,000lb (200,000kg), compared with a maximum 412,000lb (187,000kg) for the heaviest existing 767. The -400 will require runway length of between 10,000ft and 11,500ft (3,050–3,500m). Older versions need between 8,700 and 9,400ft (2,650–2,860m).

To maintain rotation angles, the 767-400ER's landing gear has been lengthened. Wheels, tyres and brakes borrowed from the 777 programme are used to accommodate the greater weights. Onboard electrical power output is being increased by one-fourth, to accommodate projected in-flight entertainment needs. A new auxiliary power unit will meet expanded air-conditioning and power requirements. The aircraft fuselage is being strengthened, and an additional outboard slat will be built into each wing to accommodate the longer wing span that will result from the addition of wing tips. The aircraft will use existing engines, giving 62,000lb (270kN) thrust, from all three manufacturers, with an eye towards more powerful future variants.

The 767-400ER's passenger cabin, with newly sculpted sidewalls, ceilings and overhead stowage bins, creates a feeling of spaciousness similar to the 777, offering greater clearance around the head and shoulders. The stowage bins offer more storage volume than existing 767s. Seat sizes will remain the same.

The newest model features an upgraded flight deck with displays similar to existing 767 models, but more in line with the 777. Six 8in square (51.6 sq cm) liquid crystal flat-panel displays are laid out, two in front of each pilot plus over and under centre panel screens for engine instrumentation, weather radar or back-up in case of failure. This set-up is called the large formal display system (LFDS), a software-loadable format that enables the cockpit instrumentation to be quickly converted to match display layouts of other Boeing transports in an airline's fleet. This is another way of reducing training requirements. For example, symbols on the screens can be switched to match the layout of older flight decks on the 737, 757 and 767 or the 777. In addition, many analogue instruments in the -400 are being replaced with flat panels, so that a pilot looking at the flat panel will see what looks like a knob. This development reduces training time for the new model and makes it an enticing investment for leasing companies whose aircraft move frequently between fleets. The configuration also accommodates future growth and enables flight crews to readily qualify for a wider range of assignments. A crew trained on the 767-400 could, with additional training, fly the next-generation 737, the 747-400 and the 777 – as well as the entire 767/757 family.

Enhancements to the -400's cockpit will eventually be shared within the 767/757 family. By the year 2000, Boeing plans to take the new, large-panel flight deck being developed for the 767-400ER, and its new electronics bay and interior, and transfer them to an improved version of the 767-300. Ultimately, the 767-400ER's new cockpit will be moved to the 757 as well.

The wing tips, made primarily of composite material, serve the same purpose as those on the 747-400 – they give the plane more lift, added range and increased flight efficiency. In testing, Boeing has found that the 767-400's patented raked wing tips will decrease fuel burn by about 3 per cent on a 3,450 mile (5,520km) mission. Rather than extend the 767's wing to get more lift, which would have cost millions of dollars, the extensions – 7ft 7in (2.3m) long – are bolted to the end of a 767-300ER wing, and no additional design changes are made to the tip or leading edges. The wing tips are known as 'raked' because, rather than sticking straight up, they lie flush with the wing and rake back, giving the plane considerable lift with

Computer-Aided Design

Hundreds of planners, tool designers, production workers and others are involved in the 767-400 programme. However, on this aircraft programme, employees are working together and communicating in new ways. Through the use of powerful computers, different areas of Boeing's scattered operations are able to work at the same time, rather than waiting for one unit to finish its work. Through computer-aided design, an engineer in one area can see whether a part will fit with another section designed thousands of miles away.

This virtual teamwork, along with valuable supplier partnerships and innovative thinking, enabled Boeing factories and suppliers in May 1998 to begin tool fabrication and parts assemblies for the new aircraft. Engineers at Boeing's Douglas division in California use computing technology that allows them to be virtually co-located with team members in Everett. The Douglas division is designing the wing tips and the aft-most section of the plane.

Computers have also helped employees to evaluate how the longer aircraft will move through the existing production line in the Everett factory. Tooling will need to be lengthened, and clearances will have to be checked if large assembled parts are to be moved by overhead cranes. Moving the aircraft from the final body join to each subsequent production stall requires precise choreography. Contact with tooling or another aircraft could cause damage, resulting in losses from rework and materials.

Boeing employees had to determine if changes in the -400's pathway would be required to accommodate the aircraft's larger size. To visualize the manufacturing requirements, Boeing used a set of computing tools originally developed to engineer the 777. Designers used computer-aided, three-dimensional interactive applications (CATIA) to define aircraft parts as three-dimensional solids. Boeing enhanced CATIA capabilities by creating a visualization tool called Fly-Thru. This software uses CATIA data to help engineers analyse the position of three-dimensional parts in relation to each other. From the comfort and safety of their desks, they used Fly-Thru to zoom in and around large assemblies to discover where parts would not match up or would interfere with other parts.

The design team used CATIA to create the aircraft shape virtually, and Fly-Thru to simulate its move through the final stages of production. Using input from factory employees, the team came up with different manoeuvring paths for the aircraft and options for altering final assembly positions. The virtual production-line simulation showed other 767s just ahead or behind the 767-400ER in the production sequence. These stationary aircraft are depicted as overlays in three different sizes, to account for all three models of the 767 on the same manufacturing line.

As the 767-400 is towed out of final body join, the driver must avoid the tooling. In the digitally designed environment, Fly-Thru allowed the team to compute the clearance, which was 24in (60cm). As the aircraft in the last stall position rolls out of the factory, it must stay clear of the aircraft parked in position No. 2 and the tooling. The virtual simulation helped designers realize that the 767-400 could be built alongside other 767s without the building being changed, but that the aircraft's right wing tip should be installed only after the aircraft has moved out of the final body join.

Once Boeing was confident that the new aircraft would move through the facility free of hazards, assembly of the first 767-400ER was able to begin in January 1999.

minimal air resistance or drag. They provide about the same range capability as other wing-tip designs, but these would have required the wingspan to be extended by another 10ft (3m). This design has the added benefit of giving the 767-400ER more gate and taxiway flexibility. It can use the same gates as the DC-10, MD-11 and L-1011, unlike the competing A330-200, which must use gates sized for larger aircraft. The -400's wing tips are being considered on future, longer-range versions of the 777.

'To improve low-speed performance and cruise efficiency, we looked at various wing tips, including winglets,' says John Quinlivan, programme manager for the -400. 'Studies showed that a raked tip provides balance in flight efficiency, maintenance, performance and reduced weight. The wing tips have a blunter leading edge and a higher sweep angle than traditional winglets.'

Because the -400's airframe stretch leads to a reduction in range of 500 miles (800km) compared with the 767-300ER, Boeing has studied ways to further extend its range even before assembly has begun on the new family member. These include increasing take-off gross weight by about 10,000lb (4,535kg) to 460,000lb (210,000kg), and adding higher thrust engines. Most of the range extension would come from extra fuel in a new tank in the horizontal stabilizer, a modification similar to one made to the 747-400. Boeing estimates that the tail tanks would hold up to 2,000 gallons (7,580 litres).

Another plan to increase range – and marketability – is to fit additional fuel tanks in the belly of the aircraft. The -400's stretch fuselage can accommodate up to three auxiliary tanks, each capable of holding around 1,740 gallons (6,585 litres) of extra fuel. The tanks would be installed in the aft belly compartment, behind the aircraft's wingbox, in the space provisionally reserved for additional cargo containers. The aircraft is being designed to carry up to five freight pallets in the forward hold and a maximum of 18 luggage containers in the aft belly. Some airlines, however, will not need to use the whole of the -400's lengthened belly for cargo, and would rather use the extra space for additional fuel.

This design would extend the aircraft's range by up to an additional 400 miles (640km). The same modification is also being considered to extend the range of new 767-300ERs. The resulting 767-300ERX would have a range capacity of almost 7,705 miles (12,400km), slightly greater than that of the Airbus A330-200.

The effort to increase range came in response to requests from British charter carrier Britannia, which operates more than twenty 767s and 757s. The airline is interested in operating the stretched version on non-stop flights to Asia. Boeing seriously considered the request, especially in the light of the fact that other UK charter carriers, such as Air 2000, Airtours and Leisure International Airways, which operate 767s and 757s, chose the longer-range Airbus A330-200 for their future needs rather than the 767-400ER.

Boeing and its customers reached agreement about the basic design of the aircraft on 9 January 1998. That gave engineers the go-ahead to begin releasing design information to Boeing factories and suppliers, beginning the fabrication of parts, tools and assemblies. The longer -400ER, like the 757-300, required Boeing to develop new tooling and make adjustments to the production line, to account for a longer fuselage. The -400 will be built alongside -300s in the same line at Everett, and will complement rather than replace the -300.

The 767-400 is the first widebody airliner to be stretched for a second time. Even before Boeing's merger with McDonnell Douglas, the two companies had signed a technical agreement to share some of the work. Douglas was to have received work on the empennage and wing-tip area. The two companies also pioneered the 'virtual teaming concept', which Boeing now uses regularly for long-distance design efforts with subcontractors and partners on several programmes.

Boeing hopes to control costs on the new derivative by establishing the certification basis much earlier than usual in the development cycle. The sooner regulatory agencies in the United States and Europe agree on requirements, the sooner Boeing can stabilize the design and test programmes. This helped Boeing develop the 767-400 into more than a simple 767-300 stretch.

The -400 will extend the life of the 767 family as it enters its third decade. To develop what is almost a new model, yet to retain commonality with previous 767s, the -400 incorporates the best of the new-generation 737, the 777 and the 717. As a result, configuration objectives included not only the use of existing 767 structures, fuselage design, engine nacelles and struts, but also the introduction of dramatically new features such as a 777-style flight deck. The new flight deck was adopted late in the programme.

In addition to the new-look flight deck, other changes include a new main instrumentation panel and glareshield, centre console, two-position landing-gear selection lever and a new air-data/inertial-reference system that integrates the air-data computer and inertial reference units.

Sales of the 767-400 were expected to grow substantially in 1999, reflecting significant interest from airlines looking to fill the capacity gap between the 767-300 and the 777.

Specification – 767-400 vs. 767-300		
	767-400	767-300
Wing span:	170ft 4in (52m)	156ft 1in (47.57m)
Overall length:	201ft 4in (61.4m)	180ft 3in (54.94m)
Height:	55ft 1in (18.79m) (due to lengthened landing gear)	52ft (15.85m)
Body width:	16.5ft (5m)	16.5ft (5m)
Passengers:	245 (3-class), 303 (2-class)	218 (3-class), 269 (2-class)
Cargo volume:	4,905 cubic ft (137.3 cubic m)	4,030 cubic ft (114.2 cubic m)
Engines (two):	PW4000 GE CF6-80C2 Rolls-Royce RB211-524G/H	PW4000 GE CF6-80C2 Rolls-Royce RB211-524G/H
Fuel:	24,140 gallons (91,370 litres)	24,140 gallons (91,370 litres)
Max. take-off weight:	440,000lb (200,000kg)	412,000lb (187,000kg)

CHAPTER ELEVEN

In Service

First Revenue Flights

The 767 and 757, designed during the oil crisis to cut fuel consumption and reduce operating costs, entered service during a recession, when serious questions were being raised about the ability of a distressed airline industry to absorb a surge of new aircraft. United Airlines, for example, asked Boeing to stop work temporarily on

The 767 era began on 8 September 1982, when a United model touched down at 1.05 pm local time to complete its first commercial flight, from Chicago's O'Hare International Airport to Denver's Stapleton International Airport; there were 175 passengers and eight crew members on board. Among those enjoying the inaugural 2-hour and 20-minute flight was 82-year-old Lucille Wright, an aviation buff who had been on 20 maiden flights, including the first DC-3 voyage some 50 years earlier. 'It's like riding in a cradle,' she said about the aircraft, which for the first time featured economy-class seating of two rows of two seats

on each side and one row of three down the middle.

During its send-off in Chicago, Mayor Jane Byrne had splashed champagne on the nose of the new jet, christening it the 'City of Chicago.' She did not break the bottle, to avoid denting the nose. Passengers in first class received leather passport

Delta Air Lines is the largest operator of the 757-200, with 110 in service or on order. Gary Liao

20 of 39 767s for delivery in 1983 and 1984. Eastern Airlines, the 757 launch customer, had threatened to cancel its order for 27 of the aircraft amid a tax dispute. Despite the early hurdles, however, the new planes quickly caught the attention of the flying public as comfortable, quiet aircraft. And it did not take long for airlines to recognize the savings that could be made by flying these new types.

cases stamped with an image of the plane and the date.

The next day, the aircraft began serving a route linking San Francisco, Denver, Chicago, New York and Boston, replacing DC-10s. A second 767 soon joined the fleet, followed by six more by December. United initially employed the new aircraft on routes from its Chicago and Denver hubs to the East Coast, but quickly discovered that

129

A Continental 757 is shown at San Francisco. The aircraft is commonly used on flights linking the east and west coasts of the United States. Ed Davies

American Airlines is the largest operator of the 767-200 model with thirty examples. Ed Davies

it was an ideal transcontinental aircraft as well. By November 1982, the 767 was a frequent visitor to Detroit, Newark, Portland, Seattle, Los Angeles and Washington.

The world's first 757 entered service with Eastern Airlines on January 1, 1983, linking the carrier's Atlanta hub with Tampa, Florida. Upon its return to Atlanta, the 757 flew a round-trip mission to Miami. Financially strapped Eastern

Once in service, Eastern found the 757 much cheaper to fly coast-to-coast than existing planes. It placed the new plane on such routes as Philadelphia–Los Angeles, Miami–Seattle, Atlanta to the West Coast, and Kansas City to both the East and West Coast. Eastern recorded a schedule reliability rate of 99.1 per cent in the first 20 days of service. During that time, the planes recorded 166 revenue flight hours during 112 flights.

plane flew non-stop from Miami to Buenos Aires, Argentina. 'On the return flight, during a refuelling stopover in Panama City, one of our directors looked up at the tail, saw the numbers "757" and said how good they looked in our own colours,' says Borman. 'So we decided that all our 757s would have the model number on the tail.'

British Airways became the first airline outside the United States to operate the 757, when it took delivery of two planes at

Delta Air Lines is the largest operator of the 767-300, with seventy-one, that are used on domestic, transatlantic and Latin American flights. Ed Davies

told reporters on the inaugural flight that the 757 would enable the airline to move one passenger 700 miles (1,120km) on 10.4 gallons (42 litres) of fuel. During the first quarter of 1993, Eastern's inaugural 757 served Boston–Miami, Miami–Nassau, Newark–Atlanta, Newark–West Palm Beach, Albuquerque–Atlanta and Chicago–Atlanta.

Eastern advertised its introduction of the 757 with the numerals '757' painted prominently on the tail in blue letters to match the double-blue Eastern cheat lines. The story behind this is recalled by Frank Borman, the airline's former chairman. Eastern's board of directors was invited on a flight test to South America on a Boeing-owned 757 bearing Eastern's colours. The

the end of January 1983. The aircraft received Civil Aviation Authority certification on 4 January, after 53 additional flight-test hours devoted to CAA requirements. BA introduced the 757 to Europe with a service on 9 February 1983.

Since their first revenue flights, the 767 and 757 have become the most versatile aircraft in the world.

American Airlines is the second-largest 757 operator, with 102 in service or on order. The 757 can operate in noise-restrictive airports such as Orange County, California, shown here. Darren Anderson

US Airways uses its fleet of thirty-four 757s on domestic routes. Chris McDowell

America West, Delta and TWA are among the US airlines operating 757s at Orange County. Darren Anderson

Market Successes

The 767 is a multi-market success, serving more city pairs over a greater variety of distances than any other widebody twin-jet. Its ability to fly between cities separated by vast expanses of water, or remote terrain far from airfields, has revolutionized air travel. More than fifty airlines log more than 14,600 extended-range flights each

a home in a deregulated US airline industry that welcomed new point-to-point service. The aircraft offers carriers a proven combination of performance, economy, flexibility and reliability that no comparably sized twin-jet can match, enabling airlines to fly both short feeder routes and intercontinental non-stops profitably. Over the years, the 757, designed for short hops, excelled in an area that Boeing had never considered –

annual average of 43 767s rolling out of Everett, and 49 757s coming off the line in Renton. For the 767, the busiest year was 1992, when 63 planes were delivered. Just 20 had been delivered in its first year, 1982. In 1998, a banner year for commercial aviation, Boeing delivered 47 767s. In 1997, Boeing received orders for 98, including 56 of the new -400 models. Of the 98 orders, 73 came from just four stead-

America West is known for dressing up its 757s in special colours. This example honours the state of Ohio, the location of the airline's smallest hub in Columbus. Darren Anderson

month, crossing the Atlantic, West, Central and South Pacific and Indian Oceans, and the Caribbean and Tasman Seas. At about half the trip cost of a 747, the 767 allows airlines to offer more frequent flights and more non-stop routes between cities that could not support regular service by three- or four-engine jets.

The 757, the most fuel-efficient airliner ever built, actually made its debut after the rise in fuel prices had subsided, but it found

long, overwater routes. The 757 transports more people and cargo farther for less money than any other single-aisle transport. It also permits airlines to serve far more of the world's airports than competing jets.

Deliveries of 767s and 757s have grown steadily over the years. Through 1998, Boeing had recorded orders for more than 860 767s and more than 950 757s, delivering more than 725 of the widebodies and more than 830 757s. That represents an

fast US customers – Delta, American, Continental and United.

On the 757 programme, 1992 was also the busiest year, when 99 planes were delivered. The slowest year was 1984, when just 18 left the lines, a result of the lingering recession. Deliveries were up to 54 in 1998. For the 757, 1989 was the banner year, when 200 planes were ordered.

Boeing produces an average of four 767s a month. The 767 family has outsold the

US Airways employs the 767-200 on its transatlantic routes. Bob Polaneczky

near-defunct Airbus A300/ A310 combination. The 757 rolls out about four times a month.

Due to its lower cost per seat, the -300 is the most popular 767 model. Airlines around the world operate 228 767-200s, but nearly 500 -300s. The largest operator of the -200 is American Airlines (30 planes) followed by Air Canada (23), Japan's All Nippon Airways (20) and United Airlines (19). Including orders, Delta has the largest -300 fleet, with 71, used both on domestic and transatlantic flights. American (49), All Nippon Airways (40) and United (37) follow. British Airways

American Airlines has a hefty fleet of forty-nine 767-300s for use domestically and internationally. Ralph Olson/Flying Images Worldwide

This Air Canada 767-200, one of twenty-three in Air Canada's fleet, bears a special livery in honour of Donovan Bailey, Olympic sprinting champion. Stephen Wilcox

flies 28 of the type, and United Parcel Service flies 30 767-300 freighters, including orders. Delta, with 86 767-200s and -300s, is the largest overall 767 operator, followed by American, with 79. American took delivery in May 1998 of the 700th 767. The 767 family has outsold the near-defunct Airbus A300/A310 combination.

Delta flies the most 757s. By 2000, it will have 110 of the type, followed closely by American (102) and United (98). Northwest Airlines is another large operator, with 73 in its fleet, including orders. United Parcel Service flies 75 freighter versions. British Airways is the largest European operator, with 57. Nearly two-thirds of 757 sales are to US airlines. In fact, seven of the top ten American airlines – United, American, Delta, Northwest, Continental, US Airways and America West – fly the model, using it both for long, coast-to-coast routes and for quick regional hops.

The 757, despite its relatively large size, is also a popular executive transport for business people willing to pay about $40

million for a used model. However, it is being overshadowed in this role by the corporate version of the 737, the Boeing Business Jet, and the Airbus A319 Corporate Jet. About a dozen 757s have been converted into executive transports, including one for Paul Allen of Microsoft and the late Sir James Goldsmith. Some professional sports teams in the United States also travel in privately owned 757s.

A Positive Response

Soon after entering service, the 767 and 757 received positive responses from pilots, who appreciated the advanced avionics, navigation and flight-management systems, and the amount of information made available to them on the CRT displays. Cabin crews found the layout of lavatories and galleys an improvement over previous aircraft for food and beverage service. Passengers were pleased with slightly wider seats, roomier overhead luggage compartments and more

leg room, and airline managers were delighted to note immediate savings in fuel costs.

'Many airlines thought flight crews would never want to fly these things, but they just ate it up,' says John Armstrong, the 757 test pilot. 'Airlines thought it would take a great deal of time to train pilots, but it didn't come down to that. The airplane is much easier to maintain with the glass cockpit.'

Eastern flight crews surveyed by *Aviation Week & Space Technology* magazine shortly after the 757's debut said that it was the best aircraft they had flown. 'I like it because greater thought has been given to both passenger and flight attendant,' Katherine Bennett, an Eastern attendant, told the magazine. 'Unlike most airplanes, lavatories are away from galleys. Service carts are well designed, unlike the Airbus A300, where you run to the galley, grab trays and serve the passengers. In the 757, the service flows smoothly, with well-designed carts.'

Because of the location of a full galley and lavatory midway along the cabin, flight attendants are able to serve food and drinks without interfering with passengers walking back and forth through the single aisle to the rear lavatory. This allows for more coffee refills and additional personal contact between passengers and crew. Having the galley and the lavatory midway in the cabin splits the coach section into two parts – a 15-seat section behind first class and a larger aft cabin.

Initially, the automated flight deck – full of high-tech equipment and mind-boggling computing power – caused enormous concern to both the airlines and reg-

Minor Problems

As on all new aircraft, a few mechanical problems cropped up in the new planes after service entry, but these were quickly fixed.

In the early days of 757 service, Delta Air Lines received letters from passengers who claimed to hear excessive rushing air sounds between rows 20 and 24, and a high-pitched noise in the aft cabin. Delta determined that the rushing air noise came from inadequately muffled air-condi-

over-sensitive yaw dampers, broken plastic sun-visor holders, cracks of composite materials, and poor air-conditioning while on ground power. Some 767s also recorded these problems, which were subsequently fixed.

The environmental-control system initially had difficulty clearing cigarette smoke from the cabin and providing sufficient cooling for equipment and subsystems. It was found that the blades on the recirculation fan were stalling and causing a reduction in the air flow. The fan was

American Trans Air is a US charter and scheduled service carrier flying the 757. Ralph Olson/Flying Images Worldwide

ulators, because it was so new. However, perhaps because of rigorous pre-delivery testing, the all-new glass cockpit did not cause any major problems when it entered service on either the 767 or 757. One small complaint was that the crew alerting system was at times over-sensitive, and gave many false warnings. Flight crews were put in the position of either choosing to ignore some warnings, or paying attention to many that were probably false.

tioning ducts. The cause of the aft cabin noise was determined to be improper drains for door seals and lavatory facilities.

Other airlines noted excessive engine noise, and this led to modified engine mounts. Some airlines also reported ultra-sensitive brakes when taxiing and making turns; this problem required a change in the metering valves in the hydraulic brake-control system. In the early days of the 757, pilots also complained of

replaced with a different design and the problem was thus solved.

One idiosyncrasy with the 757 involved a slightly swaying tail. Boeing made modifications in 1990 to reduce the side-to-side motion that passengers were feeling at the back of the aircraft. With the fix, 757s have no more wiggle than other Boeing planes. On a long aircraft like the 757, it is more likely that the ride will be bumpier in the aft portion.

Several airlines use both the 767 and 757 in their fleets, since pilots qualified for one can fly the other. TWA is among the carriers enjoying the savings of such an arrangement. Ralph Olson/Flying Images Worldwide

British Airways, which used the 757s to replace de Havilland Tridents, spent two years debugging the 757 to correct some minor problems. 'We had a lot of what you might call infancy problems, particularly during the first nine or ten months of the aircraft's operation,' Barry Booth, British Airways' project engineer for the 737 and 757, said at the time. One problem the carrier encountered was a fatigue in the engine support strut. The British Airways cabin crew was fond of the 757, but noted that meal service on the aircraft could be difficult because of the large number of passengers carried, compared with the Trident, the single-aisle plane it replaced. On short flights with meal service, the crew found that there may not be enough time to serve food if the seat belt light remains on.

Versatility and Other Attractions

The planes' versatility was quickly grasped by carriers around the world. Just as United had discovered the 767's transcontinental abilities, other carriers soon began to use the 757 on lucrative coast-to-coast services, including some new long-haul routes. Northwest Airlines, for instance, initially used the 757 to replace Boeing 727s on heavily travelled routes of 1,000 miles (1,600km), but soon expanded its scope. 'The beauty of the 757 is its versatility,' Benjamin G. Griggs Jr., Northwest's executive vice-president of operations, said at the time. 'It can do economically what the DC-10 does on transcontinental routes where loads are not large enough, and can replace the 727 on short-haul routes. It will do anything we want.' Northwest opened new routes, including New York-Seattle, a link it had had to drop in 1984 when it was served by the DC-10, which was too large for the route. The 727 did not have the range for the 2,421-mile (3,873km) flight.

The 757 was also increasingly attractive on a number of short-haul routes, which, up to two or three years earlier, had been flown with widebody aircraft. British Airways had been using L1011s on such routes, while competitors were using cheaper, smaller aircraft. When BA's 757s entered service in February 1983, they replaced many TriStars, leaving the widebodies for such routes as London-Paris and charter service. 'That is the kind of

flexibility we have always said we needed, and which the 757 gave us,' Watts said at the time. By 1984, British Airways had enough 757s to establish a shuttle fleet of five to six aircraft equipped with 220 seats without galleys. With its added size over the Tridents, the 757 eliminated the need for one back-up flight on high-density shuttle routes, saving the airline $1.2 million a year.

When it struck a deal with Boeing for 60 757s, Delta Air Lines required that aircraft cost efficiencies should exceed the original

The 767's interior features two-by-three-by-two seating. With this layout, the plane would need to be 87 per cent full before the centre row has to be used. Boeing

1980 Boeing proposal by 10 per cent. Initial operations of the 757 four years later showed a 14 per cent improvement, which resulted from engine and aerodynamic efficiencies. Delta negotiated normal guarantees for reliability, costs, fuel efficiency and total performance, and also a guarantee that its Pratt & Whitney PW2037 engines would perform better than the Rolls-Royce engine. Delta was the first airline to choose Pratt to power its 757s.

Flying the Twins

767 Configurations

The 767 has always been popular among the travel-weary. Its economy-class cabin layout – two seats on either side of two aisles and only three seats in the middle – is a welcome sight compared with 747s, DC10s, and L-1011s that have four or even five seats in the middle of the cabin. The layout ensures that six out of seven, or 87 per cent, of the seats are next to either

a window or an aisle, meaning an aircraft would have to be close to full before the middle seat is taken. It has the smallest proportion of centre seats of any airliner and the smallest body that can economically be built around two aisles.

In the early days of service, United reported its satisfaction with the 767's seven-abreast layout, which offers greater passenger appeal and comfort than six-seat, single-aisle configurations, particularly on

The 767's first-class cabin has a single seat in the middle, making the aircraft a popular choice among passengers. Boeing

(Below) A cutaway drawing of the 767's interior. Boeing

flights of more than two hours. 'We became enamoured with the 2-3-2 seating,' says Richard Ferris, United's former chairman. 'We thought that was an attractive feature, especially for the business market.'

In first class, the 767's five-abreast seating accommodates standard 747-sized sleeper seats for long-range flights, two

when a 767's cabin is configured in eight-abreast seating, for inclusive tours.

In a three-class configuration, the 767 offers more stowage volume per passenger – 3 cubic feet (84 cubic cm) – than any other widebody except the 777. The overhead bins in a -300 model, the longest in any jetliner, rise sharply and are recessed

Straight, level aisles make the attendants' work easier and meal service quicker on the 767. Doors and aisles are wide, for fast, efficient boarding and de-planing. On the downside, it takes some time to exit a -300, particularly from the back, if there is just one gangway, which can lead to frustration among travellers in the rear.

The business class section of a 767. Boeing

rows of two seats on each side and a single seat in the middle. In business class, where seats run six across, each passenger can sit next to either a window or aisle. Even those in economy class can enjoy a taste of luxury – the seats are slightly bigger than those on most widebody aircraft. Only the 777 has bigger seats. The exception is

into the ceiling for more headroom and greater perceived spaciousness. There is so much room that a passenger of 5ft 3in (160cm) could stand up straight at the window seat without hitting his or her head. Short passengers, however, need to climb on to the seats to put their bags in the overhead compartments.

Bulkheads, particularly in the -300 model, serve to divide the cabin into cosy sections, so passengers do not truly get a feel for how long the plane is. The divisions also allow flight attendants to work a variety of service stations without clogging the aisles.

There are more than 100 different interiors, both original and modified, in the

7 Galley Locations

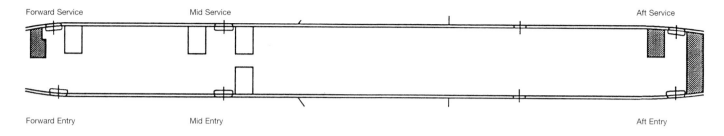

Forward Service   Mid Service   Aft Service

Forward Entry   Mid Entry   Aft Entry

12 Lavatory Locations

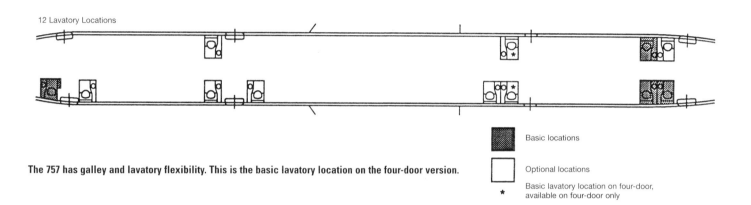

The 757 has galley and lavatory flexibility. This is the basic lavatory location on the four-door version.

■ Basic locations

□ Optional locations

★ Basic lavatory location on four-door, available on four-door only

767 fleet. A difference in interior could mean changing the location of a magazine rack, or of a lavatory. Many airlines have modified and certified their own 767s after delivery. There are too many customer-requested features to count; when a customer wants something unique to set a different standard and is willing to pay for it, Boeing will customize an airliner.

The 767-200 has five lavatories (six in the -300), two centrally in the main cabin, two aft in the main cabin and one or two forward in the first-class sections. Galleys are situated at forward and aft ends of the cabin.

Unlike other widebodies, the 767 takes to the air surprisingly quickly. The aircraft has a very high climb gradient. This is because a twin-engined plane, after reaching take-off speed, must be able to continue the take-off in the case of one engine failing. Both the 767 and 757 have twice the power needed for take-off after minimum engine-out take-off speed is reached. In comparison, a three-engined plane, like the 727, with all engines running, has one and a half times the power needed for take-off at the minimum engine-out take-off speed, and a four-engined plane, like the 747, has one and a third times the power needed. In flight, the 767 flies qui-

etly and the reassuring drone of the engines is hardly noticeable.

Distinctly narrower than the 747, DC-10, L1011, A340 or A330-300, the 767 is a treat on short hops normally reserved for narrow-body routes. Its economic hourly operating efficiency – an average of $3,324 for a 767-200 and $3,609 for a -300 – allows for short flights, which are normally an expensive proposition that is best left to smaller aircraft.

Passenger-service units on both aircraft put call buttons, air and lights at the passenger's fingertips. Both the 767 and 757, in common with most large commercial transports today, feature telephones built into seat-backs, activated by credit cards. This feature has been retrofitted into older planes. Because the 767 is a widebody, programming appears either on monitors or on large screens on bulkheads. Seat-back video screens, a feature on the 777 even in coach class, are being offered for future models. On the 757, an in-flight video system is available, with monitors positioned off the ceiling every ten rows, affording passengers an unobstructed view of movies, television shows, news or onboard safety announcements.

757 Configurations

Unlike its wider cousin, the 757 offers normal standard-body seating – two rows of three seats in economy class. (The two-by-two seating in the first-class section features wider seats than competing aircraft, giving operators a marketing edge.) However, with the coach-class arrangement the same as a 737's, the 757's cabin can seem rather long and cramped, making it among the most disliked aircraft among frequent travellers. Passengers on transatlantic or coast-to-coast North American flights lasting five hours or more can feel quite claustrophobic. The 757, the longest single-aisle aircraft in the world, can be uncomfortable when a flight is full. Boarding a full 757 can be a chore as passengers pause to put belongings in overhead bins. On the other hand, when a flight is empty, chances are that passengers will be able to enjoy a row to themselves. And, because the aircraft can operate in fog and other conditions that may ground other airliners, with the 757, passengers have a better chance of arriving on time or making connections in foul weather.

The widebody A310's seating capacity is slightly more than the 757, but Boeing

With Overwing Exits

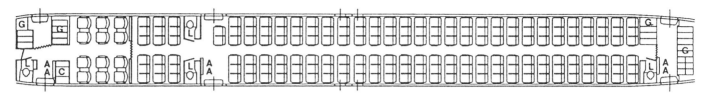

12 first class
38-in pitch

182 economy class
32-in pitch

194 passengers

With Four Doors

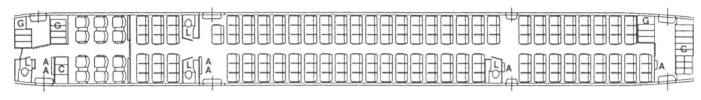

12 first class
38-in pitch

176 economy class
32-in pitch

188 passengers

With Overwing Exits

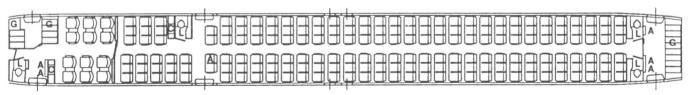

12 first class

189 economy class

201 passengers

With Four Doors

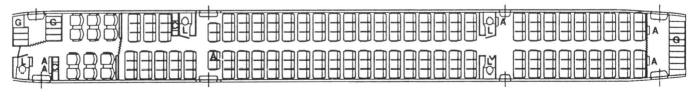

12 first class

183 economy class

195 passengers

A = Attendant
C = Closet
G = Galley
L = Lavatory

Interior arrangements on a mixed-class 757-200.

markets the 757 as a more modern, more fuel-efficient model, on which cost savings outweigh the comforts of a widebody. Boeing studies showed that, in short- to medium-haul flights, passenger preference had little bearing on the type of aircraft preferred. Company analysis also showed that, for ranges of less than 1,500 miles (2,400km), a minor preference for two aisles is more than compensated for by the 757's ability to return a profit to the airlines with substantially fewer seats occupied.

Even before its first flight, the 757 was available with two different engines, a choice of three take-off weights, two door layouts and a remarkable choice of interior arrangements. Each interior style – the fabric, the seats – is determined by airlines. They also decide on which galley and lavatory locations they prefer. Available with either three or four entry doors, the 757 offers airlines more galley and lavatory location choices than competing airliners. While Eastern and British Airways had much to do with the original configurations, Delta has driven many of the changes made since then.

The most significant characteristic a passenger notices when entering a 757 is the plane's length. When compared with other narrow-bodies, it can seem never-ending. To break up the monotony of the seating, the 757's cabin can be configured into sections, giving the airliner a club-like atmosphere. The aircraft's multi-exit configurations allow passengers to board and exit smoothly, reducing congestion at doorways and in the aisles. The mid-cabin doorways allow those travelling in first class to be seated and served while other passengers are boarding in the aft cabin. The three-door overwing-exit configuration incorporates emergency exits over the wings, with lavatories in the aft end of the cabin, just ahead of the galley. The four-door arrangement features mid-cabin lavatories, and galleys fore and aft. Airlines that fly two- or three-class transcontinental and intercontinental routes prefer four doors. This arrangement breaks up the cabin for different levels of service, and also facilitates movement within the cabin by providing more places for flight attendants and passengers to pass by food and beverage carts. There are no less than nine galley locations and nine lavatory locations, depending on the emergency-exit configuration selected. Airlines can choose from options of multiple units of each at either forward, mid or aft positions. The 757 has four lavatories.

The 757's galleys make better use of space than conventional versions. Set transversely against the aft bulkhead, their design enables a cadre of five to seven flight attendants to work side by side without interference. In contrast, conventional two-sided galleys require attendants to take turns vying for floor space. The 757 aft galley also lets cabin crews roll food and drink carts straight out the door and up the aisle. Conventional galleys require attendants to manoeuvre carts through right-angle turns into the aisle. The galleys feature large right-side service doors. Because they are located within the galleys, these doors enable provisioning to take place quickly within the galleys, leaving the aisle free for boarding.

The 757 can be configured into three classes, a four-abreast first class, five-abreast business class and six-abreast economy class. First-class seats on the 757 have a 38in (96.5cm) pitch. The pitch in economy class is 32 or 34in (81 or 86cm). The aisle is 20in (50.8cm) across. Boeing developed an attractive and functional interior for the 757's passenger cabin. Sculptured ceiling and sidewall panels made from weight-saving composite materials, and accented by recessed lighting, give the interior a spacious look; indeed, the plane has a widebody feel, even if the floor width is the same as the 727. The Kevlar-enforced overhead stowage bins provide about 1.9 cubic feet (54 cubic cm) of space per passenger, and can store flat garment bags. Each bin is 5ft (1.52m) long, and holds up to 180lb (82kg) of carry-on items.

The take-off in a 757, as in its larger sibling, is sudden and steep. Once up, the ride is quiet, except for some vibrations experienced by those seated near the engines.

The Pilot's View

In general, pilots love flying the 767 and 757, and use the aircraft as a yardstick against which to compare others. According to pilots, the aircraft are well designed, fun to fly, responsive, reliable, adaptable, and very manoeuvrable for their size. They are pilot-friendly aircraft, offering excellent performance, good navigation, handy redundancies and few, if any, recurring mechanical problems. Unlike the fly-by-wire Airbus family, the 767 and 757 offer a combination of high technology and good, old-fashioned, take-control-of-the-stick flying, which pilots prefer.

For pilots, the reliability of the aircraft is the strongest suit. Both planes will regularly operate properly more than 99.5 per cent of the time on any given day. Pilots say that even more modern aircraft, such as the McDonnell-Douglas (now Boeing) MD-88, are less reliable, despite having newer computer-controlled flight decks.

The 757 is a pilot's aircraft, says Boeing. 'It handles great, gives you all sorts of performance, and it will fly anywhere, any time, it's quiet and has all kinds of capability,' says Doug Miller. The plane is so powerful that pilots rarely have to use full engine power to take off. Throttling down saves engine wear as well as fuel.

The identical flight deck – the hallmark of these planes – can cause havoc for a pilot who is daydreaming. Although some switches and the electronic engine controls differ between the 757 and 767, and the 767's cockpit is slightly wider, even veteran pilots type rated to fly both aircraft must continually remind themselves of the type they are flying. For example, when taxiing, pilots must remember that the 767, especially the -300 model, is wider and heavier, and requires wider turns. Landing is also different, and this can cause problems unless pilots are paying close attention. Hard landings in the 757 may be in part due to the fact that the 757 cockpit is 6ft (1.83m) lower to the ground than the 767 cockpit; the pilot may forget which type he or she is flying, and be in for a quicker touchdown than hoped for. The 757 offers a clean and light landing, so much so that pilots tend to cut all engine power when the plane is about 30ft (9m) above the runway. Doing this when coming in to land with the much heavier 767 will cause a hard landing, because the 767 will drop immediately after the engine power is cut. Another difference is that the 767 has two sets of ailerons at low speed. It is more responsive on turns because of the second one, and there may be a tendency for a pilot – thinking he or she is flying the 757 – to over-compensate the controls slightly.

A pilot working for an airline that has both planes in its fleet will frequently switch between the 767 and 757, often several times a day. While there is a benefit in training just once in order to qualify for both planes, the real pay-off is the day-to-day flexibility that the airlines have. Pilots can operate aircraft seating 183 or 252 passengers, with the same crew. For example, a Delta pilot who flies from Atlanta to Cincinnati on a 757 may find him or herself on a 767-300 for a flight from Cincinnati to Los Angeles. If the pilot could fly only one of the planes, two crews would be required for the two flights – as well as two sets of reserve pilots.

Because much of the programming for the flight plan is done on the ground, the 767 and 757 give pilots more time to sit back and observe during the flight; this was a specific goal of the designers, who insisted on lower crew workloads. 'I love the technology. I love the computer systems,' says one TWA 767 pilot. 'They've engineered all the idiosyncrasies out of the airplane.'

Earning ETOPS

Perhaps the greatest legacy of the 767/757 family is an ability to cross oceans or conquer hours of barren terrain on just two engines.

In the first years of the 767's commercial service, certification authorities, such as the Federal Aviation Administration in the United States and the Joint Aviation Authority in Europe, required the aircraft to fly within an hour of a suitable airport so it could safely divert in the event of an engine failure. This was known in the

an airport, but with both engines working. Either way, the rules were made with good reason, at a time when aircraft were propeller-driven, using reciprocating engines.

Flying long routes with two engines is called ETOPS – Extended Twin Engine Operations, or, affectionately, 'Engines Turn or Passengers Swim'. Every month, the 767 alone successfully completes more than 14,600 extended-range flights. The plane has come a long way from its early days, when doubters were more comfortable with at least three engines, if not more. 'The only reason I fly in a four-

A TWA 767-200, like the one shown here, was the first 767 revenue passenger flight allowed with the 120-minute ETOPS rule. On 1 February 1985 Flight 810 departed from Boston to Paris. Ralph Olson/Flying Images Worldwide

John Armstrong, the first 757 test pilot, calls the 757 a pilot's aircraft that is great to fly by hand. 'This airplane felt more like you were in an airplane that would perform like a pilot would expect it to,' he says. 'Pilots are comfortable in it. The instrumentation and everything in there is easy and logical to understand. The logic was a big thing. We made the flight deck intuitive, and even if a pilot had never been in one before, he could still do a lot.'

United States as Federal Aviation Regulation 121.161: 'Unless authorized by the administrator, based on the character of the terrain, the kind of operation, or the performance of the airplane to be used, no certificate holder may operate two-engine airplanes over a route that contains a point farther than 1 hour flying time (in still air at normal cruising speed with one engine inoperative) from an adequate airport.' The Europeans allowed 90 minutes from

engined plane,' the saying goes, 'is because there are none with five.'

ETOPS is granted to a specific twin-engine aircraft based on design and testing. ETOPS approval is granted to a specific airline to operate an ETOPS-approved aircraft based on its pilots, maintenance, flight planning, training capabilities and history. The unique aspect of an ETOPS flight is that, for part of the flight, the aircraft is more than 60 minutes from a suitable airport.

Twin-Engines Crossing Oceans

The extended-range 767-200 was the first twin-engine aircraft capable of crossing oceans. In the early 1980s, the thought of a twin flying passengers across the Atlantic was unheard of. 'It'll be a cold day in hell before I let twins fly long-haul, overwater routes,' FAA administrator Lyn Helms told Boeing's Dick Taylor when Taylor first approached him on the issue, in 1980. Helms was actually more worried about systems failures rather than engines not working.

This allows independent systems to back up others, and contributes to a greater margin of safety. Of course, the same engineering that increases aircraft dependability creates a confusing network of interconnected systems. Failure in one component can affect operations of others.

The 767 fleet operated for more than two years before the FAA granted initial approval for ETOPS service. In May 1985, the FAA released guidelines authorizing only those 767s powered by Pratt & Whitney JT9D-7R4 engines to fly up to 120 minutes from a suitable airport. This

Just as Boeing succeeded in convincing aviation authorities that, with the right technology, two-member crews are safer than three, the reliability of high-bypass engines showed the world that two engines can be just as safe as – or safer than – three. 'We all got the failure rate data for jets and made the case that jet engines don't fail as much as they get bigger,' Taylor recalls. Today's high-bypass engines are ten times more reliable than the piston engines of the 1950s.

'We worked with the two engine companies to increase reliability. Everybody

Air Canada was among the first carriers to operate ETOPS flights with 767s. Today there are 14,600 ETOPS flights a month, most of them operated by 767s. Ralph Olson/Flying Images Worldwide

Until the early 1980s, three- or four-engined aircraft handled all long-range routes, including those over water. Twins were relegated to intracontinental travel. Since then, the twins' range and reliability have increased because of the excellent performance and fuel efficiency of the engines, and the capability and redundancy of systems, such as hydraulics and avionics, which are equivalent to or better than those of three- and four-engined aircraft. Aircraft systems are made redundant by the linking together of components.

enabled Trans World Airlines to initiate a 767 transatlantic service. Three months later, similar approval was granted to 767s powered by GE CF6-80A engines. By December 1986, twelve operators were flying 49 ETOPS-equipped 767s on long-range flights across the North Atlantic and the Tasman Sea, and trans-Sahara. Three years later, 152 ETOPS 767s flew more than 3,000 flights a month, having added the South Pacific and Indian Ocean to the list of long-range routes, as the reach of the twin-jet was extended.

had their minds on the engines being the real driver, but I took the position that all systems should be sufficient as an alternate to go as far as three hours from an airport,' Taylor says. 'That meant systems in duplicate or triplicate so that if you started a diversion, three hours later you would still be operating.'

To appease the FAA, Boeing gathered data on aircraft performance. The company compiled every failure and shutdown ever experienced in the first few years of 767 service. Boeing told the FAA that the

With fifty-seven examples, British Airways is the largest 757 operator outside the United States. Peter Sweeten/Aviation Images Worldwide

probability of both engines failing at once was once in 50,000 years. The likelihood of 767 diversions to alternate airports statistically was less than that of a 747.

In fact, even if one engine were to fail on the 767, it still has substantial power. The aircraft can take off at maximum weight, lose an engine shortly afterwards – the most critical moment in a flight – and

Engine reliability does matter, however, and it plays the most significant role in the granting, or otherwise, of ETOPS. After all, a leakage of air, the failure of a sensor in an engine, or a leak of oil or hydraulic fluid might not harm the engine, but it could lead to the eventual need to shut an engine down halfway across an ocean, and, just to be safe, the plane landing at a

rate, the FAA and Europe's JAA approved 767s for long-range flights of up to 120 minutes from a suitable airport. In 1989, the time was extended to the maximum 180 minutes.

In many ways, ETOPS transformed commercial aviation. No longer were long-haul routes the domain of larger, more expensive 747s, L-1011s and DC-

Air Mauritius operates two 767-200ERs on routes to Europe. Peter Sweeten/Aviation Images Worldwide

still climb with the remaining engine. If an engine fails at a high cruising altitude, the 767 will lose altitude for 400 miles (640km) and then can start a slow climb for the rest of the flight – without using full power. The number of engines alone does not dictate safety when it comes to earning ETOPS. For instance, at 30 degrees west, in the middle of the Atlantic, it would be better to be in a 767 than in a four-engine DC-8 in the event of a cargo fire, because the 767 has a fire-suppression system and the older DC-8 does not.

diversionary airport. When this happens, many headaches arise, including the necessity of bringing parts in and accommodating passengers, and schedules are left in disarray.

Along with advances in engines, improvements to the 767 airframe, including additional electrical sources and a fire-extinguishing system in cargo holds, convinced authorities that the 767 would be safe over long distances, first for 75 minutes, then for 90. By May 1985, after the 767 recorded a very low engine-shutdown

10s, or the remaining gas-guzzling 707s and DC-8s. Instead, smaller, more fuel-efficient aircraft carried more people to more destinations. With ETOPS, trans-oceanic flights became shorter because aircraft could fly more direct, time-saving flight paths; new routes were introduced, as airlines could profitably enter markets that could not support larger aircraft; and airlines made money through fuel savings and increased traffic. It is no coincidence that ETOPS ushered in the greatest expansion in commercial aviation history.

To demonstrate the range capabilities of the 767, Boeing scheduled a 7,500-mile (12,000km) delivery flight of an Ethiopian Airlines 767-200ER from Dulles International Airport outside Washington, DC, to Addis Ababa, on 1 June 1984. For the flight, Boeing received a special exemption from FAA rules regarding overwater operations. Two months earlier, an El Al 767

minute barrier early on, most notably Air Canada, with a 75-minute exemption to the Caribbean in 1983.

The first fully qualified 767-200ER that met US and international certification goals for extended-range aircraft was delivered to Air Canada in October 1984. The aircraft was the first to be equipped with a fourth generator independently

petitioned the agency to use twin-engine planes on transatlantic crossings. Before that could happen, the FAA required Boeing to establish 'statistical maturity' of specially equipped 767s. To gain a 120-minute rating, a fleet of modified 767s powered by JT9D engines had to log 250,000 consecutive flight hours on commercial flights, and achieve a very low rate of engine failure.

Austria's Lauda Air flies 767-300ERs from its Vienna base to charter destinations across Asia. Peter Sweeten/Aviation Images Worldwide

had flown the type's first commercial nonstop transatlantic flight, from Montreal to Tel Aviv, but that trip was within 60-minute ETOPS regulations. El Al, Air Canada and TWA began using 767s over the Atlantic in the spring of 1984 after receiving exemptions allowing them to fly no more than 75 minutes from a suitable airport, before the FAA's formal approval of such flights. Australia's Qantas and Air New Zealand did the same over the Pacific. There were several instances of 767 airlines getting approval to fly beyond the 60-

powered by a hydraulic motor, additional chemical fire-suppression capability, and equipment for cooling the 767's cathode ray tube instruments. These safeguards were recommended by the International Civil Aviation Organization, the International Federation of Air Line Pilots Association, the US Air Line Pilots Association and the FAA.

In 1985, the FAA, at Boeing's behest, extended the range from 75 minutes to 120, opening the way for transatlantic flights with twin-jets. Several airlines had

The Inaugural 120-minute ETOPS 767 Flight

The first 767 revenue passenger flight allowed with the 120-minute ETOPS rule took place on 1 February 1985, when Trans World Airlines flight 810 departed from Boston to Paris. According to *Aviation Week & Space Technology*, 'passengers on the first flight showed mild enthusiasm for participating in an aviation first and no outward concern that the aircraft was powered by two engines rather than three or four'. The new rule shortened the flight from 3,885 miles (6,216km) to 3,797 miles (6,075km). It was not a big difference, but when it was multiplied by the dozens of flights a day that would follow, the savings quickly became clear.

TWA's inaugural 767 transatlantic flight saw the Boeing model replacing an L-1011. February, with traditionally low load factors, was a good time to start any experiment. The first time that most passengers on board heard about the history-making flight was when an announcement was made from the cockpit. A commemorative postcard, writ-

that undertook the task of proving that 767 extended-range operations could be safe and reliable. Training for the first group of sixteen TWA pilots included a refresher course in international requirements, intensive simulator flying, and procedures for landing at Sondrestrom, Greenland, a new alternative airport.

As the 767 approached landfall over Northern Ireland, London Control asked if this was the first 767. The aviation airwaves exploded when the pilot confirmed it. 'You're very lucky to have made it,' one unidentified British pilot said. 'Are they

that it retrofitted five of the aircraft for extended-range flights, at $2.6 million each. The investment paid off as new routes, including New York–Munich, were later launched.

Further Range Extensions

ETOPS, an accomplishment of engineering, actually began as a marketing concept. 'ETOPS evolved through the 767, and it was our marketing department that wanted to use the 767 to travel the lucrative California–Hawaii route. They said,

Air Pacific of Fiji uses its only 767-300ER on ETOPS routes to Australia and the United States. Peter Sweeten/Aviation Images Worldwide

ten by a student and mailed from Paris, stated, 'Now they tell me it's a two-engine airplane, as if I don't have enough troubles.'

In the cockpit of Flight 810, the mood was one of accomplishment as the aircraft approached the Irish coast. The flight was the end result of more than two years of effort by pilots Walter E. Grayum, Norman Fausett and William Sonnermann. Sonnermann headed the Air Transport Association's Flight Systems Integration committee

both still running?' asked another. They ran quite well, their every vibration monitored by the crew and by eleven FAA observers who focused on the Pratt & Whitney JT9D-7R4D engines throughout the flight.

Flight time for this historic flight was 6 hours and 32 minutes. Fuel burn on the trip was about 10,000lb (4,550kg) per hour – 7,000lb (3,175kg) an hour less than the L-1011 it replaced. TWA was so convinced of the 767's cost-saving abilities

"What would it take it to get our 767s there?"' recalls Dick Taylor, who was charged with the responsibility.

While it was first used over the Atlantic, where diversionary airports exist, the 767-200ER's proven track record of 120-minute ETOPS cleared the way for Hawaiian routes, flying over nothing but water, between the US west coast and the islands.

In 1989, the FAA extended the twin-jet range to 180 minutes, making it possible

Qantas Airlines of Australia operates twenty-one 767-300s for domestic, regional and international routes.
Peter Sweeten/Aviation Images Worldwide

Far Eastern Air Transport of Taiwan flies the 757 on intra-island domestic flights. Wung Te Chu

Condor Flugdienst of Germany is among the many charter airlines operating 767-300s. Tomas Frocklin

Uzbekistan Airlines operates two 767-300ERs to modernize its fleet of ex-Soviet aircraft. Peter
Sweeten/Aviation Images Worldwide

British Airways, with twenty-eight examples, has the largest fleet of 767-300s in Europe. Kurt Roth

Delta Air Lines is the largest 767 operator, including fifteen of the -200 models. Ed Davies

for 767s to fly from the US mainland to Hawaii, a route that reached the midway point at 150 minutes. However, to gain 180-minute approval, an aircraft/engine combination had to accumulate 12 consecutive months of successful 120-minute ETOPS flights, as well as meet even more stringent engine-failure rates.

Officially, 767s won their first 120-minute ETOPS approvals in May 1995, using Pratt & Whitney JT9D-7R4 engines. The 767s powered by GE's CF6-80A won approval three months later. Due

RB211-524H engine received 180-minute ETOPS approval in 1992.

ETOPS recorded nothing but success in its early days. According to Boeing, by 30 June 1990, 767s had performed more than 100,000 ETOPS flights and only two per 1,000 had to turn back or divert to an alternative airport. During the first five years of operations, 767 crews had to make a decision to turn back, divert or continue only 279 times. Only 7 per cent of these incidents related to the ETOPS portion of the flight, when the aircraft was more than

from 15 per cent of all crossings in 1990 to 20.4 per cent. Today, more than half of all transatlantic crossings are by 767s.

United Airlines, the 767's first customer, operated its 100,000th ETOPS flight in April 1998. United's first ETOPS flight took place in spring 1990 between Washington's Dulles International Airport and Frankfurt, Germany. Newer -300s later became the backbone of the airline's ETOPS fleet for service from the United States to Europe and South America. United entered ETOPS service on the 757 in 1995. The 757

A LOT 767-300 at New York's John F. Kennedy International Airport. Michael McLaughlin

to their extraordinary reliability records, the CF680A/C2 engines were the first to receive FAA approval for 180-minute ETOPS on the 767, in 1989. The JT9D-powered 767 did not receive 180-minute ETOPS authority until April 1990. ETOPS approval (120 minutes) for the 767-200 and -300 with PW4000 engines was also granted in April 1990. The engine was certified for 180-minute ETOPS in August 1993. The Rolls-Royce

60 minutes from an airport. During that time, the 767s had achieved a 99.8 per cent non-stop arrival rate, only two flights in 1,000 having to turn back or divert.

By late 1991, the number of North Atlantic crossings by US carriers actually exceeded the number of three- and four-engined crossings. The number of twin-engined aircraft from all nations grew by 27 per cent from 1990 to 1991. During that time, the proportion of 767 crossings grew

fleet specializes in California–Hawaii operations, particularly to Kona and Maui, where load factors are lower.

'In 1985, all commercial flights across the Atlantic were operated with four- or three-engine aircraft,' says Louis Mancini, United's vice president of engineering. 'And there was some resistance to twin-engine overwater operations. It was contended that if an engine had to be shut down three hours from an airport over water, the plane might not make it to an airfield with only one engine in service. Happily, history has confounded these doomsayers.'

Steve Zigan, retired manager of aircraft programmes at GE Aircraft Engines, credits the efforts of Boeing's Dick Taylor for ushering in ETOPS. 'Had it not been for Dick, ETOPS probably would not have happened so early,' he says.

'The whole industry has moved up a notch because of ETOPS popularity,' Zigan says. 'We never thought it would be so successful. Early on, no one could possibly imagine that twin-engine aircraft would dominate the Atlantic routes. That success is a tribute both to engine technology and the 767.'

airline industry took a nose-dive and 767s and 757s replaced half-full DC-10s and 747s on many routes.

On 31 July 1990, the FAA granted 180-minute ETOPS certification for 757s equipped with the Rolls-Royce RB211-535E4 and RB211-535C engines. Those engines had received 120-minute ETOPS approval in December 1986. In April 1992, the FAA granted 180-minute ETOPS certification for the 757-200 equipped with Pratt & Whitney PW2000 engines. The FAA had certified Pratt engines for 120-minute ETOPS in March 1990.

For added reliability on ETOPS flights, the 757, like the 767, is available with extended-range features, including a

The Boeing 767 has now flown over 1 million ETOPS flights, more than any other aircraft. Since 29 May 1985, when the FAA gave its official blessing to the 767 as the first aircraft to receive approval for 120-minute ETOPS flights, more than 60 airlines have flown ETOPS flights.

Engine-shutdown rates on ETOPS routes have proven to be outstanding. Major carriers are exceeding no more than 0.02 shutdowns per 1,000 hours of flight on 180-minute ETOPS, showing that engine reliability has grown exponentially since the days of the early 707s. Typically, shutdowns occur when the plane is 30–60 minutes from an alternative airfield in the North Atlantic. Careful monitoring of each shutdown, plus

Japan Airlines operates 767-300s to augment the larger 747 on domestic and international routes. Michael Pellaton/Flying Images Worldwide

ETOPS for the 757

The success of the 767 ETOPS service led to extended-range clearance for 757s as well. Once again, marketeers played a role, eyeing the smaller twin as an ideal transatlantic aircraft for charter operators. The 757 received 120-minute ETOPS approval in 1986, and the first ETOPS flight by a 757 occurred on 1 May 1988, with British charter Monarch Airlines. The 757 first crossed the Atlantic on a regularly scheduled flight in May 1990, in time for the recession of the early 1990s, when the

back-up hydraulic-motor generator and an auxiliary fan to cool electronics. High gross-weight versions of the aircraft can fly 4,500 miles (7,240km) non-stop, with full passenger loads. These developments give the 757 the ability to serve more markets.

Shutdown Rates

Today, all new 767s and 757s are automatically certified with 180-minute ETOPS approval, a testament to hard work and engineering expertise.

the requirement that the carrier take corrective action, provides a strong incentive to manufacturers and operators to identify and eliminate problems. Maintenance is scheduled at shorter intervals and inspections are more demanding on ETOPS aircraft. Many 767s and 757s even have 'ETOPS' painted on their noses, so that ground crews will know that they need to give them particularly careful scrutiny. Operators are encouraged to conduct external inspections to find frayed wires, missing clamps and loose nuts; such pieces have all caused in-flight shutdowns on ETOPS aircraft.

Air Seychelles has one 767-200 (pictured) and a -300 model. Michael Pellaton/Flying Images Worldwide

El Salvador's TACA uses the 767-300 on routes to the United States. Michael Pellaton/Flying Images Worldwide

Asiana of South Korea is among the many Asian carriers relying on the 767-300's capacity and fuel efficiency to fly regional routes. This example is shown navigating the famous Checkerboard turn at now-closed Kai Tak airport in Hong Kong. Michael Pellaton/Flying Images Worldwide

Vietnam Airlines operates six 767-300ERs, providing some much-needed lift on growing routes. Michael Pellaton/Flying Images Worldwide

One factor that could deter the use of twin-engined aircraft on ultra-long routes is speed. While the 767-300ER cruises at Mach .80, the 747 has a speed of Mach .85, which could account for nearly an hour's difference in flight time on a flight of ten to twelve hours' duration.

Flying Around the World

Both the Boeing 767 and the 757 operate on every inhabited continent and in all

a choice of engines and thrust ratings that allow airlines to tailor their twin-jets to market requirements. Whether operated in domestic, regional or non-stop intercontinental service, each member of the family delivers economic efficiency and market flexibility. As an example, a 757 operator can use the plane on high-demand shuttle routes in the morning, then fly the same aircraft on a non-stop intercontinental service later in the day. Over the years, both planes have filled roles beyond those envisioned by Boeing: the 767 has emerged as the

with Australia. The 767 also economically serves north-south routes between North America and South America, and Europe and Africa and the Middle East. The 767 has the versatility to meet the demands of a variety of air-travel markets, on domestic, regional or intercontinental routes, opening up new routes around the world. Today's 767 routes are just the beginning of more extensive point-to-point services and the expansion of international hub networks, because the aircraft is an economical choice for small-

Royal Air Maroc is one of only three African airlines operating the 757. Peter Sweeten/Aviation Images Worldwide

climactic conditions. More than 70 airlines around the world rely on the dynamic duo for efficient, safe and comfortable air transportation.

The 767/757 family provides broad, effective market coverage. One ingredient is the wide selection of design weights, which provide range flexibility. Another is

premier long-range twin-jet, while the 757 is increasingly popular for long intercontinental flights.

The 767

The 767 is ideally suited for routes linking North America with Europe, and Asia

er international markets. As a companion to the 747, the 767 provides widebody comfort during off-peak or seasonal market demands. That means better service and schedule flexibility for passengers, and competitive opportunities for airlines.

Because of its range, capacity, reliability and fuel efficiency, the 767 is by far the

Iberia is one of twenty-five European carriers with 757s in their fleets. Peter Sweeten/Aviation Images Worldwide

The 757 has found its way into the former Soviet Union, as seen in Baikal Airlines colours. Peter Sweeten/Aviation Images Worldwide

Israel's El Al flies the 757 on routes to Europe and Asia. Peter Sweeten/Aviation Images Worldwide

Ethiopian Airlines flies to many high-altitude airports in hot climates, a hindrance for many aircraft, but not the 757. Peter Sweeten/Aviation Images Worldwide

most popular aircraft employed on the heavily travelled North Atlantic corridor. More than thirty airlines make more than twice as many transatlantic crossings per month with the 767 as with the Airbus A300-600 and A310 twin-jets combined. Among the airlines that fly the 767 across the Atlantic are Aeromexico, Air Canada, Air France, American Airlines, Avianca, Britannia, British Airways, Canadian Airlines, Delta Air Lines, El Al, LanChile, LOT, Malev, SAS, TWA, United and US Airways.

The 767 also links primary and secondary population centres in Europe,

Thanks to 180-minute ETOPS, the aircraft is also popular from North America to Hawaii, from Australia to Asia, and from Japan to points in south-east Asia, or even from North America to Asia. Across portions of the Pacific, the 767 is flown by Air Canada, Canadian Airlines, Air China, Air New Zealand, Air Pacific, All Nippon Airways, American Airlines, Asiana, EVA, Gulf Air, Japan Airlines, LAN Chile and Qantas. Air Canada, Canadian, Air New Zealand and Qantas are operating between Honolulu and the west coast of North America. Air New Zealand and Qantas also fly more than

and 767s also fly such routes as New York–Los Angeles, Vancouver–Honolulu, Seattle–Seoul, Washington–Frankfurt, Vienna–Bangkok, Tokyo–Hong Kong, Sydney–Singapore, Santiago–New York and Miami–Rio de Janeiro.

With its range advantage, and as a result of the economics of operating a twin-engined plane, the 767 is used by airlines constantly to open up new non-stop flights. The 767 connects smaller cities, where traffic is not heavy enough to justify larger widebodies. In recent years, such routes as Hamburg–Atlanta, Manchester–Chicago and Washington–Munich

Taiwan's EVA Air operates four 767-300s (pictured) and four -200 models. Peter Sweeten/Aviation Images Worldwide

Africa and Asia with direct intercontinental services. Among the airlines using the plane to connect Europe with Asia and Africa are Air China, Air France, Air Mauritius, Air Seychelles, Air Zimbabwe, All Nippon Airways, Britannia, Condor, Egyptair, El Al, Ethiopian Airlines, EVA, Gulf Air, Lauda, LOT, Malev, Martinair, Royal Brunei and SAS.

2,000 ETOPS flights a month between New Zealand and Australia, and to Singapore, Japan and other points in Asia.

The 767-300 is an important plane in Asia, where jumbo jets are widely used on domestic flights. The type is also used on densely travelled intra-European routes. British Airways, for instance, uses the 767-300 on short routes such as London-Paris,

have emerged simply because the 767 seats just enough people, and flies efficiently enough for the route to be profitable. Delta Air Lines has also used the 767, replacing L-1011s, to aggressively expand its international network.

767s are used with 757s to provide the bulk of transcontinental service within the United States. By far the most non-stop flights between the east and west coasts are operated by the family.

The 767 has carried more than 800 million passengers on more than 3 million flights, for more than 18 million fight hours. The 767-300 is in the air for an average of 11 hours per day. The dispatch rate, a measure of fleet reliability, is about 99 per cent, as is schedule reliability, an industry measure of departure from the gate within 15 minutes of scheduled time.

more efficiently than any other single-aisle twin-jet.

The plane is both an intercontinental airliner and a rugged, dependable transport that meets rigorous demands of commuter schedules. The 757 flies farther for less money per trip than any other airliner. Its seat- and ton-mile operating costs are lower than those of any aircraft of comparable size. The plane addresses the spectrum of mission requirements –

altitude or hot weather. The 757 can depart from high, hot airports such as Denver, Mexico City and Nairobi, with full payloads and virtually without compromising range capability.

Airlines fly the versatile 757 on a wide variety of routes. The plane can serve city pairs as far apart as 4,636 miles (7,417km), and as close together as 41 miles (65km) with equal aplomb. The 757 flies an average of nine hours a day. Like its larger

A Japan Airlines 767-300 takes off from Tokyo's Haneda Airport on a high-density domestic fight. Ito Noriyuki

The 757

Although originally designed as a replacement on hub-and-spoke systems, the 757 is used today to bypass crowded hubs and offer point-to-point service on lower-demand routes that many competing jetliners cannot fly because of economic or performance reasons. The 757 can fly more passengers to more destinations

whether point-to-point, multiple-stage regional, non-stop transcontinental or inclusive tour.

The 757 serves busy hubs and small airports with equal ease; wherever the 737 can operate, so, too, can the larger 757. No other airliner in its class can maintain its range and passenger capability when operating into airports limited by runway length, strength, weight restrictions, high

cousin, the 757 also has a dispatch reliability of about 99 per cent.

The 757 can easily fly non-stop from the US East Coast to any city on the West Coast. From London, the 757 can cover all of eastern Africa and well into the Middle East. Out of Bahrain, the aircraft can reach Europe, and from Hong Kong the 757 can cover all of India, and touch down in Australia.

Another example of a Japan Airlines 767-300, taxiing at Haneda Airport. Ito Noriyuki

Japan's All Nippon Airways operates twenty 767-200s, seen here taking off from Haneda. Ito Noriyuki

In the United States, the largest commercial aviation market in the world, the 757 has helped to spur new routes, such as Boston–Portland, Oregon, and New York–San Diego; before, connections would have been needed in order for passengers to complete their journeys. Today, it is the most popular plane on coast-to-coast routes, an economical alternative to a widebody. A

Cologne, Germany. Mexicana employs the aircraft on its Cancun–Buenos Aires run of 4,281 miles (6,849km). TWA, having disposed of its ageing fleet of 747s and L-1011s, uses the 757 from St Louis to Honolulu, a route spanning 4,121 miles (6,593km). Russia's Transaero flies the 757 from Moscow to Yuzhno Sakhalinski, covering 4,134 miles (6,614km).

Africa and points in the Middle East. It is also popular from the United States to South America, where many of the airports are in hot and high locations.

Some of the 757's diverse array of regularly scheduled routes are Boston–Seattle, New York–San Francisco, Miami–Cali, London–Cairo, Hong Kong–Beijing, Orlando–Reykjavik, Chicago–San Diego,

All Nippon also flies forty 767-300s to go with twenty -200 models, making the carrier the largest 767 operator outside the United States. This version is shown in Pocket Monster colours. Ito Noriyuki

dramatic increase in international service has led US carriers to shift their 767s to overseas routes instead of long domestic flights. In 1982, only one daily transcontinental flight was flown with a narrow-body aircraft. Today, more than 100 of these flights are served by single-aisle transports, and the bulk of them are 757s.

Despite its billing as a medium-range airliner, the 757 can serve a unique variety of long-haul routes. Germany's Condor uses the plane on its longest regularly scheduled flight: 4,636 miles (7,417km) from Puerto Plata, Dominican Republic to

Because the 757 is economical on shorter routes, it is employed on such hops as Sarasota–Tampa (41 miles, or 65km) and St Croix–St Thomas (45 miles, or 72km) by Delta Air Lines; from Tenerife–Las Palmas (73 miles, or 117km) by Spanair; and by United Airlines from Denver to Colorado Springs (74 miles, or 118km), and San Francisco–Monterrey (78 miles, or 124km).

The 757 can serve routes from North America to Hawaii, South America to Easter Island, Brazil to Europe, Australia to Southeast Asia, and from Europe to

Pittsburgh–Los Angeles, Los Angeles–Hawaii, Newark–Shannon, Toronto–Manchester, Bogota–New York and New York–Madrid.

On the heels of the 767, 757s are increasingly popular across the Atlantic. New city-pairs are opening up with the aircraft, and one of the new cities is Birmingham, England. British Airways started a daily 757 service from Birmingham to New York's John F. Kennedy International Airport and Toronto in 1996, while Continental Airlines opened an additional service to Newark, New Jersey,

The 757 is found in the fleets of six Chinese airlines, including China Southern, shown here on final approach at Hong Kong. Carlos Borda

Avianca of Colombia is one of six Latin American airlines flying the 757, shown here landing at Los Angeles. Kristian Damboulev

767s and 757s are popular among charter carriers because of their fuel-efficiency, passenger capacity and schedule flexibility. Brittania is among those flying 767-200s, with six examples in its fleet. Ralph Olson/Flying Images Worldwide

Air 2000 is among a handful of British charter carriers operating the 757, which can reach North and South America. Michael Pellaton/Flying Images Worldwide

with a 757 in 1997. This city in the Midlands is an example of the trend towards new non-stop transatlantic services from regional cities using medium-sized twin-jets.

The 757 is also commonly used by airlines to enter new markets with lower demand – the so-called 'long, thin routes'. One of these is Cleveland–London, a

The 757 is a favourite aircraft among European charter carriers, which employ the type from northern Europe, particularly Britain, the Netherlands and Germany, to the sun-drenched beaches of the Canary Islands, Spain, Italy and Greece. All six of Britain's major charter carriers – Britannia Airways, Airtours International, Monarch Airlines, Air 2000, Caledonian and Air-

to Izmir, Munich to Mali, or Zurich to Luxor.

The 757 is a perfect fit for two northern European airlines, Icelandair and Finnair. Both airlines take advantage of the aircraft's size and range to fill market niches. Icelandair, a 757 operator since 1990, works its aircraft hard, logging an average 14-hour daily block times. The airline has

LTU, a German charter airline, flies 757s from Germany to southern Europe, Africa and the Middle East.
Thorsten Eichner

route which, in the past, would have been impossible to inaugurate profitably with a larger aircraft. The 757's efficiency and low operating costs make launching a new route an easier proposition.

The 757 is the perfect aircraft for Continental Micronesia, a Pacific carrier that feeds Asian cities to its hub on Guam, on routes on which larger aircraft are simply too expensive to operate for relatively light loads. The 757 is also reliable enough to fly over thousands of miles of open ocean, without a dot of land – let alone a landing strip – in sight. For Continental Micronesia, which covers far-flung destinations scattered across the vast South Pacific, the 757 is efficient and reliable.

world – operate 757s. The type is equally well adapted to flights from the US to the Caribbean islands, which have notoriously short airfields. It is a workhorse of the leisure-travel industry. Tour operators choose the 757 because it gives them low operating costs, exceptional range and 180-minute ETOPS ability, and they are able to change the aircraft's interiors.

As charter airliners, 757s can fly from Edmonton to Maui, Los Angeles–Montego Bay, Toronto–Havana, New York–Aruba or Boston–Tenerife. From Europe, virtually any major city can be reached along the US East Coast and the Midwest, as well as Caribbean resorts. The 757 can fly from Glasgow to Las Palmas, Hamburg

one of the top three utilization rates in the world, with an average stage length of 3.7 hours. Because of Iceland's location, in the middle of the Atlantic, the airline serves both North America and Europe. One of Icelandair's 757s is used for Greenlandair, ferrying passengers between Denmark and Greenland. Icelandair achieved a record engine time-on-wing milestone for a Rolls-Royce RB211-535E4, of more than 32,000 hours.

Finnair received its first 757 in 1998, to fill the seating gap between its MD-80s and MD-11s, and to add additional leisure-traffic capacity. One popular route is Helsinki–Las Palmas, a route too small for an MD-11, and too far for the 757's prime

The 757 is a perfect fit for Icelandair to fill niche routes. Miguel Snoep

competitor, the A321-200. For Finnair, the 757 was the right solution.

Besides the Concorde, the 757 is the most-sought-after aircraft for round-the-world charter flights, for which passengers pay £10,000 or more. It is used frequently on routes that include stops at Easter Island and Mongolia, places where the Concorde or larger aircraft cannot land. Its range makes it an ideal choice for such a mission.

Because it can land on short runways and operate efficiently at high altitudes, the 757 has also been used to open new, seasonal routes into ski resorts in the American Rockies in the state of Colorado. American Airlines uses the 757 on flights from New York, Dallas, Chicago and Miami to such resorts as Aspen and Vail. Delta and Northwest also use the 757s for the same purpose from their hubs in Atlanta and Minneapolis, respectively. The service bypasses busy Denver airport, getting passengers to the slopes more quickly, eliminating a commuter flight or avoiding a long, hazardous drive along icy highways.

The 757, like the 767, is a good neighbour, particularly in Europe, where the most

stringent noise restrictions are imposed. Since the 1960s, high-bypass engines have reduced jetliner noise by about 75 per cent, or 20 decibels. To put that in perspective, 20 decibels represents the difference in volume between a large truck passing nearby and wind rustling through trees. Noise impact of a 757 take-off is typically confined within airport boundaries. Because it is so quiet, its operators can serve even the most restrictive airports, day or night, and it has, as a result, helped to open up routes to such noise-sensitive airports in the United States as Washington's National Airport and Orange County California's John Wayne Airport.

Coupled with the 767, with its larger capacity and longer range, the 757 offers airlines a 'one-type' solution for medium- and long-range markets. The fuel and operating efficiency of both aircraft is most important to airlines. Trans World Airlines, which teetered on the verge of bankruptcy twice in the 1990s, made the 757 and 767-300 a vital part of its fleet-renewal plan, replacing ageing 747s and L-1011s on transcontinental and transatlantic routes. The newer jets helped improve TWA's on-time performance and

beefed up a meagre bottom line, and they have been a major weapon in the airline's hard-fought recovery from bankruptcy. Through much of the 1990s, TWA had the oldest fleet of the major American carriers, but it is now able to catch up quickly. The 757 is about 25 per cent cheaper to operate than the L-1011 it replaced. A 757, for instance, costs an average of $2,571 per hour to operate, compared with $2,470 for a 727, but can carry 35 more passengers, or $3.42 per available seat-mile against $4.67 for a 727-200. This includes crew cost, fuel and oil, taxes, insurance, depreciation and maintenance.

Not all 757s are the low-cost jets that Boeing's marketing people like to talk about. Royal Brunei Airlines' three 757s feature leather seats, and have gold and crystal adorning the interior. The oil-rich sultanate employs the 757s on routes to south-east Asia and one-stops to London. The airline's order in 1985 was the first of the 757s to feature three-class configuration. The lavatory, twice the standard size, has a marble-look counter, gold-and-crystal fixtures, laser-carved walnut trim and a leather bench to hide the toilet.

CHAPTER TWELVE

Continuous Improvement and Records

Designers and engineers constantly strive to improve the products we use. From cars to computers, light bulbs to lenses, virtually every product on the market has improved over time, as developments in technology have gathered pace. Commercial aircraft are no different. The 767s and 757s produced today are, on the inside, completely different from the aircraft that rolled off the assembly lines in the early days of the programmes. New technology and designs, and cost-saving measures have all been incorporated into this dynamic duo, with more changes planned in the future. This aircraft, which was introduced at the time when vinyl 45s were still popular, must keep up with a world that craves the portable CD player.

Boeing works closely with airlines to identify technologies that might enhance the aircraft. Since the introduction of the 767 and 757, hundreds of improvements have been built in, or added as options. As well as systems and performance enhancements, which increase safety, simplify operations and maintenance, and reduce costs, interior flexibility has been improved in order to increase the revenue potential of the aircraft and passenger convenience.

Changes to the 767

Changes in the 767 have helped to enhance its ability to fly over oceans, lowered its weight, reduced maintenance costs, improved electronic engine controls, increased safety standards, extended the aircraft's life, and improved communications. Since the aircraft entered service in 1982, some of the changes have included: 120-minute ETOPS ability (1985), windshear detection (1986), carbon brakes (1987), 180-minute ETOPS (1988), improved fire-worthy interiors (1990), improved fuel system (1991), provisions for Global Positioning System (1992), improved autopilot (1992), expanded and improved corrosion protection (1992), take-off performance

improvement (1994), improved acrylic passenger windows (1994), and a SAT-COM communications system (1997). The precision of GPS – which can tell pilots the aircraft's position within feet – along with automated air traffic control functions and advanced guidance and communications features, was made available as part of the new Future Air Navigation System (FANS) flight-management computer, introduced in 1998.

To improve the model's capabilities, Boeing introduced the 767-200ER in 1984, the 767-300ER in 1988 and higher gross-weight -300ERs in 1991 and 1993. The first flight of the -200ER took place on 6 March 1984. The model featured a larger centre fuel tank and increased gross weight of 345,000lb (156,490kg). The first ER was delivered to Ethiopian Airlines on 23 May 1984. Optional higher gross weights offered are 351,000lb (159,200kg), 380,000lb (172,400kg) and 387,000lb (175,500kg).

Development of the 767-300ER began in January 1985, offering increased gross weights of 380,000lb (172,400kg), 387,000lb (175,500kg) and 412,000lb (186,900kg). The type was certified in late 1987, with delivery to American Airlines beginning in February 1988.

As well as these improvements, which changed the scope of the family, other changes were made to keep the aircraft safe. In one example, Boeing redesigned the latch mechanism on the overwing emergency escape hatch after three incidents in which the slide came loose from the aircraft during flight. The slide is stowed in a small hatch in the wing-body fairing, just aft of the overwing escape exit. It was designed so that when the emergency door is moved, a spring is released, popping the hatch open and deploying the slide. Boeing also had to redesign a removable cover for the recess containing the handle that activates the escape slide after a de-planing passenger inadvertently deployed the slide, using the handle to help himself out of his seat.

New Brakes

The 767 family has new carbon brakes. AlliedSignal Bendix has been developing them for three years, using a material called CARBENIX 4100. They are expected to have a longer life, offer smoother operation and be quieter than existing brakes. The brakes, to be installed on new 767s or retrofitted on older ones, are a step beyond the advanced carbon system found on the 777, and a far cry from the first 767 brakes, which were made of steel.

To certify the brakes, Boeing borrowed an American Airlines 767-300 and flew it to Edwards Air Force Base in California. There, a team performed a maximum brake-energy rejected take-off (RTO) test, one of many tests required to be undertaken before certification.

What pressure did these brakes face? The force of a 767-300 landing at nearly 200mph (320km/h) – far faster than the average landing – creates intense heat exceeding more than 3,400°F (1,649°C). In the first 15 seconds after stopping, the brakes generate enough energy to power a home for three to four months. After such a violent event, the carbon brakes glow white hot and the tyres deflate, for safety reasons. The brakes passed the test and were certified for service.

Changes to the 757

Much has changed on the 757, too. Boeing introduced overwing exits and carbon brakes in 1984; a new, wide-aisle interior in 1987; freighter improvements in 1989; 180-minute ETOPS, a cargo conveyor system, a higher gross-weight version and improved fire protection, all in 1990; enhanced flight-data recorder capability and a better thrust-management computer in 1991; an improved flight-control computer, a new movable class divider, passenger service unit and ceiling-mounted videos in 1992; an improved flight-deck lining in 1993; and communications enhancements in 1997. New avionics, provisions for GPS, a new fuel gauge and new leading-edge wing flaps are among hundreds of changes in an ongoing improvement process. The electrical cooling system has been updated, and insulation blankets were resealed because they were retaining moisture. Cockpit windows, as on the 767, have also been replaced with glass, because the acrylic ones showed fine cracking. Recent developments include an improved flight-deck lining and floor-beam corrosion protection. Boeing introduced the extended-range version of the 757 in May 1986, with delivery to Royal Brunei Airlines.

'The airplane today is not the same plane by a long shot,' says Doug Miller, chief engineer on the 757 for seven years. 'The changes have been subtle, aimed at increasing reliability, maintenance and passenger appeal.'

New passenger service units (PSUs), which contain the oxygen masks and reading lights, are among the most noticeable improvements in newer 757s. PSUs on older 757s were dedicated left- or right-hand units. The new ones, with slight changes to the latches, are used on both sides of the aisle. The new units save money because all bulbs – whether for reading, flight attendant calls or passenger information – can be changed without opening the unit. They also weigh less and last longer; the reading bulb's life is twice that of the old unit. Many airlines prefer to stow life vests in the PSUs to reduce the chances of passengers walking out with them as souvenirs, a problem common in the early days of the 757. Each PSU can include an optional stand-alone life-vest module, with the capacity for one life vest per seat. Each module has three transparent lenses to verify quickly that the vests are in place. A passenger-operated push-latch mechanism in the door allows the door to drop open 45 degrees to remove the vests.

In addition to saving money, the new PSU complements adjustable-pitch seating, another feature of newer 757s. Each unit can easily be repositioned to match changes in seat pitch. When changing from three-abreast economy to two-across business seating on each side of the plane, one of the passenger reading lamps is turned off and the other two are re-aimed, and this is done entirely from below without special tools. This versatility permits the same plane to fly hub-and-spoke operations during the week, and high-density charters on weekends.

Likewise, seat sizes on the 757 can be changed, so that the same plane can be used for multiple markets. A flexible-pitch quick-release mechanism for the seat-track fittings makes it possible to change seat-row pitch and add or remove seat rows

within hours. A handle releases the seat-track attachment fittings, allowing the seat to move freely in the track, and it can be locked in any 1in (2.5cm) increment. Telescoping seat-track covers attached to the seat leg extend or retract to maintain a consistent floor surface. When the seat is in the desired location, closing the handle pushes pins into the gaps in the seat track. A locking device prevents any tampering with the seat handle. To remove the seat from the track, the handle is fully rotated to completely release the attachment fitting, and the seat is lifted away. Seats can be added or removed by just one person.

Newer 757s also feature a movable class divider that lets airlines adjust the ratio of premium- to economy-class seating. Designed not to bind or jam, this improved unit rolls smoothly on recessed tracks mounted beneath the overhead stowage bins. To move it, an airline employee simply unlocks the divider, rolls it to the desired location and locks it into place. By combining the divider with any or all of these features, airlines can gain cost-effective cabin flexibility tailored to their specific operational requirements. This flexibility enables operators to adjust available business-class seating capacity to meet business travel demand on a flight-by-flight basis, increasing revenues and passenger satisfaction. These features can be retrofitted on older models. Video screens on newer 757s are 13in (33cm) wide, and mounted under stowage bins. Unlike ceiling-mounted screens, under-bin screens make it easy to adjust class dividers.

In 1986, a mechanized cargo-handling system was developed to enable airlines to fill excess space on 757s with revenue-producing cargo, even with short turnarounds. The system had been used for years on 747s and 767s, but until then had been absent from standard-body aircraft. Instead of having to be loaded by handlers scrambling on their hands and knees through a cramped hold, the system sends a container up a belt and into the aircraft, where lateral belts engage and move the cargo through the hold. The 757 was a natural for a mechanized system. Its cargo doors open outwards and up, whereas the doors of the 737, for example, open into the hold, presenting an obstacle to bulky cargo. With the conveyor system, a complete load of containers can be offloaded and loaded by just one person in 10 minutes – it would take three people about 45 minutes to do the same job manually.

Using the system to unload baggage means that passengers will be able to claim their belongings about 13 minutes earlier.

Re-contoured sidewall panels became available on the 757 in 1987. The new panels provide greater clearance at the head and elbow for passengers and give the entire cabin a more spacious appearance. Another change made to 757s was a 2in (5cm) increase in the width of the aisle. This move, also incorporated into 737s, was aimed at increasing the aircraft's competitiveness with the Airbus A320 family, which offered a 20in (50cm) aisle when the aircraft entered service in 1988. That small increase can make a big difference, for example, allowing a passenger to slide past a food cart in the aisle. The wider aisle could have been achieved simply by shoving the seats outwards, but that would have limited head and shoulder room. Instead, it was decided to re-sculpt the sidewall panels. The air-conditioning outlets were relocated, the overhead inward curve of the plane was shaved and lights were recessed behind stowage bins. The change also reduced the perceived mass of the stowage bins, so the interior appeared larger. The change became standard in mid-1987 at a cost of $10 million; half was spent on moving the air-conditioning system and half on the new sidewall tooling. Legroom was not affected.

In response to airline requests, newer 757 interiors offer continuous handrails extending the length of the passenger cabin, along both sides of the aisle. Designed to help cabin crews work efficiently and safely during turbulence, these rails also provide support during such routine tasks as serving window-seat occupants.

The 757 received some flak in the early 1990s when a popular American magazine, *Consumer Reports*, told the public to avoid the aircraft because of poor cabin-air quality. Boeing countered by saying that, as on any of its aircraft, 50 per cent of the air on board a 757 is filtered and combined with fresh air. The 757 changes its air every two minutes, which is better than most buildings.

Safety Records

The 767 and 757 have been exceptionally safe airliners, which have undertaken millions of hours of service with just a handful of fatal accidents. Both the 767 and 757 completed their first eight years of airline service with a perfect safety record, and one of their most significant achievements was proving the reliability and enhanced safety of the glass cockpit.

The perfect safety record was broken when a 757 found itself at the wrong place at the wrong time. On 2 October 1990, a China Southern Airlines 757 was waiting to take off from Guangzhou, China, when it was hit on the left wing and top fuselage by a hijacked Xiamen Airlines 737. The 737 touched down hard, the result of a struggle in the cockpit, clipped a parked 707, and then collided with the China Southern jet. One hundred and thirty-two people perished on both planes.

Lauda Air Flight 4

On 26 May 1991, Lauda Air flight 4, a 767-300 en route from Bangkok to Vienna, crashed in a remote jungle hillside 130 miles (210km) north-west of the Thai capital. All 213 passengers and 10 crew members were killed. The plane was nearly new – it had completed just 95 cycles.

The new plane was climbing at 25,000ft (7,620m), in good weather conditions, when it disappeared from radar screens. Whatever caused the crash struck swiftly, leaving the crew no time to report trouble. Later, the reason for the crash was determined to be an in-flight deployment of the port-side engine thrust reverser, which helps to slow down a plane after it has landed. Investigators were not able to determine what caused the uncommanded deployment of the thrust reversers, but concluded that either the hydraulic or electrical systems could have been at fault. The destruction of the aircraft, plummeting straight into the jungle, was so extensive that no determination could be made.

The reverser is powered from an engine's hydraulic system and is controlled by two valves. The isolation valve is normally off, to depressurize the reverser except when it is needed, and mechanical locks keep the fan sleeve in the stowed position. The directional control valve applies the hydraulic power to either open or close the reverser. Most 767 thrust reversers are commanded by mechanical cables from the cockpit, but newer models have engines with electronically commanded reversers. The Lauda 767 was one of these. In a simulation conducted during the crash investigations, the engine thrust automatically returned to idle when the reverser was deployed. The accident

prompted the FAA to order airlines to disable thrust reversers on all 767s with electronic controls.

Two 757 crashes involved pilot ignorance of some aspect of the automated flight-control or flight-management systems.

American Airlines Flight 965

On 20 December 1995, an American Airlines 757 collided into a mountain near Cali, Colombia, bringing into question how much pilots rely on the automated flight systems that the plane helped to pioneer. Flight 965 from Miami crashed 38 miles (60km) north of Cali during descent under instrument flight rules. The flight was operating in a radar surveillance environment until a few minutes before the crash. The plane was on autopilot, and it was a clear night. Only four of the 156 passengers and eight crew members survived when the plane flew wildly off course.

The 757 crashed at 8,900ft (2,713km) more than 10 miles (16km) off course. Air traffic control read-outs left no clue to any malfunction or difficulty in the flight deck. The flight data recorder, however, gave a better picture of what had happened during flight 965's approach to Cali. When the flight was cleared for approach to Runway 19, it was just north of the town of Tulua. As the crew was entering the approach into the flight-management computer, the aircraft passed over Tulua continuing southbound. Because Tulua marks the beginning of the approach, once the computer was programmed, the plane's autopilot attempted to turn the aircraft back to Tulua, resulting in the plane flying east for about one minute. The crew then re-oriented the aircraft to proceed directly to another nearby town, Rozo.

By this time, they were far enough off course to the east that proceeding directly to Rozo would mean hitting the surrounding high terrain. Examination of the cockpit flight recorder shows that there was confusion both between the crew members, and between the crew and the air traffic control centre. The approach to Runway 19 follows a course down a narrow canyon. The approach only just meets minimum criteria for safe margins. The crew was apparently unaware of its position when the plane turned east after passing Tulua, otherwise they would have known they were entering an unsafe flight path. The crew made no mention to Cali approach that they had deviated from course. They also

seemed unable to orient themselves or properly programme the flight-management system. From the beginning of the easterly turn, it was four minutes to impact. Transcripts of the cockpit voice recorder leave many questions about what the crew was attempting to do and exactly where they believed themselves to be. The crash brought to light just how much crews place their trust in the 757 and 767 flight system.

Birgenair and Aeroperu

On 6 February 1996, a 757 carrying 176 passengers and 13 crew members for the German-based Turkish charter airline Birgenair, bound for Berlin via Gander, Canada, crashed into the Caribbean Sea near Puerto Plata, Dominican Republic. The impact broke the plane apart. The aircraft was climbing through 7,000ft (2,100m) when it was observed on radar starting a right descending turn. It then disappeared. The US National Transportation Safety Board determined that the crash was the result of a mechanical deficiency. The cockpit voice recorder and flight data recorder showed that the static port system aboard the flight, which is responsible for calculating airspeed, transmitted an erroneous indication. The discrepancy led to confusion in the cockpit, and pilot error was a contributing factor. The cockpit crew simply showed lack of comprehension of what the aircraft was doing, and why. The pilot, on discovering that one of the plane's airspeed indicators had malfunctioned, failed to switch to one of the other indicators. He had thought the 757 was flying too fast. In response to the erroneous reading, the crew slowed the plane down until it stalled, causing it to plummet from the sky. The sensor in question may have been blocked by an insect nest. The plane's black box, in 7,200ft (2,195m) of water, had to be recovered by unmanned submersible. Ultimately, the crash was blamed on both system malfunction and crew error.

The safety board found that the operations manual for the 757 did not contain procedures either to identify an erroneous airspeed indication, or to select the alternative air data source as a corrective manoeuvre. The plane's EICAS system, which provides alert messages to advise the pilots of system failures and abnormal operational conditions, does not produce a message to alert pilots regarding an unreliable airspeed indication. Following the

Liveries

Both aircraft are often used by airlines to display interesting or unique paint jobs. Several 757s in the fleet of US carrier America West Airlines are painted in unique designs to reflect the major states they serve, including Arizona, Nevada, California and Ohio. Two of its 757s also bear the colours and trademarks of two sports teams, the Phoenix Suns basketball team and the Arizona Diamond Backs baseball team.

To honour the 1996 Olympics in its home city Atlanta, Delta Air Lines repainted a 767-200, renaming it Spirit of Delta. The plane, N102DA, was re-dedicated with the striking blue, red, and violet colours of the 1996 Summer Olympic Games before an emotional gathering of 7,000 employees. It was the only aircraft painted in the special livery, although other Delta aircraft did sport a smaller Olympics logo. Delta's new livery, unveiled in 1997, was first spotted on one of its 767-300s. After 35 years, a new colour scheme was introduced on N190DN. The aircraft was ferried in white from Seattle on 26 March, painted in Atlanta and photographed prior to rollout on 2 April. The full 'Delta Air Lines' title replaced 'DELTA' on the fuselage. New shades of blue and red were also selected, and the Delta widget logo was retained only on the fuselage, not the tail. When Delta, in common with other airlines around the world, faced economic difficulties in the early 1990s, employees purchased a 767 through payroll deductions. Delta is not the only airline to promote the Olympics on a 767.

United Parcel Service, in celebration of being a corporate sponsor for the 1998 Winter Olympics and the 2000 Summer Games, has applied a dozen athletic images in the five Olympic colours against an all-white fuselage on several 767-300 and 757 freighters.

As a leading aircraft among charter carriers, both types are frequently painted in vibrant, colourful hues reflecting holidays. Condor, for instance, has painted a 757 with a mural depicting fun-loving, sunglass-wearing holidaymakers surrounded by stars, birds and hearts. This 'Rizzi-Bird' design was painted to mark the airline's 40th anniversary.

Delta Air Lines introduced its new livery on the 767-300 in 1997. Michael Pellaton/Flying Images Worldwide

SAS painted its largest aircraft, the 767-300, in the colours of the Star Alliance, the global airline partnership of which SAS is a founding member. Andreas Mowinckel

Liveries *(continued)*

America West uses a 757 to depict teamwork. The aircraft is pictured at the airline's hub in Phoenix. Bill Dellinges

accident, the safety board recommended that Boeing should revise its flight manuals to alert pilots to conditions that forward an erroneous airspeed indication, and include a detailed emergency procedure addressing the identification and elimination of an erroneous airspeed indication. As a result, a 'caution' alert is now emitted when erroneous airspeed is detected.

Another 757 crashed shortly after take-off on 2 October 1996. The Aeroperu 757 plummeted into the Pacific Ocean after taking off from Lima on a flight to Santiago, Chile. All 70 people on board were killed. The crash occurred because maintenance workers forgot to remove the tape-and-paper covers they had put over pressure sensors while polishing the plane. As a result, safety officials recommended that airlines should be required to use 'only standardized, highly conspicuous covers with warning flags attached' to cover static ports when planes are serviced. Shortly after the crash, Boeing began to manufacture brightly coloured covers for the pressure sensors, which are about 1in (2.5cm) in diameter.

Just before the crash, the pilot radioed air traffic controllers to say that he did not know where he was, and that his instruments had gone haywire. The National Transportation Safety Board found that, because of the partial blockage of pressure-sensing instruments, one automatic system in the cockpit was indicating that the plane was flying too slowly and would fall out of the sky, while another sounded an alarm that it was flying too fast. According to the safety board, a partial blockage in the static port would create a lag in airspeed and altitude readings, 'that will cause the readings to be too low while climbing and too high while descending'. Aeroperu said that pre-flight procedure called for the first officer to make sure ports and vents are not obstructed.

Running Out of Fuel

Perhaps the most dramatic crash of a 767 was caught on videotape and shown around the world. On 23 November 1996, an Ethiopian Airlines 767-200 en route from Addis Ababa to Abidjan, Ivory Coast, crashed just off the beach at Moroni, Comoros Islands, after running out of fuel during a hijacking. One hundred and twenty-seven people aboard died, including the hijackers. The captain and co-pilot were among the 50 people who survived.

Three unemployed Ethiopian youths had hijacked flight 961 and demanded that the crew fly the plane to Australia. It was running out of fuel when the captain decided to ditch the plane in the water off a resort beach on Grand Comoros Island.

Another 767 was the subject of an embarrassing and dangerous – although not fatal – mistake. Early in its service, an Air Canada 767 had to land at a remote glider field in Manitoba because it ran out of fuel. Why? The cockpit crew mistook pounds for kilos of fuel, and did not notice until it was too late. Thanks to the 767's large wings, the aircraft was able to glide for half an hour and make an emergency landing.

Minor Incidents

Both the 757 and 767 have had several minor problems which have required action from regulatory agencies. The FAA ordered operators of older 767s to inspect all take-off and landing flaps in 1997 after a 21ft (6.5m) flap ripped off a Delta Air

Lines model while the plane was preparing to land. Three of the six heavy titanium bolts holding the 32ft (9.75m) flap to the wing had failed.

In July 1996, worn electrical systems may have triggered the explosion of a TWA 747. 747s were inspected for this problem, and, in 1998, 231 US-registered 767s were inspected to uncover any chafing of fuel-tank wire insulation inside the metal conduits that enclose those wires.

Several incidents have been reported in which small, general-aviation aircraft following a 757 in a landing pattern have crashed, due in part to the wake turbulence behind the 757. The accidents prompted the FAA to determine whether it should change separation distances for aircraft landing behind a 757. One explanation for this problem is that, since the 757 can land at much smaller airports than most large aircraft, it interacts more with smaller aircraft. Another problem is its size, which makes it difficult to classify – it is not a heavy widebody nor a small 737.

Completing eight years of airline service with a perfect safety record – proving the reliability and enhanced safety of the digital cockpit – was one of Boeing's most significant achievements with the 767 and 757. And Boeing learned from the dynamic duo, and made further improvements in the 747-400, whose two-member crew

digital flight deck has 606 fewer lights, gauges and switches than the standard 747, 22 fewer than the 757 and 767, and 100 fewer than the much smaller 737.

Aviation Records

The efficient and versatile 767 and 757 hold a number of aviation records.

On 1 June 1984, the first 767-200ER for Ethiopian Airlines set a twin-jet airliner distance record, flying 7,500 miles (12,082km) from Washington, DC, to Addis Ababa, Ethiopia, in 13 hours 17 minutes. That mark was topped on 18 April 1988, when an Air Mauritius 767-200ER flew 8,893 miles (14,309km) from Grand Rapids, Michigan, to the Seychelles in 16 hours 49 minutes. On 10 June 1990, a Royal Brunei 767-200ER set a new distance record for twin-engined aircraft, with a 9,253 mile (14,890km) flight from Seattle to Nairobi, Kenya, in 17 hours 51 minutes.

Air New Zealand set a speed record for a 767 when its 767-300ER delivery flight set a world speed record from Everett to Christchurch, New Zealand, on 28 October 1997. The four-person crew and 18 passengers made the 6,627 nautical mile (12,273km) journey in 14 hours 54 minutes.

The 757 has demonstrated remarkable performance at high-altitude airports,

where the air is thin and conventional aircraft must limit payloads in order to take off. In 1995, China Southwest Airlines inaugurated regular service to the world's highest-altitude commercial airport (14,219ft, or 4,334m) at Bangda, Tibet, from Chengdu, China, using a 757. Boeing, China's Civil Aviation Administration and China Southwest Airlines completed a survey flight in October 1994 to prepare for regular service. Prior to the route, people travelling from Chengdu to Tibet had to travel for three to five days by road to reach Chengdu, between Chengdu and Lhasa, Tibet. The trip by air takes one hour. The 757's performance at such a demanding altitude convinced the Chinese aviation authorities to order additional planes for various airlines in China.

In one remarkable 1991 demonstration, a 757 took off with the power of just one engine from Gongga Airport in Lhasa, Tibet. Gongga, one of the world's most challenging airfields, is the second-highest commercial airport in the world. It sits in a box canyon 11,621ft (3,542m) high in the Himalayas. The 757 showed its ability to serve the airport safely by circling within the canyon and landing again. Even with one engine out, the 757 out-performed the four-engined 707 that the Chinese use on such difficult, remote routes.

Air New Zealand set a speed record with a 767 on 28 October 1997. The 767-300 extended-range model took off from Boeing's factory in Everett on a non-stop flight to Christchurch. It completed the 6,627 nautical-mile (12,273km) flight in just under 15 hours. Boeing

CHAPTER THIRTEEN

The Competition and Other Uses

Following Boeing's absorption of McDonnell Douglas, airlines today have just two choices to fit their needs for jets seating more than 100 passengers: Boeing and Airbus. The industry has always been highly competitive, and, over the years, aircraft were developed as much to beat the competition as to satisfy the customer.

The A330-200 and A321-100

The 767 entered service partly to compete against the Airbus A300, the world's first twin-engined widebody, of which about 500 have been sold. In 1988, Airbus stopped developing the A300 family because the plane could not compete with

the range of the 767-300ER, and only a trickle of longer-range A300-600s are built today. The 767 also affected sales of the A310, a shorter, longer-range version of the A300.

The 767's latest version, the 767-400ER, was developed largely as a response to a new medium-sized widebody aircraft from

The Airbus Industrie A330-200, which entered service in 1998, is the 767's newest and fiercest competitor.
Airbus

Specification – A330-200

Dimensions:	Length 193ft 6in (59m); wingspan 197ft 10in (60.3m); width 17ft 4in (5.28m); tail height 58ft 9in (17.89m)
Passengers:	253 in three classes, 293 in two classes and 380 for charter
Fuel capacity:	36,750 gallons (139,100 litres)
Weights:	Plane weight 265,000lb (120,200kg); max. take-off weight 507,100lb (230,000kg)
Performance:	Range 7,422 miles (11,900km)
Service entry:	1998

Airbus, the A330-200. The Airbus A330-200, touted as the 767's greatest competitor, has had the advantage of flying for two years before the 767-400ER is scheduled to take to the air. The verdict among many airlines is that the A330-200, dubbed the 'jet of the 21st century', is the best and most efficient plane ever developed and built by the Europeans. The A330-200 is a shorter, longer-range version of the A330-300. It was developed as a replacement for the A300-600 and launched in November 1995. The A330-200 entered service with

The Airbus Industrie A321 — a stretched version of the popular A320 — was introduced in 1994 to compete in the same capacity as the 757. Airbus

Specification – A321-200

Dimensions:	Length 146ft (44.5m); wingspan 111ft 10in (34.1m); width 13ft (3.96m); tail height 38ft 9in (11.81m)
Passengers:	185 in two classes, 200 in single class
Fuel capacity:	6,261 gallons (23,700 litres)
Weights:	Plane weight 106,130lb (48,140kg); max. take-off weight 196,200lb (89,000kg)
Performance:	Range 2,992 miles (4,815km)
Service entry:	1997

Canada 3000 airlines in May 1998. Even before the model's first flight, ten customers had ordered 99 aircraft, compared with three customers who ordered 56 767-400s. The A330-200 poses a serious threat, it seems, to the 767's undisputed leadership in transatlantic travel.

'The A330-200 is a magnificent airplane,' says Dietmar Kirchner, deputy chairman of Germany's Condor. 'It will force Boeing to come out with its new 767-400 as quickly as possible, in order to remain competitive.' Engineers at LTU, another German charter company, calculated in 1996 that the A330-200 would show nearly 25 per cent lower operating costs compared with the 767-300ER. The A330-200 has a range of 7,500 miles (12,000km) in its standard version, which seats 256 passengers. The number can be increased to 350–380 seats to accommodate charter companies. The 767-300ER, by comparison, has a range of about 7,187 miles (11,500km), and the -400 even less.

The introduction of the A330-200 – which looks a lot like the 767, except for winglets on the wings – provides Airbus Industrie with yet another family member with a different capacity and range to compete effectively with Boeing. Airbus sees the plane as a replacement for ageing DC-10s and L1011s, as well as MD-11s and earlier A300s and A310s.

The A330-200 is closely related to the A330-300 on which it is based, and shares near-identical systems, airframe, cockpit and wings. The only difference is that it is 16ft (4.7m) shorter than the A330-300. To achieve the shrink, Airbus took out two fuselage plugs fore and aft of the wings. Because of the decreased length, the A330-200 features enlarged horizontal and vertical tail surfaces and a centre fuel tank, which gives it a greater fuel capacity than the -300. As Boeing did when it used lighter material on the 767, Airbus has introduced the aviation world to something new – the A330-200's rudder is made of carbon fibres.

The A330-200 has 35 more seats than the 767-300ER, in a three-cabin layout, providing airlines with a suitable aircraft to accommodate traffic growth for routes now served by 767-300ERs. The A330-200's increased range allows transatlantic routes from central Europe to the West Coast of North America. Just as the 767-300ER is an ideal long-haul aircraft for the inclusive-tour market, since the combination of its size and range makes it ideal for many charter carriers, the A330-200 is also a suitable long-haul aircraft. It offers these carriers an additional 55 seats in single-class layouts and 300 miles (500km) extra range over the 767-300. The A330-200 has eight more seats than the new 767-400.

The A330-200 and 767-400 are entering the market at a time when some operators are considering L-1011 or DC-10 replacements to absorb growth on the networks that first-generation widebody twins had pioneered.

John Quinlivan, the 767-400ER programme manager, maintains that his model is more efficient to operate than the A330-200 because it is easier and cheaper to stretch an aircraft than to shrink it. The A330-200 weighs more, adding to fuel costs and maintenance. Quinlivan claims that the 767-400 will be 4 per cent to 7 per cent cheaper to operate than its chief competitor. The A330-200 may also be too big for some airlines, providing an opportunity for the 767/757 family. Airbus will have to work hard to sell the new type to existing 767 operators because of the advantages of commonality.

Until recently, the 757 has had no direct competition in the 180-passenger market, but, on 18 March 1994, Airbus introduced the A321-100, a stretched version of the popular A320 twin-jet. The A321-100 seats 185 passengers in a two-class layout or 200 in a single class, a capacity fairly similar to that of the 757, but it offers less range than the 757. To address that deficiency, in 1995 Airbus launched the A321-200, an extended-range version that features a reinforced structure, higher-thrust CFM56 engines and an additional centre fuel tank holding 766 gallons (2,900 litres) of fuel. The changes increased maximum take-off weight to 196,210lb (89,000kg), slightly less than the 757, and increased range by 402 miles (648km) to more closely match the 757. Airbus had hoped that the changes would give the A321 increased market appeal on North American domestic routes, charter routes from northern to southern Europe, and on flights between Europe and the Middle East. The first flight of the A321-200 took place on 12 December 1996. The A321 does not quite match the capacity or performance of the 757, and is a slightly smaller aircraft, including overall length, weight, height and wing span.

The Tu-204

At first glance, the Russian Tupolev Tu-204 looks very much like the 757, except for winglets extending upwards from the wings. The Tu-204 was designed to replace the Tu-154 and Il-62 airliners, stalwarts of the former Soviet fleet. While not a major threat to the 757, the Tu-204 is expected to sell at least 500 units in Russia and other parts of the former Soviet Union over the next twenty years. There is also massive sales potential in China as both nations modernize their fleets and rid themselves of accident-prone and inefficient equipment. While Russian-made planes may not attract much interest in the Western world, some European airlines are eyeing the new plane for use as a medium-haul freighter.

The original Tu-204 first flew in 1989, but the model only began to attract attention when it made its first flight with Rolls-Royce RB211-535E4 engines – the first Russian plane with Western engines – on 14 August 1992. The aircraft can seat 184 passengers in two classes and up to 212 passengers in a single class, compared with

Specification – Tu-204-200	
Dimensions:	Length 150ft 11in (46m); wingspan 137ft 9in (42m); width 13ft 5in (4.1m); tail height 45ft 7in (13.9m)
Passengers:	184 in two-class, 212 in single class
Fuel capacity:	6,261 gallons (23,700 litres)
Weights:	Plane weight 130,070lb (59,000kg); max. take-off weight 244,155lb (110,750kg)
Performance:	Range 3,930 miles (6,330km)
Service entry:	1996

THE COMPETITION AND OTHER USES

up to 239 for the 757. The Tu-204, available in cargo and combi versions, has a maximum range of 4,100 miles (6,600km), a good 400 miles (640km) less than the 757. Compared to the 757, the Tu-204 has a longer wing-span and is wider. The Tu-204 entered revenue service on 23 February 1996.

While it does not match the 757's performance, the Tu-204 offers one favourable factor – the price. Sized between the A321 and 757, it has a list price of $36.8 million – half as much as a 757 or A321. Still, the plane has a credibility issue to overcome, something which does not affect the proven Boeing and Airbus models.

In many ways, Boeing's biggest competitor is Boeing itself. As it develops more derivatives to fill every conceivable market, Boeing is giving airlines more options to order different types of models. The longest version of the next-generation 737 family, for example, the stretched 737-900, is expected to seat around 180 passengers, just a handful fewer than the 757. The 737-900 is a response to the Airbus A321, but it will seat nine fewer passengers than the A321. Airlines flying 737s will undoubtedly prefer this model over a new 757, for the sake of commonality with the 737 family.

Cargo and Military

The 767 and 757 can do more than fly passengers and their belongings. Their range and reliability make them excellent as all-cargo aircraft, and the models are also used on a variety of military missions.

767 Freighter Models

As the world's largest all-cargo airline flying an extensive fleet of ageing DC-8s, United Parcel Service (UPS) looked to the 767-300 as a less expensive alternative for its short- and medium-haul routes. The first 767 freighter took off from Everett on 20 June 1995, carrying a load of flight-test equipment rather than parcels. The flight kicked off a relatively short test period of 60 flight-hours and an additional 300 hours of ground tests.

The 767 freighter has the same airframe and engines as passenger models. At issue during certification were the requirements for unique hardware and flight systems. Those systems include air flow and smoke detection in the main and lower

cargo holds, the capability to dispatch the aircraft with the cargo areas unpressurized, and an evacuation demonstration for crew members.

The flight-test programme for the 767 freighter involved three aircraft. The second rolled out of the factory on 18 July 1995, and the third followed a month later. Boeing launched the cargo-carrying derivative when UPS announced an order for up to sixty of the new freighters in January 1993, powered by GE CF6-80C2 engines (only thirty were delivered). Detailed design engineering began immediately following the order, with design reviews completed in July 1993 and April 1994. It entered production in January 1995, and was rolled out in May of that year. UPS took delivery of its first 767 freighter on 12 October 1985, for service between its base in Louisville, Kentucky, and Cologne, Germany, UPS's main European hub. This purchase by UPS was the largest order for all-cargo aircraft ever received by Boeing.

The 767-300 freighter is designed to accept 11,990 cubic ft (339.5 cubic m) in cargo containers on its main deck, plus 3,282 cubic ft (92.9 cubic m) of cargo in lower holds. A large cargo door on the main deck on the forward fuselage is used to load goods. Flight crews enter the plane through a single door just aft of the cockpit. The 767 freighter can carry 59 tons (53.56 tonnes) of payload for 3,450 miles (5,520km), or 45 tons (40.85 tonnes) as far as 4,600 miles (7,360km).

Unique to the 767 freighter are a 140 × 105in (350 × 262cm) main-deck cargo door; a rigid barrier between the larger-than-normal flight deck and main-deck cargo compartment; a manual cargo-loading system; smoke detection; and other environmental control system considerations. Below deck, the 767 can carry any of today's widebody cargo containers, including irregular shapes. Altogether, the 767 freighter can carry 24 modified A-2 containers, seven LD-9s, two LD-2s and 430 cubic ft (12 cubic m) of bulk cargo.

The 767-300 is also available with powered cargo-handling equipment both on the main deck and in lower holds. The system provides complete automation of the cargo-loading process. An operator navigates the system with control panels and joysticks. The aircraft's main deck has both interior and exterior master control panels, as well as local panels to provide maximum flexibility.

This version offers environmental control system changes that make the 767-300 suitable for transporting live animals and perishable goods. Plenty of fresh air is delivered, and temperatures can be controlled to cool or heat the freight appropriately. The main-deck cargo system offers the flexibility of accepting virtually all types of pallets and containers, from those used on 747s to those used on 757s.

In 1998, Boeing began offering a version of the shorter 767-200 to replace more DC-8s still flying with cargo carriers around the world. If successful, the development of the 767-200 could considerably alter the dynamics of the mid-sized freighter market. The first version is due to be delivered by the year 2000. The programme would involve converting older 767-200s. Modifications, to be done at Boeing's plant in Kansas, would involve completely removing the existing floor and replacing it with a strengthened main deck designed originally for the 767-300F. That version's freight door would be inserted in the front left section of the fuselage. Boeing decided to offer 767 conversions to counter efforts to transform older Airbus A300s, Lockheed L1011s and McDonnell Douglas DC-10s into freighters.

Older 767-200s are finding new life as cargo airliners. Instead of buying new aircraft, many cargo airlines are converting passenger aircraft. Airborne Express became the first cargo airline to convert a passenger-200 model, giving Airborne an aircraft with 35 per cent more capacity than its primary workhorse, the DC-8.

All 767-300ER models boast a larger cargo door than -200 models. As the -300 supplemented or replaced other widebody aircraft on long-distance passenger flights, the larger cargo doors had to accommodate larger air freight shipments, some connecting from larger aircraft.

The larger door gives airlines the option of carrying both standard containers and large pallets. Freight is loaded on the pallets, which are specially designed metal sheets, restrained with straps and netting. The larger door enables bigger shipments to be consolidated for easier handling, and not mixed with passenger baggage.

757 Freighter Models

The 757 has also found a home in the air-cargo industry, and has become a valuable workhorse, hauling both large container shipments and overnight express packages. The first derivative of the 757 was announced on 30 December 1985, when UPS ordered 20 freighter versions. Since then, the cargo carrier has ordered 60 more, with deliveries beginning in September 1987. The 757F, as it is known, has no windows, doors or interior amenities. A large main-deck cargo door is installed in the forward area of the fuselage's left-hand side. The flight crew boards the plane through a single entry door immediately aft of the flight deck on the left side of the aircraft.

for bulk loading. These provide a combined maximum revenue payload of 87,500lb (39,690kg), including container weight. With the maximum load, the 757 can fly 2,900 miles (4,020km).

The interior of the main-deck fuselage has a smooth fibreglass lining. A fixed rigid barrier installed in the front end of the main deck serves as a restraint wall between the cargo and the flight deck. A sliding door permits access from the flight deck to the cargo area. The 757F keeps costs to a minimum with its two-person

dard-body cargo airliner still in production. For airlines that do not want new ones, more and more older 757s are being converted to package freighters, as an economical way to increase cargo capacity.

In March 1986, Boeing launched the second derivative of the 757 with an order from Royal Nepal Airlines for a 757-200 Combi with mixed main-deck cargo and passenger capacity. In an unusual move, Boeing launched the Combi version despite only one firm order. Unlike the freighter version, the Combi retains all passenger

United Parcel Service found the 757 to be an ideal package freighter. Darren Anderson

Up to 15 containers or pallets, each measuring 88 × 125in (223 × 317cm) at the base, can be accommodated on the main deck of the 757F. The total container volume is 6,600 cubic ft (187 cubic m). The two lower holds of the aircraft provide an additional 1,830 cubic ft (51.8 cubic m)

flight deck and twin engines. This contrasts with older cargo-carrying aircraft in the standard-body class, such as 707s and DC-8s, which have three-person flight crews and are powered by four, old-technology engines that consume much more fuel. The 757 freighter is the only stan-

windows and doors. It is equipped with a cargo door on the left forward side. The Combi can carry two or three 108in (274cm) standard containers on the main deck. In a three-container configuration, the Combi can carry 9 tons (8.17 tonnes) of cargo and 123–148 passengers.

(Above) **The first 757 freighter for UPS was introduced in 1987. It has no windows and a single cargo door.** Boeing

(Below) **A cutaway drawing shows the 757's cargo capacity.** Boeing

Technical characteristics of a 757-200 freighter.
Boeing

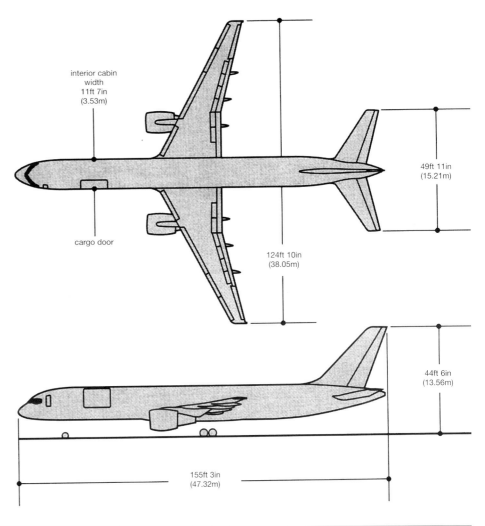

interior cabin
width
11ft 7in
(3.53m)

cargo door

49ft 11in
(15.21m)

124ft 10in
(38.05m)

44ft 6in
(13.56m)

155ft 3in
(47.32m)

An example of what the 767-300 freighter can carry.
Boeing

Royal Nepal operates a 757-200 that is the only combi version – passenger and cargo on the main deck – ever made. Carlos Borda

Military Applications

The 767 and 757 are used on a variety of military missions, including radar and weapons monitoring, refuelling, aircraft testing and government transportation.

Military Applications of the 767

The size and range of the 767 make it a logical replacement for AWACS, the Airborne Warning and Control System. Boeing began to study the adaptation of the 767-200ER for AWACS missions in December 1991, after the 707 production line was closed.

The first two AWACS 767s, designated E-767s, were delivered to the Japan Air Self-Defense Force in March 1998, with two more in January 1999. The aircraft is equipped with a rotodome-mounted antenna measuring 30ft (9m) in diameter and 6ft (1.8m) thick. The plane carries a crew of 21.

The first 767 AWACS aircraft flew on 9 August 1996, and completed flight testing in February 1997, three weeks ahead of schedule. Take-off performance tests were done at Edwards Air Force Base in California and at Moses Lake, Washington. Cooling capabilities were put to test under the hot desert sun in Yuma, Arizona. Tests were also performed on a new electrical system, and on a special fuel that will be used by the Japan Air Self-Defense Force. In addition to normal government qualification tests,

the aircraft went through the same FAA certification process as Boeing's commercial aircraft.

AWACS is the world's standard for Airborne Early Warning (AEW) systems. It fills the need of both airborne surveillance and command, control and communications functions for tactical and air defence forces. The 767 has the potential to replace more than 60 AWACS now in operation in the United States, Britain, France, Saudi Arabia and with NATO. AWACS offers countries self-defence capabilities well beyond the range of current ground-based systems. Its maritime surveillance ability allows long-range monitoring of ships in regional and territorial waters. The surveillance system includes a flexible, multi-mode radar, which enables AWACS to separate maritime and airborne targets from ground and sea clutter that limit other radar. Its radar has a 360-degree view of an area, and at operating altitudes it can detect targets more than 200 miles (320km) away.

The 767 has several advantages over the 707 for radar missions. Because of its wide-

Another military derivative of the 767 is a tanker/transport to replace ageing KC-135s, military versions of the 707. As a tanker, the 767 is an efficient, long-range aircraft suitably sized for a wide range of refuelling and airlift missions. The type also has the potential, like AWACS, to serve as a common platform for a large number of future military missions previously carried

distribution lines below the main cabin floor. This concept leaves the main cabin free for cargo or passenger transportation, allowing for simultaneous refuelling and airlift operations, or successive sorties without time-consuming reconfigurations.

In 1987, the original 767-200 was modified for the US Army's Space and Missile Defense Command as the Airborne

The size and range of the 767 make it a logical replacement for AWACS, the Airborne Warning and Control System. Boeing began studying adapting the 767-200ER for AWACS missions in December 1991 after the 707 production line was closed. The first two AWACS 767s, designated E-767s, were delivered to the Japan Air Self-Defense Force in 1998. Boeing

body configuration, the 767 offers 50 per cent more floor space and nearly twice the volume of the 707. It can carry a heavier payload, has greater range and flies higher than the 707.

out by 707 derivatives for the air forces of the US and many other nations.

Reconfiguring a commercial 767 for the tanker/transport mission involves the addition of pumps, auxiliary fuel tanks and fuel

Surveillance Testbed (AST) project, a technology demonstration programme that supported development and evaluation of defence systems to counter intercontinental and theatre ballistic missiles (ICBMs

One of the 767's most unusual uses. In 1987, the first-ever 767-200 was modified for the US Army's Space and Missile Defense Command as the Airborne Surveillance Testbed (AST) project. The plane features a large cupola on top of the fuselage containing infrared sensors capable of tracking missiles at long range.
Boeing

and TBMs). The plane features a large cupola on top of the fuselage containing infrared sensors capable of tracking missiles at long range. AST test flights continued through 1991, before the Cold War came to an abrupt end. Initial research was aimed at evaluating whether an airborne infrared sensor could reliably provide early warning using detection, tracking and target discrimination. The programme later changed its scope to gather data for ballistic missile defence development, and to resolve issues associated with target characteristics.

The sensor housed in the aircraft's cupola is made up of more than 30,000 detector elements. It is sensitive enough to detect the heat of a human body at a distance of more than 1,000 miles (1,600km) against

the cold background of space. In testing, the sensor successfully demonstrated the capability to detect, track and discriminate warheads from missile components, debris and decoys, from both the ambient temperature of an object prior to launch and from the heat generated during re-entry into the Earth's atmosphere. Hughes Aircraft Electro-Optical Data Systems Group designed and built the sensor.

While originally designed to track nuclear missiles, the AST was used during the 1991 Gulf War to support the US Army's studies on theatre missile defence systems. With the threat of nuclear war removed, the AST today observes missiles launched across the United States and in the Pacific, recording scientific data. The

AST is based in Seattle and can deploy to any national test range in a day. It carries a flight crew of 15, with room for observers. Missions last from six to eight hours, and the aircraft usually flies somewhat higher than commercial aircraft, at an altitude above 42,000ft (12,800m).

Military Applications of the 757

The smaller 757 also has a role in military aviation. It is the designated replacement for the US Government's fleet of VIP 707s, which includes Air Force Two, the plane that carries the vice-president. These planes, known as VC-137s, have been used since the late 1950s. Recently, the US Air Force has selected four 757-

200s – designated C-32As – to meet its requirements to transport the vice-president, cabinet members and members of Congress when on Government business. The C-32As are operated by the 89th Airlift Wing at Andrews Air Force Base in Maryland, outside Washington, DC. Two of the planes were delivered in March 1998, followed by another two in October. The first version made a two-hour first flight on 11 February 1998. The US Air

sophisticated navigation equipment, a military transponder, a UHF satellite communications radio, and secure voice and data transmission capability. The planes are configured for 45 passengers and 16 crew and baggage space. The planes are designed for a 4,150 mile (6,640km) mission, the distance between Washington and Frankfurt. The C-32's paint scheme is similar to that of the Air Force One 747 – white, black, gold and light blue. The C-

757's interior was gutted and replaced with console positions, data recorders and avionics racks. Among the features is an onboard mock-up of an F-22 cockpit. The 757's auxiliary power unit runs continuously during each flight, to provide all electrical power for F-22 avionics and test systems. The flying testbed, dubbed the 'Catfish' because its nose bears the F-22's front end, should save hundreds of flight hours and millions of dollars by pre-flying and debugging critical

The C-32A, a slightly modified 757, entered service in 1998 to transport US government officials.
Boeing

Force bought the C-32As for $365 million under a new acquisition procedure, which allows the service to buy the aircraft off the existing production line in Renton.

The C-32As share commonality with their commercial cousins. The aircraft meets FAA requirements relating to its certification, design and airworthiness, as well as its equipment for navigation, instrument approach and overwater operations. The C32As differ from other 757s only in that they are equipped with more

32As are powered by two Pratt & Whitney PW2037 engines.

The military has found other uses for the 757 besides transporting people and goods. The first 757 ever built is being used as a flying testbed to test features of the world's newest fighter, the Lockheed Martin-Boeing F-22 Raptor. The testbed is fitted with the forward fuselage section of the F-22 as well as the fighter's wing, placed on top of the 757 fuselage just behind the cockpit. To prepare for this unusual assignment, the

F-22 electronic systems in real time. The converted 757 can operate for up to five hours in the air at once.

One 757, still wearing the silver and blue livery of Eastern Airlines, is now being used by the National Aeronautics and Space Administration's Langley Research Center as a flying testbed. NASA uses the plane to test new technology to make low-visibility ground movements safer and more efficient. This 757 replaced an old 737 as Langley's prime research plane.

CHAPTER FOURTEEN

Into the Future

The development of the 767 and 757 has touched every other Boeing model in production. The glass cockpit, first introduced with the dynamic duo, was brought over to the 737 and 747 lines. Fuel efficiency and low noise, once a trademark of the 767 and 757, are now vital to every commercial aircraft made by Boeing.

The 767's legacy has gone beyond that, however, and has eventually inspired an entirely new aircraft, the giant twin-engined 777. When Boeing's latest model debuted in 1995, it filled a niche demanded by customers for an aircraft bigger than the 767, but smaller than the 747-400. The 777, in fact, first began as a potential derivative of the 767. In late 1986, just as the 767-300 was introduced, Boeing was researching larger variants of the 767. The reaction from airlines was that the size was right, but the range was too low, then that the size and range were right, but that the 767 wing too small to generate the necessary lift. The wing was redesigned and a new version of the 767 – stretched by 46ft (14m) – was put in the works, to offer a range of almost 7,000 miles (11,200km). In all, seven product scenarios were offered, all based on the 767 design.

At this point, the decision was made to launch a new plane, freed from the constraints of being a derivative of the 767. The all-new 777 emerged, with new wings, larger engines, more seats and greater length. As it happens, many of the 767's characteristics are visible in the Triple Seven, including a similar shape, two engines and the same nose section. Without the 767's proven twin-engine track record, particularly on long-haul flights, this new plane would never have taken off.

With their efficiency, reliability and relatively low capital cost, the 767 and 757 will remain strong-selling products well into the 21st century, although competitive pressures and new technology are forcing Boeing constantly to make changes to the models to keep them marketable. As outlined, the Airbus A330-200, a larger alternative to the 767-300ER

and a replacement for the 767-200ER, DC-10s and the A310s, is a serious threat to the 767's market share. Airbus hopes to sell 500–600 of the aircraft. Boeing's response is the larger 767-400ER. Both new aircraft are catering to market forecasts that predict a 30 per cent increase over the next twenty years in average per-aircraft capacity requirement, from 179 to

235 seats. Forecasts indicate that aircraft seating 350 passengers or more, including the 767-400 and A330-200, will account for 40 per cent of commercial transport sales over the next twenty years.

The 757 has less direct competition, and is expected to remain in demand. A boom in the British charter market should translate into renewed interest for the 757,

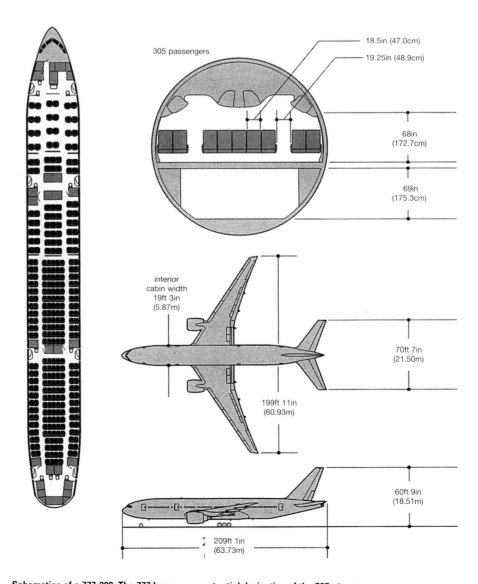

Schematics of a 777-200. The 777 began as a potential derivative of the 767. Boeing

especially since the type is already the cornerstone of the European charter fleet. Although the A321-200 is starting to make inroads, 757 sales have not been hurt badly by this model. The 757-300 and the upcoming 737-900 are both in response to the A321. In the future, therefore, the airlines will have a choice between a 737/757 mixed fleet and the A320 family.

Older 767s and 757s will continue their service well into the 21st century. They address the future needs of the air-transport industry – extending commonality, reducing pilot training, maximizing mixed-fleet operations, increasing on-wing times for engines, and reducing maintenance costs. Both members of the dynamic duo are durable. Both 767s and 757s are designed to fly for 40 years, or about 100,000 hours of service. By 1998, the average aircraft had been used for just one-fifth of that time.

In the meantime, Boeing sees plenty of demand for its aircraft. Growth in air traffic and airline profitability are the principal factors driving demand for new planes. Air travel within and between different regions of the world has grown at a consistently faster rate than underlying regional and global economic growth. In the five-year period from 1993–97, the average annual growth rate for worldwide passenger traffic was about 5.7 per cent. Boeing's twenty-year forecast of the average long-term growth rate in passenger traffic is about 5 per cent. This growth in traffic, combined with the need to replace older aircraft in service, is expected to generate demand for 17,650 new aircraft by the year 2017, valued at about $1.2 trillion. According to Boeing's market forecast, seven out of ten of the new aircraft will be the size of the 757, 737 or 717, including the Airbus A320 family. Intermediate-sized aircraft, including the Airbus A330/340 family, and the 767 and 777, will represent one in four future deliveries. Only 15 per cent of the new aircraft demand will be for aircraft of the size of the 747, or larger.

To meet its projections, Boeing is working to become more productive.

With airline deregulation spreading around the globe, with post-Cold War military budgets trimmed and Airbus Industrie becoming a powerful competitor, Boeing is making sure that it keeps its place as leader in the marketplace. At a time when it should be celebrating a strong surge in demand for its jetliners, it has been forced to take a series of expensive

and embarrassing steps to keep its over-taxed factories operating.

Despite the boom in orders, in 1997 the company recorded its first loss in 50 years. The problem was not that the aircraft-building business is turning down; in fact, Boeing has never been busier. The problem has been learning how to keep up with a surge of orders. During 1998, Boeing's factories in Renton, Everett and Long Beach turned out 47 aircraft a month. In mid-1996, that monthly figure was just 18.

Faced with what it called the 'steepest production increases since the dawn of the jet age', Boeing's factories seized up under the strain. While the 767 and 757 programmes were not affected, the company had to halt 747 and 737 assembly lines to make adjustments. Boeing was midway through a $1 billion programme to update its manufacturing when it was hit by the surge in orders. It could not cope because its systems of ordering and handling parts, and the manufacture of several of its models, were still too inefficient and old-fashioned. Every alteration, even a seemingly minor one, such as moving the location of an emergency flashlight holder, consumes thousands of hours of engineering time, involving hundreds of pages of detailed drawings, and costs hundreds of thousands of hours to execute. It is amazing that Boeing, a titan of American industry and an admired exporter, has survived and, indeed, prospered using such archaic methods.

In the future, 85 per cent of aircraft parts will be standard, with airlines specifying the rest. In addition, aircraft components, previously tracked through a mass of papers and 400 separate computer systems, will be followed on a single computer system. Boeing has also begun to ask its suppliers to design parts on computers, so that the aircraft are easier to assemble. Thanks to technology jumps made with the 767 and 757, the Boeing 777 and the new-generation 737 were designed on computers.

The overall goal of the changes is to reduce the time it takes to launch a new aircraft from 60 months to 12, saving billions of dollars.

The 767 and 757 can help Boeing to become more productive, cost-efficient and profitable, providing revenue stream for years to come. The two newest members of the family, the 767-400ER and 757-300, will fill the needs of airlines which need a big aircraft that is inexpensive to operate. Large airlines looking to replace their fleets of older widebodies will be looking to these

aircraft to fit their needs, but may wait to see how well the aircraft fare in service. Boeing studies show that sales of the new 767-400ER will increase overall sales of the 767 model, but could detract from the number of -300ER deliveries. Meanwhile, 767-200s may be falling out of favour, but they have excellent potential as used aircraft or as freighter conversions.

Although it is more than fifteen years old, the design of the 757 and its proven systems will keep the type at the forefront of the world's fleets for another ten years. Environmental issues, which affect the 727 in particular, may generate demand for used 757s among operators seeking a replacement for the tri-jets. Boeing projects that by 2010, more than half of 757 orders will come from outside the United States. There is a concern that the 737-900, a stretched version and the latest next-generation 737 offering nearly the same seating capacity as a 757, will close the gap between the two models, hurting 757 sales. However, Boeing's view is that it prefers to get an order for any model as long as that order does not go to the competition.

Looking ahead to the future, Boeing is considering longer-range versions of the 767-400ER. There is also talk of an extended-range version of the 757-200ER, dubbed the 757-200X, increasing range by as much as 690 miles (1,100km).

Further developments of the 767-300 and -400ER are under consideration. The extended range 767-300ERX would have the aerodynamic and structural changes of the -400 – except for the lengthened fuselage and additional fuel capacity. These changes would increase range by about 540 miles (900km) to around 7,000 miles (11,250km). The range of the -400 model also can be increased in what will be known as the 767-400ERX. With this model, an additional tail fuel tank, further weight increases and more powerful engines would increase range to 7,500 miles (12,000km).

These projects will depend on how the world's airlines welcome the 767-400ER and 757-300, the future of this fine family. With these new models, offering an increasing array of seating capacities and arrangements, Boeing will be better prepared to compete with Airbus. This commitment will ensure that the dynamic duo will continue to set standards in the new millennium.

William Boeing wouldn't have wanted it any other way.

Operators of the Boeing 757 and 767

This is a list of airlines and cargo carriers operating Boeing 757 and Boeing 767 models; it does not include private or military operators. Numbers in parentheses reflect aircraft on order. Information as of November 1998.

Boeing 757-200

Aero Peru	4		Flying Colors	5	
Aeromexico	6		Greenlandair	1	
Air 2000	12		Guyana Airways	1	
Air Alfa	1		Iberia	12	(8)
Air Europa	2		Icelandair	5	(1)
Air Holland	4		Istanbul Airlines	3	
Airtours International	5		LAPA	2	
Air Transat	5		Leisure International Airways	1	
America West Airlines	13		LTE International Airways	3	
American Airlines	96	(6)	LTU	11	
American Trans Air	7	(4)	Mexicana	5	(1)
Arkia	1		Monarch Airlines	6	
Avianca	4		North American	2	
Azerbaijan Airlines		(2)	Northwest Airlines	48	(25)
Britannia Airways	25	(2)	Qatar Airways	1	
British Airways	51	(6)	Royal Air Maroc	2	
Canada 3000 Airlines	7		Royal Aviation	2	
Challenge Air Cargo	3		Royal Brunei Airlines	1	
China National Aviation	1		Royal Nepal Airlines	3	
China Southern Airlines	18		Shanghai Airlines	7	
China Southwest Airlines	12		Spanair	1	
China Xinjiang Airlines	3	(1)	Star Air Tours	1	
Condor Flugdienst	18		TACV Cabo Verde	1	
Continental Airlines	29	(4)	Trans World Airlines	16	(7)
Continental Micronesia	3		Transaero	5	
Delta Air Lines	96	(14)	Transavia Airlines	4	
DHL International	1		Turkmenistan Akhal	1	
El Al	8		United Airlines	96	(2)
Ethiopian Airlines	5		United Parcel Service	73	(2)
Far Eastern Air Transport	4	(4)	US Airways	34	
Finnair	4	(1)	Uzbekistan Airways	1	
			Xiamen Airlines	5	

TOTAL 807 (90)

757-300

Arkia	(2)
Condor Flugdienst	(13)
Icelandair	(2)

TOTAL (17)

767-200

Aeromexico	2
Air Canada	23
Airborne Express	5
Air China	6
Air Europa	2
Air Gabon	1
Air Mauritius	2
Air New Zealand	3
Air Seychelles	1
Air Zimbabwe	2
All Nippon Airways	20
American Airlines	30
Ansett Australia	9
Avianca	3
Balkan Bulgarian Airlines	2
Britannia Airways	6
Continental Airlines	(10)
Delta Air Lines	15
El Al	4
Ethiopian Airlines	2
EVA Air	4
Japan Airlines	3
LOT Polish Airlines	2
Malev	2
Qantas	7
South African Airways	3
Swiss World Airlines	1
TACA International Airlines	1
Trans World Airlines	12
Transbrasil	8
United Airlines	19
US Airways	12
Varig	6
TOTAL	**218 (10)**

767-300

Aeroflot	2	
Aeromexico	2	(1)
Air Algerie	3	
Air Canada	6	
Air China	4	
Air Europe	6	
Air France	5	
Air Madagascar	1	
Air New Zealand	9	
Air Namibia	1	
Air Nippon	2	
Air Pacific	1	
Air Seychelles	1	
Airtours International	3	
Alitalia	8	(1)
All Nippon Airways	40	
American Airlines	45	(4)
Ansett Australia	1	
Asiana Airlines	12	(4)
Avianca	1	
Britannia Airways	7	(2)
British Airways	28	
Canadian Airlines International	11	(2)
China Yunnan Airlines	3	
City Bird	2	
Condor Flugdienst	9	
Delta Air Lines	68	(9)
Egyptair	2	
Ethiopian Airlines	1	
EVA Air	4	
Gulf Air	11	
Hokkaido International Airlines	1	
Iberia	2	
Japan Airlines	17	(1)
Japan Asia Airways	4	
KLM Royal Dutch Airlines	10	(1)
LAN Chile	14	(2)
Lauda Air	5	(1)
Leisure International Airways	2	
LOT Polish Airlines	3	
LTU	6	
Martinair Holland	6	
Qantas	21	
Royal Brunei Airlines	5	
SAS	14	
Shanghai Airlines	2	(2)
Skymark Airlines	2	(1)
Sobelair	2	
Spanair	2	
TACA International Airlines	1	
Transaero	1	
Transbrasil	3	
Trans World Airlines	4	
United Airlines	27	(10)
United Parcel Service	27	(3)
Uzbekistan Airways	2	
Varig	6	(6)
Vietnam Airlines	6	
TOTAL	**494**	**(50)**

767-400

Continental Airlines	(26)
Delta Air Lines	(21)
TOTAL	**(47)**

Source: *Flight International.*

Deliveries

Numbers of 767 and 757 models delivered by year. Source: Boeing.

767			**757**	
1982	20		1982	2
1983	55		1983	25
1984	29		1984	18
1985	25		1985	36
1986	27		1986	35
1987	37		1987	40
1988	53		1988	48
1989	37		1989	51
1990	60		1990	77
1991	62		1991	80
1992	63		1992	99
1993	51		1993	71
1994	41		1994	69
1995	37		1995	43
1996	43		1996	42
1997	42		1997	48
1998	47		1998	54
TOTAL:	**729**		**TOTAL:**	**836**

Index